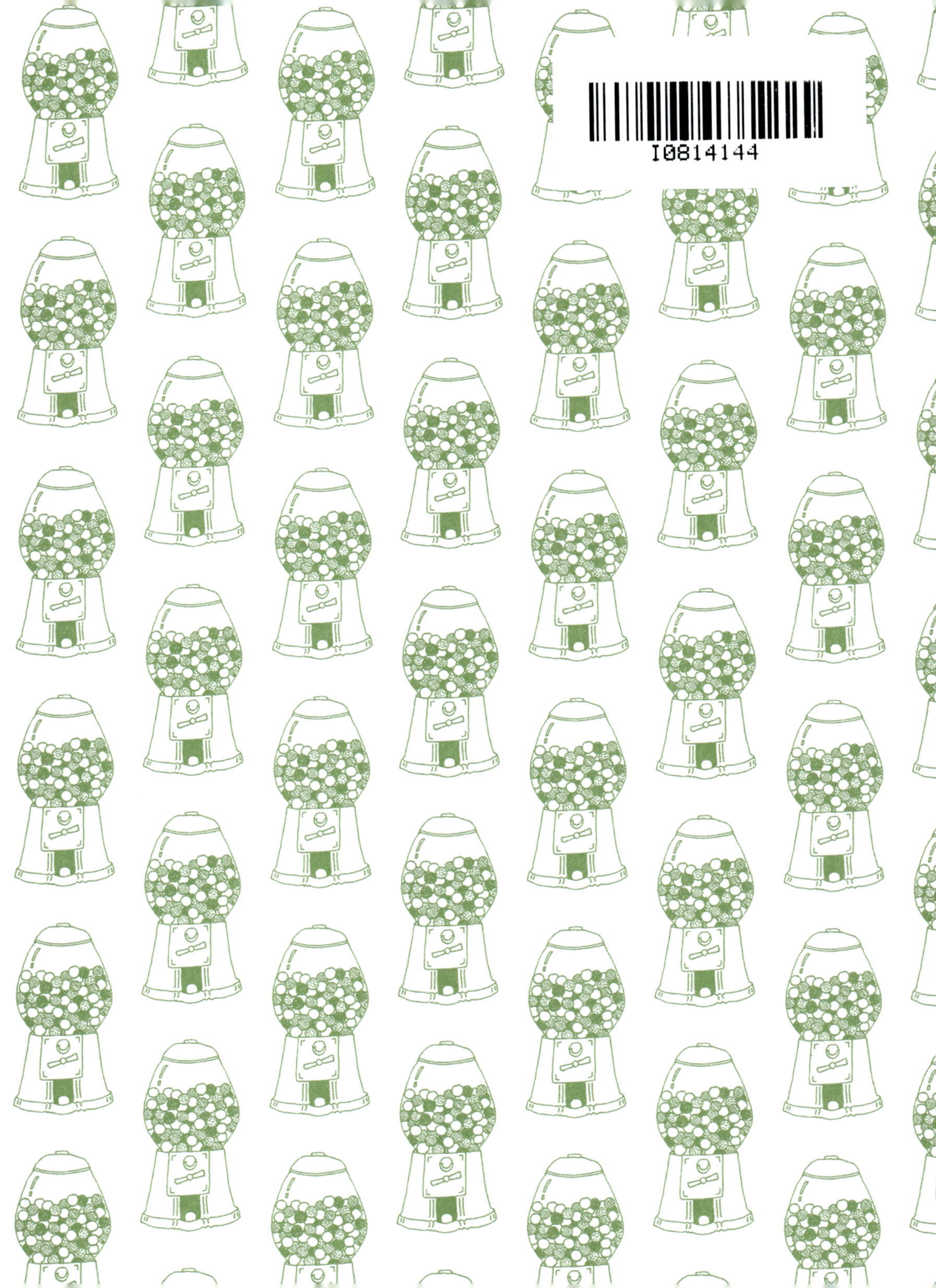
I0814144

This Is for You

This Is for You

GIFT-GIVING AS A WAY OF LIFE

Lea Redmond

Illustrated by the Author

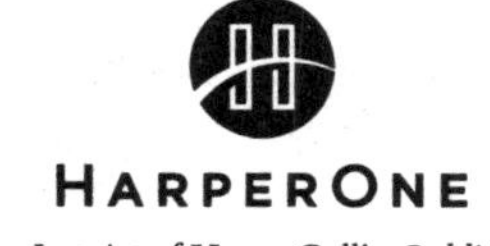

HarperOne

An Imprint of HarperCollins*Publishers*

For information, address HarperCollins Publishers, 195 Broadway, New York, NY 10007. In Europe, HarperCollins Publishers, Macken House, 39/40 Mayor Street Upper, Dublin 1, D01 C9W8, Ireland.

HarperCollins books may be purchased for educational, business, or sales promotional use. For information, please email the Special Markets Department at SPsales@harpercollins.com.

harpercollins.com

FIRST EDITION

Design by Elina Cohen
Illustrations copyright © 2025 by Lea Redmond

Library of Congress Cataloging-in-Publication Data has been applied for.

ISBN 978-0-06-328371-8

25 26 27 28 29 LBC 5 4 3 2 1

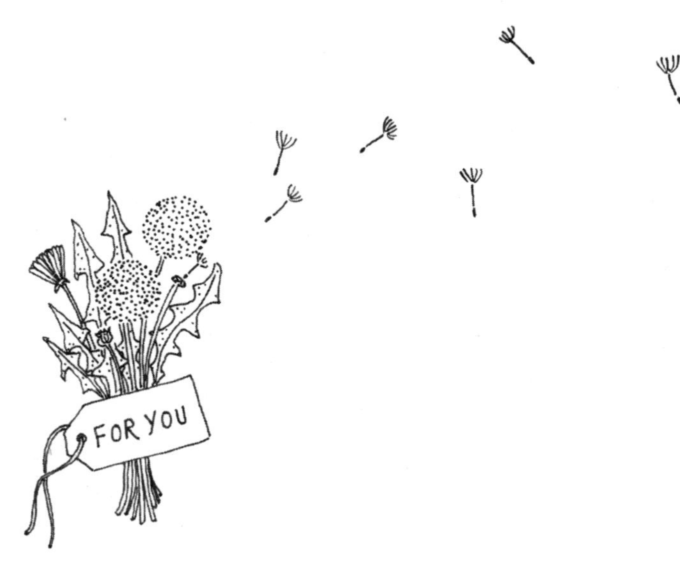
FOR YOU

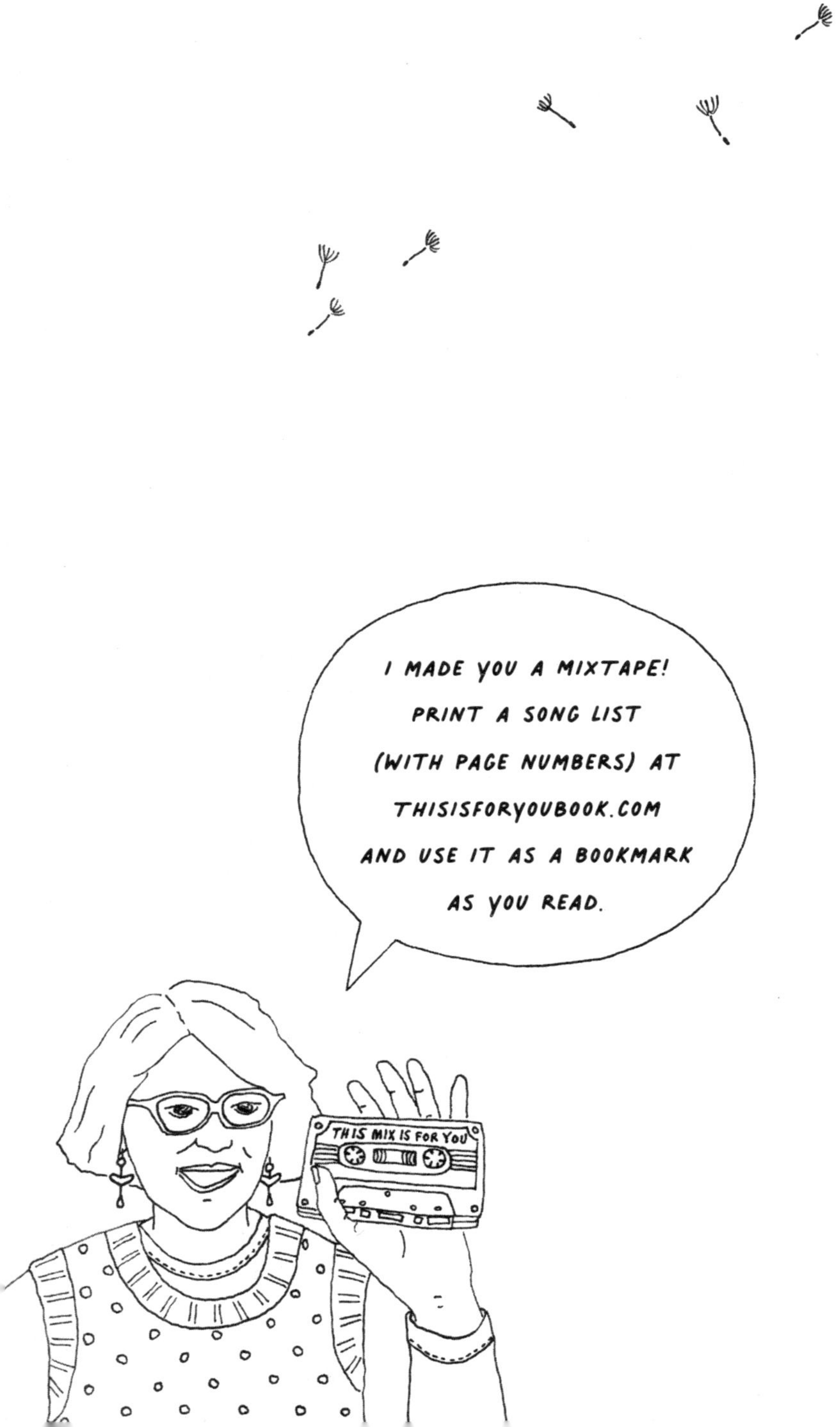

I MADE YOU A MIXTAPE!
PRINT A SONG LIST
(WITH PAGE NUMBERS) AT
THISISFORYOUBOOK.COM
AND USE IT AS A BOOKMARK
AS YOU READ.

THIS MIX IS FOR YOU

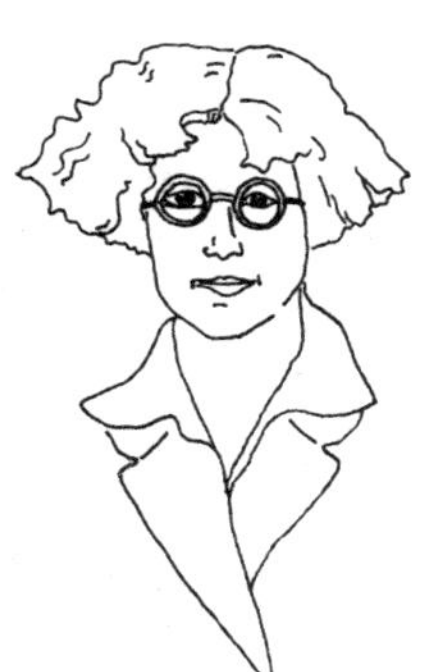

Attention is the rarest and purest form of generosity.

—SIMONE WEIL, *FIRST AND LAST NOTEBOOKS*

All flourishing is mutual.

—ROBIN WALL KIMMERER, *THE SERVICEBERRY*

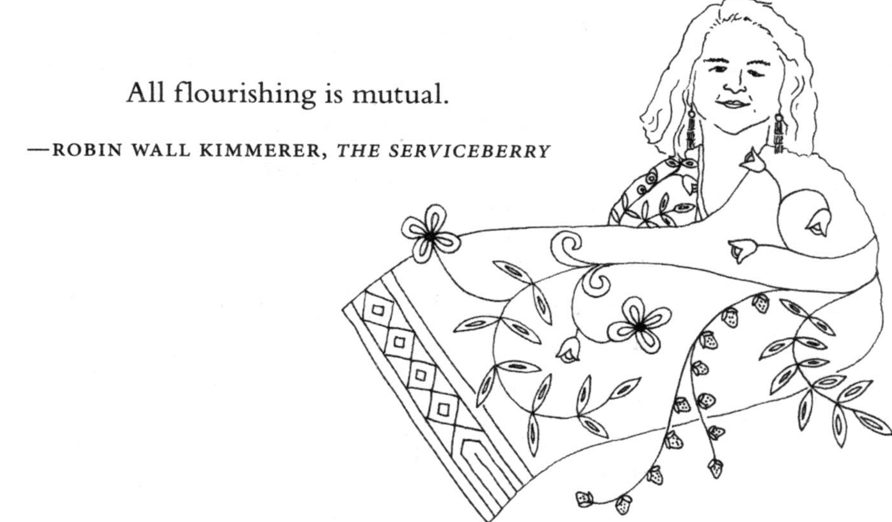

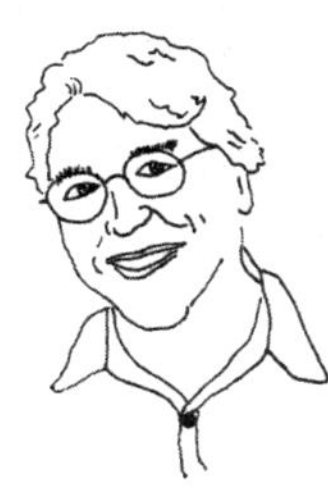

The only essential is this: *the gift must always move.*

—LEWIS HYDE, *THE GIFT*

Contents

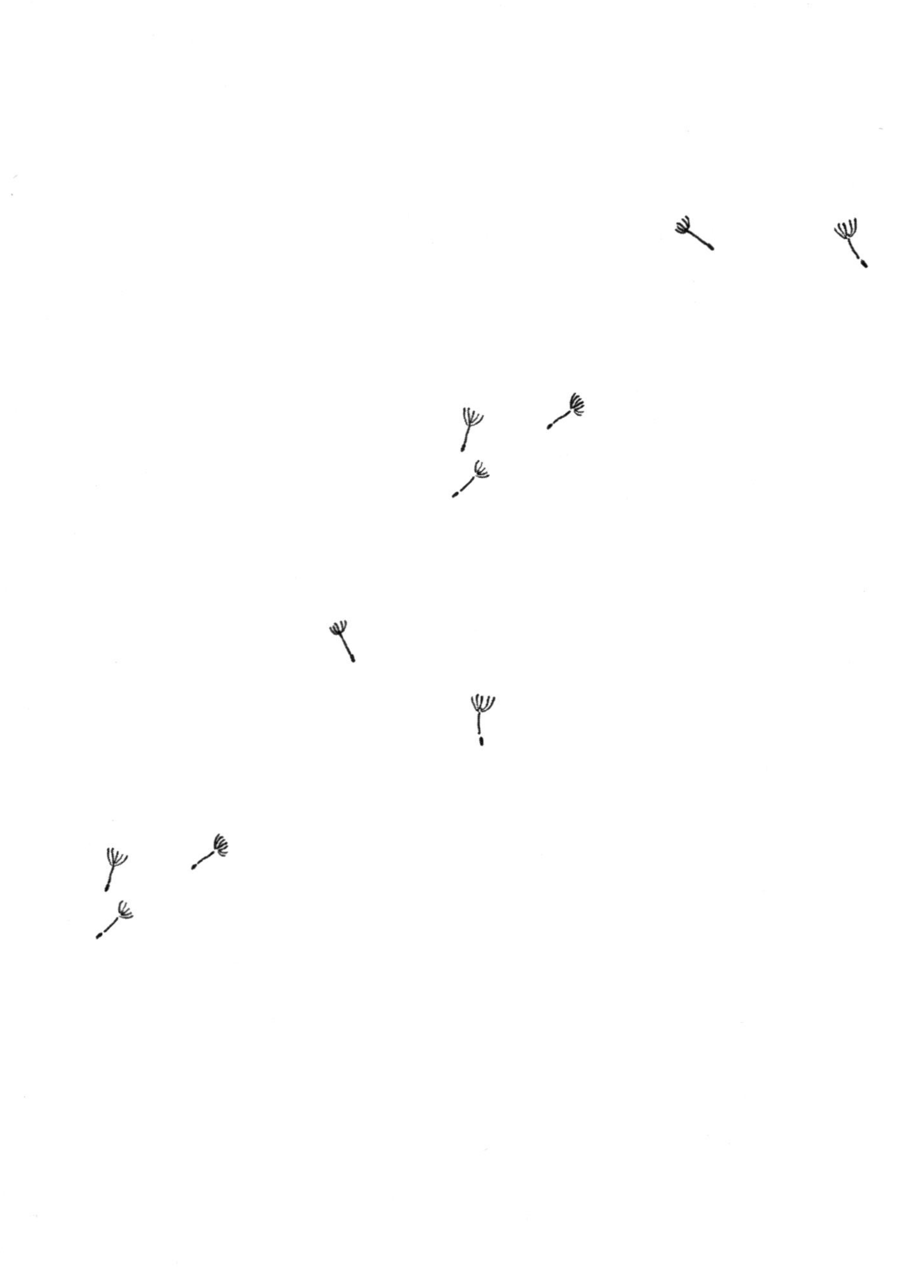

Author's Note

Writing a book is a huge joy and a great responsibility. I have done my best to treat the subject matter at hand with the utmost care and love. I have worn my heart on my sleeve, just as I do in my daily life. I invite you to meet me on the page with your heart open too. Whoever you are, I am glad you are here.

Thank you to all the people who have shared stories about gifts with me over the years. It was an honor to listen, learn, and be in conversation with you. I am moved by your creative and courageous acts of love. Some names and details have been changed to protect privacy.

In this book, I often use *we* and *you.* My intention is to be welcoming and inclusive, not presumptive. This is not a "royal we," but the "we" of me and you, dear reader—sharing a pot of tea—both of us seeking to get better at giving and receiving. I trust that you will opt in and out of this "we" in whatever way feels aligned for you.

WELCOME

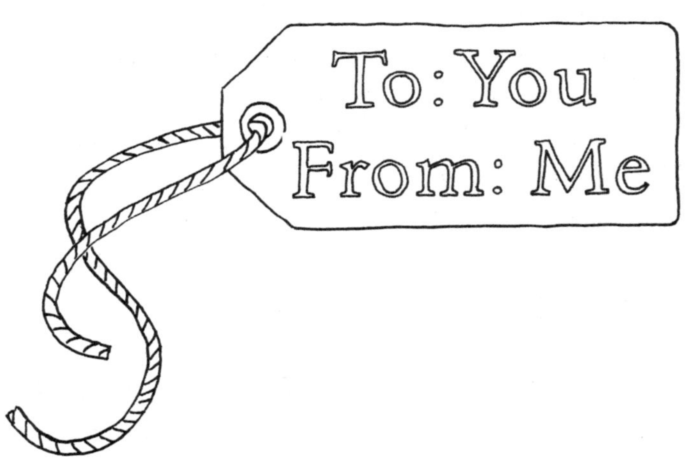

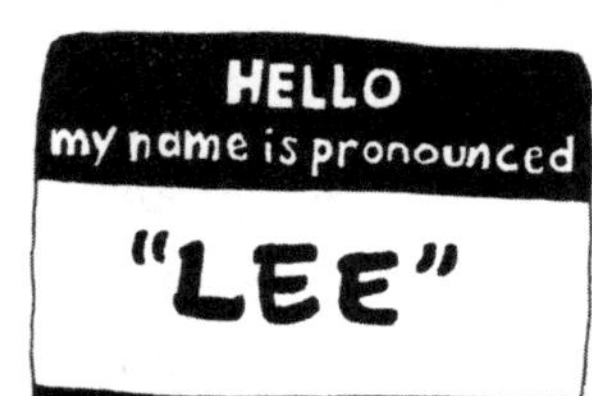

Good gifts are all about relationships, so let's begin with this one. My name is Lea, pronounced *Lee*—just like *tea*, *sea*, and sugar snap *pea*, three of my favorite things. Nice to meet you!

I'm guessing you might already be a good gift giver and are looking to shine even brighter in your gift-giving. Or perhaps gift-giving has always baffled you, and you're looking for some guidance. In any case, this book is for you! Perhaps you picked it up because you're fed up with the ecological impact and waste of consumerism, and you hope there might be more to gifts than shopping and obligation. (There is!) Maybe you're looking for meaningful ways to love on a budget. (Amen! Some of the best gifts are free!) Maybe you have been disappointed by the gifts you've been given or the lackluster responses of people who have received your gifts. Are you curious where things veered off course, and if there's a remedy? Me too.

This is not an etiquette book; we're here to explore what *could be*, not mandate what *should be*. As you'll soon see, hard rules don't apply, and there's plenty of room for you to find your own way. Most of all, we're here to discover the possibilities that exist in the sacred spaces between us. Gifts can activate these spaces in service of love and care. If we take the practice to heart, we can tap into an ancient and ongoing dance of generosity that keeps us in touch not only with each other, but also with ourselves, the world, life on Earth, and—if you wish—a sense of the divine. A great gift is a deep acknowledgment that we are here, together. It is a touchstone, a tangible remembrance of our mutual belonging and a loving response to a weariness around feeling alone in an aching world.

To give and receive is nothing less than the essence of relationship: seeing and being seen, listening and observing, communicating, supporting, celebrating, making mistakes and mending. If we let it, giving and receiving gifts invites us into the dance of connection, the tapestry of interdependence, the shimmer of interbeing. This book is designed to support and inspire you to give good gifts, yes, but also to enrich relationships between people, planet, and the kinship we all share. We'll brave the spaces between us to find small outlets for big love through good gifts, and all of this helps us practice the openhearted living that makes life good too.

You might be wondering, *Who is my guide?* I am a maker at heart and always have been. My first word was *pretty*. I would point at flowers and just say "pri." As a toddler, I stacked pink wooden blocks into a tall tower at the Montessori preschool where my mom taught. In elementary school, rainy days were my favorite because I could eat lunch in the classroom and do art at my desk. To this day, the scent of rain on asphalt makes me feel calm and crafty. In middle school, I listened to my Walkman on the school bus and wrote a fifteen-page, illustrated book titled *The Perfect Gift*, binding it with duct tape. In the story, my quest for a Mother's Day gift leads me, unsuccessfully, through a series of stores, only to find a pretty rock on the way home, for free, and decide it is just right for my mom. In high school, I practically lived in the ceramics classroom, where I learned how to make teapots and gifted them to my friends and family. I got a ceramics scholarship to a tiny liberal arts college in the middle of a wheat field where I then proceeded to fall in love with beautiful ideas, big and small.

Since then, I've mostly been making things in my art studio, making friends around town, making peace with the difficult parts of life, and trying my best to love the world. These days, I can be found at my old barley-twist oak table doing things like mocking up a moon-shaped children's book, designing a poetry game out of paint chips, or going down another teacup rabbit hole on eBay. I have a special shelf for gifts in progress. Sometimes I have helpers in the studio, employees who help me distribute big love in the form of handcrafted tiny letters and packages, all by way of a project I started in 2008 called the World's Smallest Post Service, or WSPS. You can compose a letter on our website and then we make it teeny tiny and tuck it into a one-inch-wide envelope, complete with itsy postage stamp and wax seal. We send it to your recipient with a magnifying glass. As the postmaster of the WSPS, I have witnessed tens of thousands of sweet, creative, and clever messages, convincing me this world is full of love.

Why do I love gifts so much? First, I come from a long line of good gift givers—people who are always scouting for the perfect thing and sometimes make it themselves. Second, I have always loved doing crafts. It was a lot more fun to give my pinch pots and friendship bracelets to people than to hoard them in my childhood bedroom. These days, I'm still always making something to give away in one form or another: a sweater, a handwritten letter,

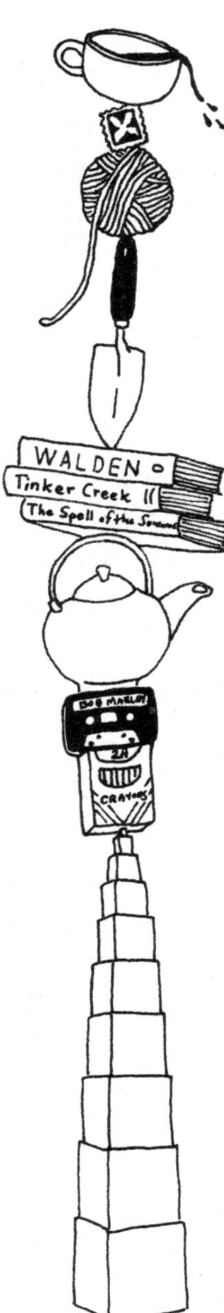

a spot of tea. I like to think of myself as a matchmaker between people and this big, beautiful world. Even though I am fed up with consumerism, I still believe in beautiful things. As an artist, I believe that objects (and experiences) are an important part of *precisely how* we inhabit this planet well.

Until recently, most of my gift-giving has been intuitive. But writing this book invited me to better understand my inner workings so that I could reflect upon them and share them with you. I also knew that if I wanted to be genuinely helpful, I needed to talk to people, to explore the full range of gift experience. Over the past few years, I've conducted over a hundred interviews with gift givers and recipients, chatted people up in coffee shops, hung out in bars with a sign soliciting stories, and compared notes with friends and family. I caretake a treasure trove of gift stories and am overjoyed to share some of these souvenirs of my own education in gifts. These stories warm my heart and give me hope.

In chapter 1, we begin with an exploration of what gifts are and then move on to where to source a gift and what a gift might be made of (objects, words, experiences). Next, we look at how to determine what gift a recipient might enjoy and how to develop a gift idea to make it even better. Last, we discuss what to do when a gift doesn't go well and how gifts might help heal a fractured world.

Gift-giving is not a hard science. I write not as a historian or sociologist, but as a working artist who loves the world and is endlessly curious about it. While the gift as a cultural form has innumerable expressions, this book's stories and insights come through the lens of a quirky gal named Lea with a big, goofy heart who loves to make things and give them away. I grew up in the socially diverse state of California in a secular family that valued art, science, sports, and the great outdoors. I am neurodiverse. I'm a hopeful romantic. I care deeply about my relationships. My way to give—to love—is one of many. I am eager for you to bring *your way* to these pages as you read, and to see what we can do together.

This book is a gift from me to you. It is also a gift to you from every person, every place, every book, every thing, and every living being I have ever touched or been touched by. It is what I have made of the myriad gifts of my life so far. What you, dear reader, make of it all in turn is up to you. I hope you find a few gems to carry with you moving forward. Please make them your own, re-facet and polish them however you see fit. May you bring them to bear on your own widening circles, letting love ripple out in all directions and circle back to you.

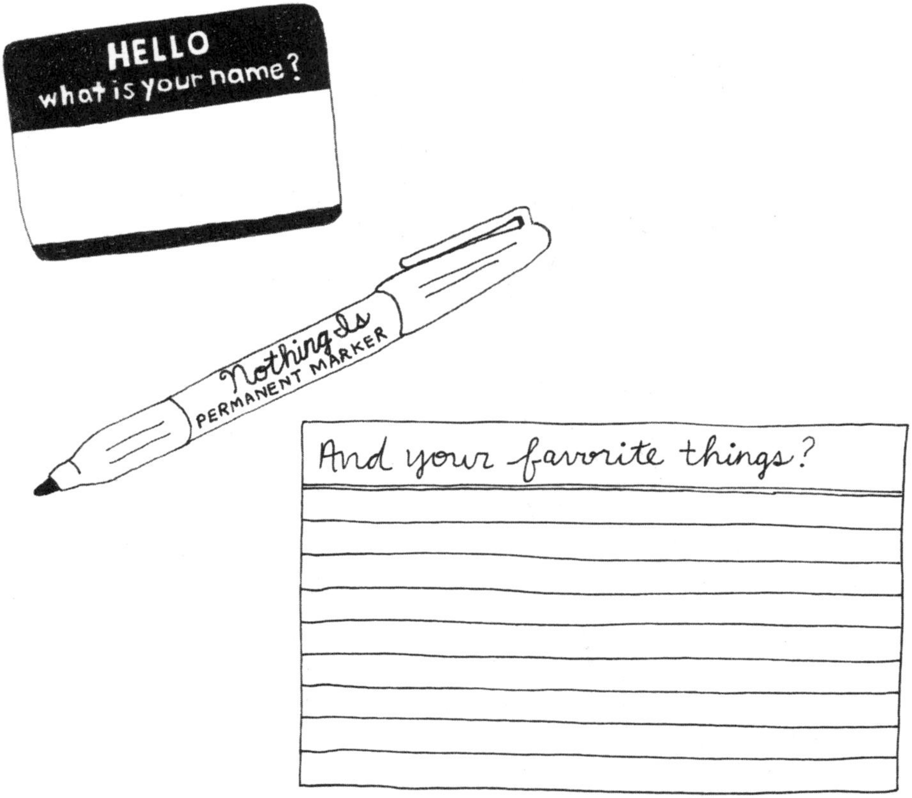

1

What Is a Gift?

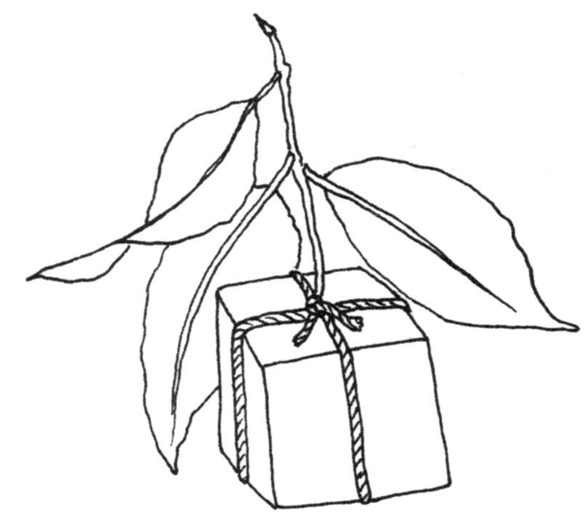

WHAT IS THE ESSENCE OF A GIFT?

WHAT ARE GIFTS FOR?

WHAT IS THE RELATIONSHIP BETWEEN A GIFT AND THE WORLD AROUND IT?

It is love alone that gives worth to all things.

—ST. TERESA OF ÁVILA

A Good Turn

A lemon on my tree ready to pick. A scattering of pink blossoms on the sidewalk. The crosswalk signal turning green just as I approach. I am the constant lucky recipient of lovely things I don't have to pay for. There are also larger lovely things, like the air I draw into my lungs, the water coming from my kitchen faucet, and the sunshine that not only feels good on my face but feeds the photosynthesis that is the base of every food chain. When I am awake to the world, it is clear to me that my being here at all is not something I earned or am entitled to. This life is pure gift. For me, all the splendid details of life are forever and always gifts from a mysterious universe. And yet, hard times are everywhere. But even those times can unfold gifts we could never have imagined but find ourselves grateful for.

At its basic level, a gift is an offering transferred willingly from one entity to another without the expectation of receiving anything in return. The implication is that the gift is something good—an item of value, a favor, a kindness or generosity that the receiver welcomes. This book takes that definition and runs with it. A gift is doing someone a good turn *on purpose* and *with a purpose.* It involves a conscious effort of consideration. A gift is a creative act to honor a person, a place, a moment, sometimes a special occasion. Gifts pause the passage of time and draw our attention to the fact: *We are here. Isn't it amazing?* In the steady flow of the more mundane happenings of our lives, a gift can re-enchant us with the magic of the world. From silly gifts to serious ones, a good gift is at least a little bit extra, a tad extraordinary.

On the one hand, I'm here to help you choose an awesome birthday present for your bestie or a great graduation gift for your eighth grader. If you are wondering what on earth you might do for your sweetie on your twenty-fifth anniversary that could adequately convey the depth of your feeling, take heart! I got you. On the other hand, I'm here to dismantle the whole category, to explore the edges of the word *gift* with an eye open to the missed opportunities for generosity and care that surround us. I also want to know: Can I dream up a fun treat for my mail carrier to leave for them on top of my mailbox on a random Tuesday? How can I put together an aesthetically compelling birthday surprise for a friend without spending a single dollar? And even: How might gift-giving and receiving open my eyes—and my heart—to the whole world?

A necklace. A book. A new bicycle for a child. A bouquet of flowers or a bottle of wine. It can be tempting to picture an *object* when we think of a "gift." A box with a bow. But a gift's determining qualities are never to be found in the physical object. The essence of a gift is the *verb,* the *gesture,* the *act.* It simply requires a "to you," a "from me," and an intention to positively impact or benefit someone. We pay attention, gather our thoughts, reflect on our feelings, concentrate our resources, and *do something* to wish each other well.

Another word for gift is *present,* a noun that traces back to a phrase from Old French, "to put a thing into the presence of a person." This etymology reveals verbs, actions. I believe gifts are about *being present* in our relationships and showing up with *presence.* A good gift is a process of making-special, *relationally,* that involves some of the loveliest human instincts—an impulse to acknowledge, understand, honor, encourage, celebrate, inspire, support, and hope. Gifts let us peek into each other's hearts. They lift spirits, nourish intimacy, and build trust. Gifts can help us express ourselves when we are at a loss for words. A good gift says, *I see you. I hear you. I am with you.*

I want to breathe new life into the idea and practice of the gift. I'm hoping to get the air circulating in patterns that are both very old and sparklingly new. The possibilities for loving each other well through gifts are infinite, and I hope you'll join the fun in your own unique way.

Little Outlets for Big Love

Many of my favorite gifts border on the ridiculous, containing a delightful unreasonableness that, to the heart, makes perfect sense. In the classic children's series *Frog and Toad,* two amphibious friends bake cookies, write letters, rake leaves, go sledding, and more, all while sporting adorable 1970s tweed and corduroy. In one story, Toad gives Frog a delightful gift, a plaid green coat. It is covered in buttons, none of them alike or having a practical function. So, what's the meaning?

The previous day, after one of Frog and Toad's long walks, Toad notices that he has lost a button on his favorite green coat. This inspires Frog to spearhead a button search party. Toad grumbles and mopes as the two of them retrace their steps. One by one, they find buttons on the ground or are offered a possible match from another forest animal, but the buttons are all wrong: too small, two-holed, square-shaped. They aren't his round, white, four-hole button, but he tucks each one in his pocket anyway. An increasingly frustrated Toad finally screams, "The whole world is covered with buttons, and not one of them is mine!"[1] He gives up, goes home, and slams the door. His eye immediately catches on something tiny on the floor—round and white. "Oh," says Toad, suddenly appreciating Frog's kind patience.

Finally at peace, reunited with his lost button, Toad gets an idea. Then he gets to work, with needle and thread. The next morning, Frog opens the gift box from Toad and knows exactly what it means. He puts on the button-covered coat and jumps for joy. In each button is a memory of care from Frog and their forest friends. What I love most about this story is that Toad was originally devastated to lose just one button off his coat, and then, one day later, he finds himself delighted to let go of his entire coat—his favorite one!—in the form of a gift.

I thought of Frog and Toad when I heard a kindred story from Laika and Robot. Hiking along the Rio Chama in New Mexico together, Laika lost a beloved handcrafted pocketknife. Several days later, Robot set out to find the knife, borrowing a metal detector and repeating the entire overnight hike solo, scanning each campsite and lunch spot. No luck. Unlike Toad's story, the knife was truly lost. So Robot commissioned a new knife from the same Santa Fe bladesmith who had made the original one. Laika loved the new knife, of course, but told me that it was Robot's thoughtful act of slowly retracing their steps, a tiny pilgrimage of sorts, that was the main gift.

A few years ago, I was inspired to pluck a few flowers and tuck them under the windshield wiper of a truck. The truck belonged to Oscar, my crush. The parking lot had only a few weeds in bloom to offer, but I made do. I didn't want to miss the moment. A week later, we were dating. The windshield bouquet initiated an ongoing game of flower ping-pong. A sprig of sidewalk jasmine tucked behind my ear on our first date. A bachelor button back to him from my yard.

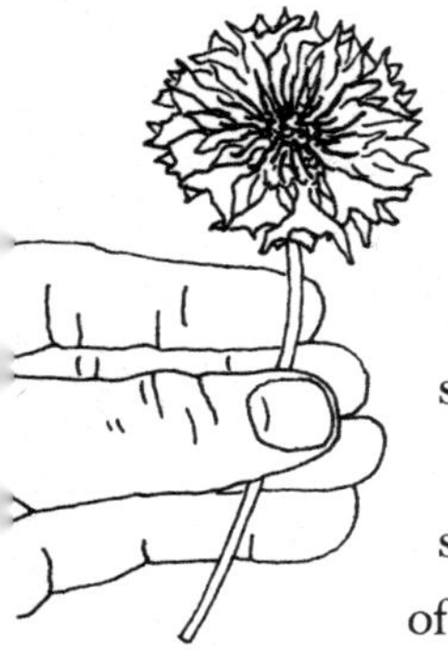

A week later, a calla lily presented to me on my stoop. On a walk together one afternoon, we harvested nigella seedpods after the woman gardening in front of her house encouraged us to take some. We planted them in Oscar's yard. We didn't spend a dime.

I did, however, drop a bit of cash on an idea. I turned our sweet game into an herbarium of the heart. I obtained a bunch of small see-through boxes and started collecting the dried specimens. In the base of each box is a white card with a few notes in pencil. Specimen No. 6 might be my favorite: a burst of bright pink preceding a kiss at a curb, both of us on bicycles. It must have looked dramatic; a woman in a passing car hollered "BEAUTIFUL!" out her open window. Specimen No. 18 is a single snapdragon blossom I plucked during a difficult conversation. Oscar didn't know you can pinch a snapdragon to make it "talk." They are basically tiny puppets, and I like to give them a voice. As we walked together down his street, the blossom participated in our difficult conversation, lightening the atmosphere as we tried to recover. And we did. Specimen No. 19: a rose, the next morning as I left for my studio.

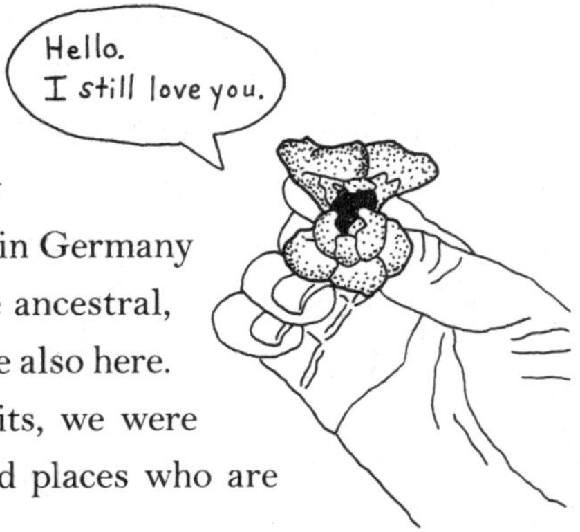

Part of what I love about this record of our courtship is that it is about us, but not *only* about us. This ongoing back-and-forth gift situated me, my beloved, and our relationship into a larger field. Neither of us is from around here. He was born in the tropics of El Salvador where, he tells me, mangos dangle from wild trees as plentifully as the lemons here in the East Bay. I was born in Ohio, but if we look back a few hundred years, my family is all over Europe, one line in Germany working an apple farm. And yet, here we are, on the ancestral, unceded land of the Muwekma Ohlone people, who are also here. As Oscar and I gifted each other these botanical bits, we were learning about what grows here, and the people and places who are supporting that growth. The foraged flora collection pulls me a little closer to feeling like I could be a responsible inhabitant of this place. When my sweetheart held out a nasturtium to me, it felt like the Earth itself—maybe even the universe or a great spirit—offering me a nasturtium *through* him. And the nasturtium was not merely *for* me. Even as it went into our herbarium, we kept the flower's gift essence moving. It was also *for* everyone in our widening circles of relations as the love between us overflowed our edges and was soaked up by our surroundings.

Button. Pocketknife. Snapdragon. We need small outlets for the big love we feel inside. To be clear, I'm not talking about just romance here. I love that the ancient Greeks had seven different words for love! Beyond romance, these included versions for platonic, familial, casual, and long-lasting love as well as self-love and universal love. When I find myself in love—any of the many kinds, and there are surely more than seven—I need to say something, do something, make something, give or receive something, to let the love energy out and express my affection. And so a gift is born.

Practicing Our Humanity

As we know, gift-giving does not always go well. A gift can push people apart rather than bring them together. A gift might overwhelm, underwhelm, or confuse, making people question the status of a relationship. Given for misguided reasons or received without an open mind or heart, a gift can offend, annoy, embarrass. A gift can be oblivious or ignorant, revealing how little someone actually knows us. Hidden motives sneak in. Gifts that impose, obligate, try to control or compete never go well. If a particular gift item is something a recipient wants very much in and of itself, it still might not be something they want *from that person.* If unnecessary or inappropriate expense is involved, a gift can make a recipient uncomfortable or even put the giver into financial trouble. All positions—giver, receiver, innocent bystander—can be stressful and awkward.

I agree with the household wisdom "How you do anything is how you do everything." Problems in gift-giving line up with the patterns of our inner struggles, the challenges in our relationships, and even the problems of the world. But caring has a pattern too. Love has a shape. I believe that we can revitalize this dynamic cultural form and that the gifts we share between us can enrich our relationships while bringing a better world into being. Gifts are a special opportunity to start small, to practice thoughtful ways of being together. I wonder, Can the way we love one thing become the way we love everything? Everyone?

Whether a particular gift is a *good* gift cannot be determined by assessing the gift on its own. The Dutch oven, the cheeky greeting card, tickets to the ballet—context matters. In first-century Rome, the stoic philosopher and gift guide Seneca advised, "Nothing is in itself a fitting gift for anyone. What matters is who gives it and to whom, where, why, when, and the other factors without which one cannot make a true accounting of the deed."[2] Gifts with an awareness of context, given by way of observation and understanding, are much more likely to be well received.

Even if the primary benefit of gifts belongs to the recipient, the creative processes that serve up the most dazzling gift ideas pair *empathy* with *introspection.* Gift-giving, then, requires *looking within.* The giver meditates on the who, where, why, and when. The giver, too, is a *who.* In gift-giving, looking within is not like looking into a mirror, but like looking through a window where you catch a glimpse of your own reflection while looking out. In turn, to receive well, we also look both out and in. The role of receiver is not a position of passivity—quite the contrary. Whether a gift becomes a truly *good* gift is partially in the hands of the recipient, in how they choose to respond to what has been offered.

I believe that with attention, intention, and practice, we can all become good gift givers. To ask how to be a good giver or receiver, though, is nothing less than to ask how to be a good human. A *good life* involves a conscious and creative consideration of who, and *how,* each of us wants to be in our relationships. These include the ones we have with people, planet, ourselves, and—for some of us—the divine. I agree with the psychotherapist Esther Perel in her belief that the quality of our lives ultimately depends on the quality of our relationships. Meaning and well-being come from the connections we caretake.

A Gift from the Sea

When I was growing up, my family always made sure the giver was watching when we opened a gift, so they could be part of the process. At age ten, after catching my parents' eyes and carefully removing the scissor-curled ribbon and patterned paper, I removed the lid from a two-inch-square box and peeked inside: a silver ring in the shape of a whale tail—my favorite animal! I slipped it on and immediately loved it.

I now see how wonderfully validating it was for my thoughtful parents to celebrate my favorite animal in the form of a piece of jewelry as substantial as this. I felt special when I learned that my parents had the ring resized just for my child-size hand. Knowing the ring had originally been intended for an adult made me feel grown up and mature, and implied that my parents saw me that way too.

As good gifts often are, this one was connected to a larger story. When I was a child in the early 1990s, a Greenpeace coral reef poster hung on my bedroom wall, and a mobile of silk-screened paper whales—humpback, grey, orca—dangled above my bed while I slept. Raised on the Discovery Channel and *National Geographic,* I was concerned about the state of the planet and the future of life on Earth.

After my parents moved us from Ohio to Southern California to be close enough to the ocean for my father to keep a sailboat, that boat became my home away from home. On weekends, if I wasn't playing in a soccer game or doing crafts in my room, I was on the boat. Sometimes, a pod of bottlenose dolphins would visit us, playing and diving at the bow. Whale sightings were much rarer; from a distance, I would see a salty spray geyser up from a blowhole or a tail slam through the water's surface. Seeing a whale was always a reminder that under the swells were all sorts of living things as well as a vast darkness. A whale, able to hold its breath for almost an hour, could breach the surface practically anywhere at any moment. Whales remind me that mysteries big and small are always nearby.

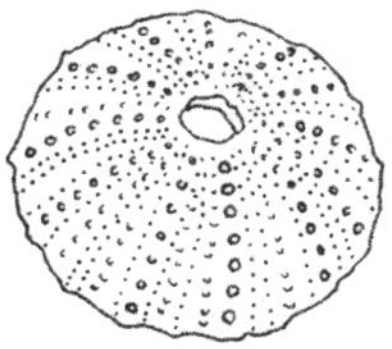

From my father's hands arrived many gifts from the sea over the years. When his head would break the surface of the water after scuba diving, he would hand me treasures from below, such as an intricately patterned sea urchin shell, before removing his mouthpiece. The wordless message was clear: *Look at this wonder. Isn't this beautiful world worth caring for?* When I reached for the shell, I speechlessly answered, *Yes.* My answer remains the same as I reach for the whale tail ring on my dresser today. It is a true *souvenir*—meaning "to remember" in French and tracing back to the Latin *subvenire,* with *sub-* meaning "up from below." The ring has the power to bring things back to the surface. It is a portal. Perhaps a promise.

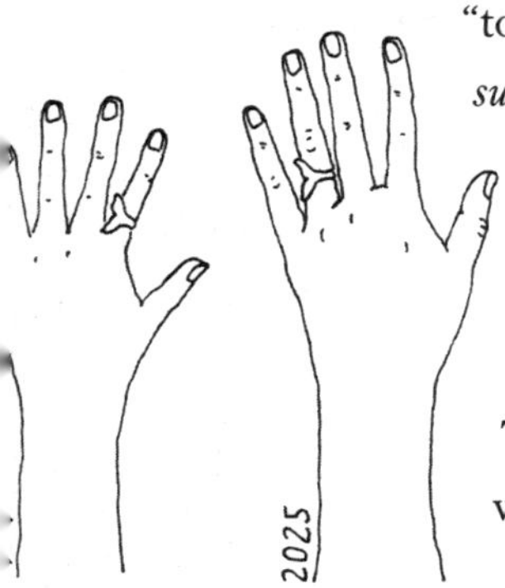

The whale ring is mine, but the belonging goes both ways. The ring belongs to me; I belong to the sea. The ring no longer fits the finger I wore it on when I was ten. These days, the ring fits my left ring finger

2025

best. The significance is not lost on me. The marriage and children I always imagined for myself have thus far eluded me. Only time will tell if the ring is a placeholder or a permanent fixture. But I am okay. I can be deeply disappointed without closing my heart. From the ocean that helped raise me, I learned to tolerate the cold, to embrace the unknown, to dive into mystery.

As a child, I nervously held my father's hand while snorkeling through sun-streaked towers of kelp bursting with life: anemone, urchin, bat ray, seal, sardine. The orange flash of a garibaldi! The iridescent rainbow I knew was hiding inside every abalone as it gripped its rock, and the soft, squishy bodies behind all those tough abalone shells. Today I see the lesson that lingered in the dancing shadows of all that seaweed: *If you are willing to breathe through vulnerability, to meet mystery and difficulty with courage and creativity, everything will be even more beautiful than you can imagine.* Life, when I stay open to it, is an exquisitely textured shell upon my fingertips, the swirl of a seal close enough to feel it, a whale getting ready to breach.

I am still learning how to care for the whale tail ring, for myself, for the world. Sometimes I like to listen to recordings of whale songs. When I do, I am hoping the deep breaths and slow heartbeats of these ancient creatures find their way into my being. I try to respond with deep breaths of my own because I want to stay awake to the world—to the beauty, all that could be lost, the people and places who are suffering as well as the joy that remains. As I slip the ring on and off my finger, it reminds me that life on Earth is a gift. *My life* is a gift. Again and again, I renew my vows.

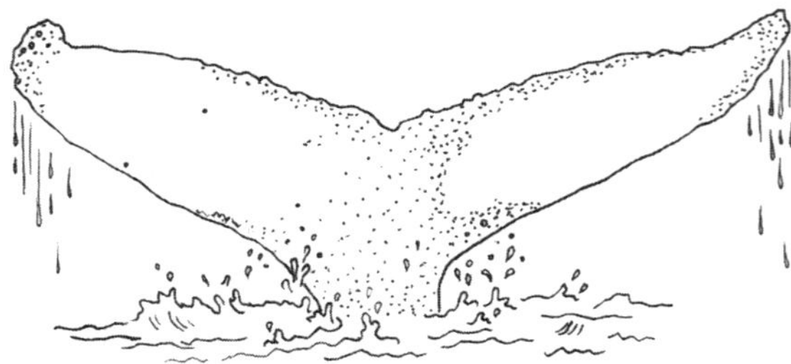

Reflect

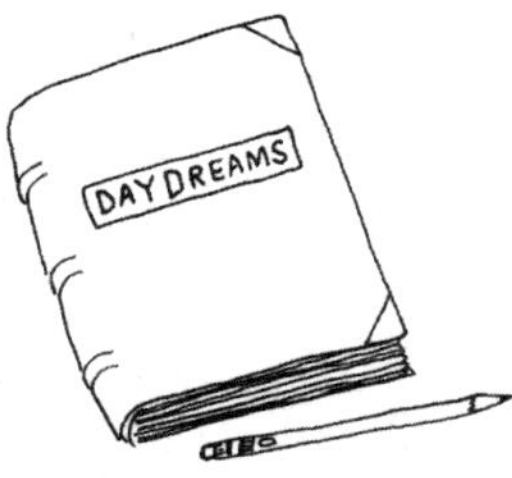

1. Have you received a delightfully unreasonable gift? Have you ever given one? What made it magic?

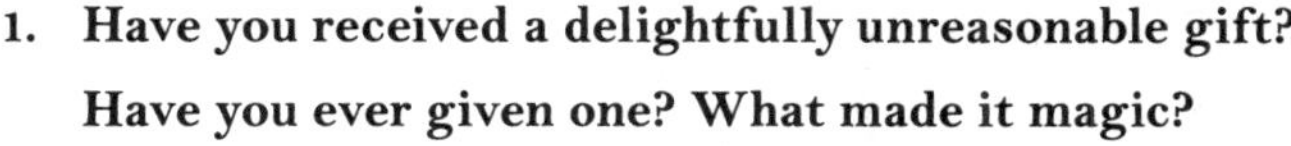

2. Make a short list of gifts you have given and received over the years. Next to each one, jot down any words that come to you that say something about the purpose of the gift and what benefit it provided or hoped to offer.

3. Like my whale tail ring, have you received a gift that has stood the test of time and maybe even evolved with you over the years? How so?

2

Relationships in Miniature

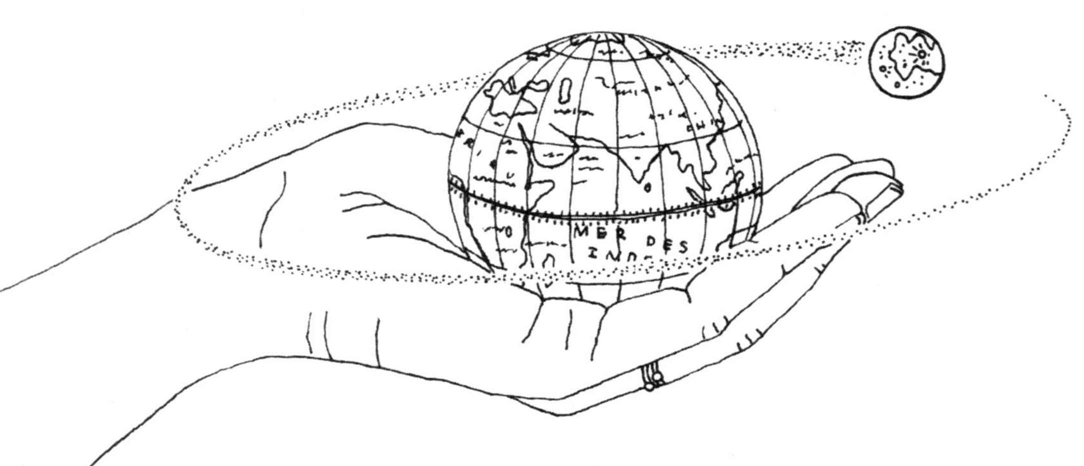

HOW DOES A GIFT EMBODY AND NURTURE MY RELATIONSHIPS?

WHAT DOES A GIFT REVEAL, AND WHEN SHOULD I TAKE IT TO HEART?

WHICH RELATIONSHIPS WOULD I LIKE TO GIFT TOWARD, AND HOW SO?

Under the microscope, I found that snowflakes were miracles of beauty; and it seemed a shame that this beauty should not be seen and appreciated by others. Every crystal was a masterpiece of design and no one design was ever repeated. When a snowflake melted, that design was forever lost. Just that much beauty was gone, without leaving any record behind.

—WILSON "SNOWFLAKE" BENTLEY, 1925

Life-Size Love

Denise tells me there wasn't a lot of money growing up in small-town Iowa in the 1970s, but she was rich in other ways, mostly related to her family. For four generations, family members had been tossing good, old things up into the attic. Why throw away a perfectly good chair, button, or toy when it might come in handy someday? When Denise got into Barbies as a child, her mom, Linda, pulled down her own childhood stash from the attic. She let Denise turn their dining room into a dedicated Barbie haven. Denise rarely had the hot new release from the stores like some of the other kids at school, but she had cool vintage accessories no one else did, including her mom's old foldout Barbie Goes to College playset. Her mom would sometimes play along, joining her with a Barbie in the "dorm room" or the "soda shop."

Leading up to Denise's fifth Christmas, a large, wrapped box appeared under the tree with her name on it. *It must be something grand*, she thought, so she started to make guesses. Linda was a single mom, age twenty-three, with a $3.85-per-hour job at a farming equipment factory. She had splurged so Santa could bring Denise one new store-bought Barbie so her daughter wouldn't think Santa loved her less than the other kids, but the gift from Mom would need to be homemade. She worried, *Would it be good enough with all of Denise's grandiose guesses of what this present could be?*

When Christmas morning came, Denise eagerly opened the box, sank her hand into a sea of packing peanuts, and pulled a tiny, gift-wrapped bundle to the surface. And another. And another. One by one, she unwrapped them to find a whole series of new Barbie clothes, including a cheerleading outfit, a dress, and a tuxedo for Ken, complete with bow tie and ruffle-edged shirt. There was even a formal gown with a glittery green halter, like the one she'd shown her mom in the catalog a few months before. Denise was over the moon about all these new garments to play with. Charmingly, some of the clothes' details didn't match the pictures in the Barbie catalog. Denise noticed that, unlike the "M" for Mattel on the store-bought ones, the cheerleading outfit had an "S" for Denise's school, Sentral, stitched across the front.

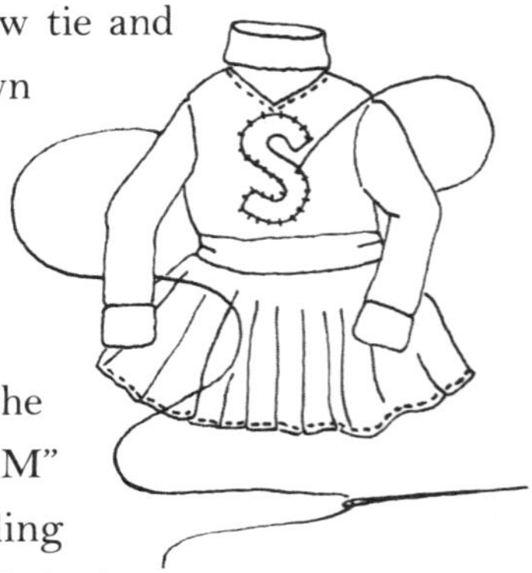

This is the kind of beautiful extravagance possible when *making* and *making do* are fused. Denise remembers lacking for nothing. Doing more with less had been her family's MO for generations. Want something? Make it!

Decades later, the Barbie clothes gift popped up in conversation among family members at the Thanksgiving table. Denise declared that it was hands down the best gift she had ever received. Each little one-of-a-kind garment created *just for her* made her feel extremely special. Soon enough, tears started running down her mom's cheeks. Listening to her grown-up daughter at the table, Linda realized that while she had been feeling inadequate, her daughter had been feeling supremely loved. This gift, this mother-daughter relationship in miniature, is a touchstone of the love between them.

Little Worlds

A gift is a relationship in miniature, a microcosm of a whole, complex system. And a "microcosm" is a situation in a nutshell—an encapsulation of the characteristic qualities or features of something much larger. A tabletop solar system model works like this, as does a dollhouse. Something about a situation becoming smaller makes it feel stronger, like boiling down a whole pot of apples to a thick, sweet apple butter. Just a teaspoon on your tongue and you're back in the orchard. The miniature conjures the whole; it concentrates our attention. The word *microcosm* traces back to the Greek *kosmos*—"order" or "world." A microcosm is essentially a "little world," and so is a gift.

It is impossible to make a miniature version of something without simplifying it. In the distillation process, much must be left out. A well-crafted microcosm is one that preserves the essence and emphasizes the most salient qualities. A skilled maker of miniatures chooses wisely as they work to ensure that the smaller version retains the truth of a situation, exemplifying the reality of the corresponding world beyond the nutshell. Like a core sample of earth, a cross section of an ancient redwood, or a single seed, a good mini is an excerpt that says it all. Therein lies its potency.

The gift that miniaturizes your relationship can still be physically large, of course; it can be the size of a whole town and adjacent forest! Grandparents Sharon and Sam organize a special project for their grandchildren during the winter holiday every year instead of showering them with presents. When I spoke with Sharon, they were well on their way to building a "bug hotel" in

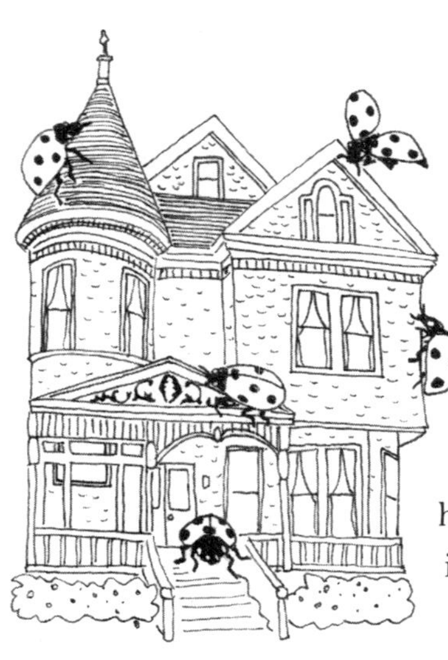

the yard of the bed-and-breakfast they run out of a big old Victorian in Arcata, California. This B&B for bugs embodies the notion that we can happily coexist with our insect neighbors. Sharon and Sam live in the same town as their grandchildren, so this gift involves dozens of walks together around town and on forest trails to collect materials. It gives them a fun treasure hunt all winter long, a reason to get excited about scouting for twigs. Sharon told me a grandchild will identify a small stick with potential, show it to her, and ask, "Do you think the bugs will like this one?"

The bug B&B doesn't just miniaturize a human-scale B&B. Most importantly, it condenses some of the key qualities of their whole grandparent-grandchildren relationship. The miniaturization process preserves its essence—quality time together, nature appreciation, health, curiosity, play, building, community—and displays it in a memorable form that celebrates and solidifies the family culture. We might dream up a gift as good as this by reflecting on the key qualities of our gift relationship, bringing them close together where we can see them all at once, and then getting creative with what we have gathered. We can ask: *What remarkable gift—thing, activity, words or combination thereof—can reference and further activate these qualities?*

Get a Bird's-Eye View

A gift offers a perspective on a relationship. Like a globe on a desk, a gift is intimacy and distance at once—something within reach that offers a bird's-eye view. A gift invites us to take a reflective step back. A whole relationship becomes palpable, activated by information and emotions.

Like a map, a meaningful gift is orienting: *We are here.* It might even reveal: *You think we are here, but I am way over there.* Sometimes the tone is more invitational: *Would it be fun if I joined you over there for a bit? Would you prefer coming my way? Is there somewhere midway we can meet?* I daydream about gifts being so aligned with our thoughts and feelings—about each other, as well as ourselves—that we can count on them to show us the truth of our lives, where we are and where we want to go.

Years ago, one month into a romance with a sweet man named Dan, I found myself daydreaming about a cookie I'd never eaten or even seen. Soon enough, I was sketching this dream cookie in my notebook, adding dimensions and color specifications. You see, Dan loves games, I love tiny things, and we both have a sweet tooth. It wasn't just a cookie I was sketching; it was a tiny game of checkers. The cookie itself was a two-inch-by-three-inch rectangle covered in white icing. The game board in the center was a grid of black and red iced squares. And the game pieces? Sixteen red and black disk-shaped cupcake sprinkles. Soon enough, we were playing at my dining table. I provided tweezers to move the itty-bitty pieces. When I proclaimed "King me!" Dan had to balance a sprinkle on top of another sprinkle to make a powerful king. Dan's delight and gratitude were obvious from his huge smile. Green flag—let's go!

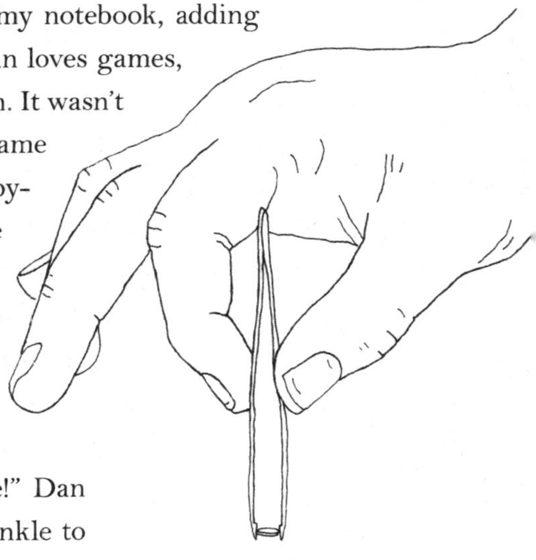

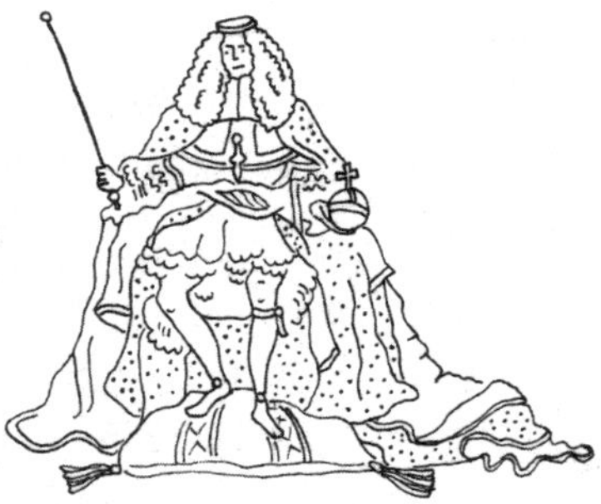

The spark to dream up this gift had been Dan's frequent, and cute, reminders that our one-month anniversary was approaching. I could tell he was eager to mark the moment, so I tried to meet him there. I commissioned the cookie from a wonderful local baker to ensure that it was aesthetically exquisite and easy to play on.

So. Dan loves games, his robot vacuum cleaner, and takeout. I love forest trails, a real broom, and home cooking. Dan does not like sweaters because they are itchy; I am a devoted knitter who wished I could knit for him. Despite our differences, we made a good run of it. We found this checkers game cookie in the sweet spot of overlap in the middle of the Venn diagram of *us.* We could meet in the middle, literally sharing space and time, even when the middle wasn't the same ground, metaphorically speaking. People don't need to be on the same page about everything. They just need to enjoy spending time together so that they might share something—a pot of tea, a swimming hole, a bed, a good laugh. When it comes to gift-giving, the most important choice isn't choosing a gift. It is choosing the *relationship*, and truly opting in to showing up, again and again.

The edible game of checkers revealed: *There is enough here, at least to keep going.* Years later, Dan told me that he came away from our whimsical game inspired to figure out how to be worthy of my gift. On game night, he thought to himself something like, *Oh boy, this is something really extraordinary, and I need to be extraordinary for this.* Dan could have just walked away with the sense that "she made this cool thing for me. I'm awesome." Instead, he paused, took it all in, and chose to see it as a growth opportunity. He felt the momentum in my gift and wanted it to work some more magic, to keep going.

When dreaming up a gift, I try to align the scale and emotional intensity of the gesture appropriately with the relationship. The checkers cookie was light enough of a gift for having been together for only a month, but significant enough to say *I really like you.* I had upped the ante, but not by too much. Even if the cookie had been "too much" for him—too much generosity, too much vulnerability, too much excitement—that would have been okay. Yes, disappointing, but not a failure—just helpful information. If the gift was too much for him, then *I* was too much for him, and I would rather be with someone who thinks I am just the right amount.

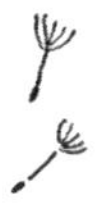

One good gift can inspire another. By the time my fortieth birthday rolled around, Dan had whipped up a present. He built me an app, from scratch, which blew my mind because I have no clue how to code. We'd been playing a lot of the word game Boggle at the breakfast table, so he made a version for on-the-go gameplay and installed it on my phone on my birthday. I am guessing an official Boggle app already exists, but holy cow, *he made one*—and mine was called *Bogglea*, a portmanteau. On my gift version of Boggle, the letters all faced the same direction on my screen, as opposed to the scramble of cubes in the tabletop game. Dan said that while designing it, he pictured us sitting side by side, leaning in close with all the letters legible to both of us. *Hot damn.* What a good nerd. The "little world" I peeked into by way of this gift was one in which Dan and I could be great playmates, keeping each other engaged, and the relationship enriched, by small wonders we dreamed up and made real. I took it as a very good sign.

Taking Gifts Seriously

I am much less interested in whether a gift is "good" or "bad" than I am in the question, *Is it interesting?* A litmus test, an experiment, an invitation, or even a wake-up call, a gift is one of the chances we get to invest in and improve our relationships. A gift is an opportunity to take stock, to savor, to wonder: *What is the nature of our connection? What have we been through together? Where are we going? Where might we choose to go if we are intentional about it?*

A librarian in New York City named Ashley told me a wonderful story of a gift that lead to personal growth. The bird's-eye view the gift offered clarified her feelings about the fellow she had been dating for a few months. Christmas was nearing. Ashley had been trying to "keep it casual," as the relationship was new, and he, Eddie, was fresh out of a marriage. Cooking new recipes and mixing cocktails at home was a big part of their courtship, so for this gift, Ashley got the idea of creating a namesake drink for him, a play on the ones at bars named after famous people. She included the ingredients Eddie would need to make it, but the main gift was a recipe card she designed with an art deco border for a speakeasy vibe.

Ashley's custom cocktail was a spin on Eddie's favorite drink, the French 75. The recipe card was playfully personalized and satisfyingly specific: one part surprise, two parts of the best feeling in the world, two parts laughter, sweetness, garnish with a candied citrus wheel if you're feeling fancy. She deciphered each ingredient on the card. The "surprise" was yuzu juice (because he had told her how much he loved traveling in Japan). The "best feeling in the world" was the best gin in the world, Monkey 47 (because he had once told her that being with her was the best feeling in the world). "Laughter" was for the sparkles of Prosecco. "Sweetness" was for agave nectar (because he is sweet, and they are sweet together). The garnish was just for fun.

At the bestowal, Ashley tried to play it cool: "I got you a little something." In truth, she was nervous and feeling vulnerable. To her relief, Eddie loved the gift. He was also stunned by the thoughtfulness. The gift caught them both by surprise, but in a good way: *Here we are!* Reflecting afterward, Ashley realized the gift essentially said "I love you" to him without literally saying it. She hadn't realized how strong her feelings had become until she witnessed herself giving him such a heartfelt gift. Meanwhile, Eddie put the recipe in a place of honor in his kitchen and started making his namesake cocktail for friends when they came over, telling them all about his amazing new girlfriend. Neither of them had said the three words aloud yet, but even their friends all knew they felt them. The gift became a turning point, a moment of mutual insight that led them to switch gears into the serious relationship mode they both truly wanted. Before too long, they were expecting a baby, and it would be mocktails for Ashley for a while.

Gift-giving and receiving is complex enough and capacious enough to become a significant personal practice, maybe even a spiritual one. Every gift can be a chance to check in with ourselves, to challenge our assumptions, and to ask questions about who we want to be in our relationships. The self-awareness a gift invites is a great prompt for a journal, for a brainstorm, for coffee dates with friends, for processing in a therapy session, or for a walk. The inspiration to give a gift can draw our attention to the fact that a particular person is important to us or starting to become so. As the recipient, when we savor a gift, it might mean the same. At every phase, there's something to notice. Instead of just rushing off to the next thing, we can pause and reflect. If we take it play-by-play and infuse the process with commentary and curiosity, we will see more. We can be here now, we can portal to the past, and we can envision futures we want to work toward.

A gift that doesn't go over well can still be an accurate little world, a truth-teller offering helpful information. When artist Leah Rosenberg was a high schooler in Saskatoon, she received the gift of her grandmother's vintage Jell-O mold and had fun with it in the kitchen. The young aspiring artist took a molded creation—salmon mousse garnished with "roses" sculpted from carrots—to a high school potluck and was then crushed when no one paid it any attention. Not a bite. It just jiggled there while the partygoers danced and drank. This was the moment Leah realized the importance of finding a receptive audience, finding her people in the world, and reading the room before she was even in it. The dish wasn't well received, but it was *good* for Leah to learn this about both art and herself. The gift was still a microcosm, clarifying reality. In this light, we can see that her "failed" gift was actually a huge success, ushering in an expansion of her horizons. These days, Leah's home base is San Francisco, and she creates her artworks all over North America. I would drop everything for one of her gorgeous desserts.

A gift can reveal the truth of a relationship; it can also obscure it. In relationships that are on the rocks, sometimes people use a gift to avoid doing the emotional labor that the relationship is calling for. They try to love someone with a special object or thoughtful gesture rather than doing the work of improving the relationship itself. No gift of any form—things, words, experiences—can make an unhealthy or unhappy relationship suddenly work. Such a gift is eclipsed by its context. A gesture of love that feels confusing, empty, or incongruous with one's experience of a relationship as a whole *might be* (but is certainly not necessarily) a palpable reflection of a relationship needing attention, or perhaps evolving into a new phase. If we can get a bird's-eye view, though, a gift that hides the truth might show it to us after all, if we're ready to see it.

So yes, let's take a gift seriously when it has something important to show us. Along the way, however, let's remember: Not every gift must move mountains. Each gift has its place and purpose. We don't need to create—or search for—a "big wow" in every gift for it to be a meaningful microcosm of a relationship. The *aha!* facilitated by Ashley's cocktail recipe bolstered a turning point; the bug B&B simply maintained a grandparent-grandchild bond that was already strong. It cheered, *Let's keep it up!*

Taking Gifts Lightly

It is important not to mistake a mini for the real thing: the actual, real live relationship. Any gift, even a really good one, is not the full story, a perfect replica in miniature. Not every gift is put together with thought and skill. So before we all go getting our hearts broken because we are expecting the world from a gift, let's keep in mind that giving great gifts doesn't come naturally to everyone, especially in a consumeristic culture. A gift that doesn't seem to carry a lot of significance doesn't always mean the corresponding relationship is also lacking in significance. The same goes for a gift in which the meaning feels off. I spoke with a couple in Michigan who had a gift gaffe in the early days of their marriage. A communication mix-up resulted in the bestowal of an unwanted blender from husband to wife, along with some hurt feelings. But they were resilient; they learned to love each other better. Decades later, the same husband gave his wife an amazing keepsake "book" for her fiftieth birthday, an online, animated world she could explore like a video game, sprinkled with personal notes from friends and family. She swooned and cried happy tears. As time went on, their gifts became better-crafted microcosms, more accurate expressions of their happy marriage.

While some gifts deserve to be taken seriously, there are many others that do not call for such weighty consideration. As such, it can be wise to sometimes not read too much into a gift. Maybe the giver is overwhelmed at work right now and had to choose something in a rush. Maybe their main "love language" isn't gifts. Maybe they're sick of consumerism and don't realize they can give gifts that don't come from stores. Or perhaps you are so incredibly important to them that they are frozen in fear that they won't come up with something awesome enough, so they flounder. Someone who loves you can misstep. We can be generous with each other as we learn to pack the real-deal love we feel into the gifts we give. I try to be humble in my giving and gracious in my receiving. Sometimes it really is just the thought that counts.

When people don't know us very well, they might try to give us something beyond the carrying capacity of the relationship, which can be off-putting even if they have the best of intentions. In these cases, the gift condenses the truth of the relationship by calling attention to the lack of familiarity or intimacy between the people involved. Oops! When a gift does not go over well, I think it is only worth taking it to heart if the gift reveals something truly problematic about the relationship and, furthermore, only if the relationship is worth the energy and emotional labor required to sort it out.

Thankfully, all gifts—wanted or unwanted—can be interesting, informative, and catalyzing if we meet them with curiosity and creativity. A gift is an opportunity to get to know each other better, or at least to get to know ourselves better. We can tap into our own agency and respond with joy, humor, tears, or whatever might meet the moment well. With a creative regift, for example, a recipient can redirect an unwanted gift from one relationship to enrich *another* relationship. A friend of mine who is nonbinary once received a tube of red lipstick from their aunt who, quite thoughtfully, remembered saying no to my friend when they had asked for something similar as a child, decades before. The aunt was aiming to please, but she did not understand that my friend had grown up into someone who no longer wanted such a feminine item, especially not as a gift. At the time, my friend didn't want to explain their gender identity to their aunt, so they gracefully accepted the gift and then let it go. Indeed, they literally kept the gift moving. My friend passed the lipstick along to another friend where the meaning was a match, a trans woman who was happy to have it. In the relational context of the regift, the lipstick had been transformed. It was not just a great shade of red but a gesture of solidarity. The gift found its way home.

A Gift's Center of Gravity

In a cringeworthy scene in *The Simpsons,* the whole family is dressed up, celebrating Marge's birthday at a fancy restaurant. At the end of the meal, Homer declares, "Your mother hasn't opened *my* present yet," cues the singing waiters, and hands a wrapped present across the table. A bowling ball immediately slips out the bottom and smashes the birthday cake in front of Marge. The problem is transparent from everybody's facial expression except that of Homer, who swoons over the gift, almost mesmerized: "Beauty, isn't she?" Marge is livid, and immediately snaps, "Well, it's hard for me to judge, since I've never bowled in my life!" Homer still doesn't get it, or, worse, maybe he does: "Well, if you don't want it, I know someone who does." The metaphorical icing on the cake is that the bowling ball is already engraved, "HOMER."

This gift revolves around Homer, and blatantly. He misses Marge completely as he steals the show. Yes, the scene is pure Homer, and perfect *Simpsons* humor. But after I laugh, I can't help but feel for Marge. When I put myself in her shoes, I long for Homer to truly see me, not just himself. I want my relationship to feel more balanced, for us to meet in the middle. Marge doesn't play along. With her outburst at the table, Marge takes her birthday back. She lets us know that she matters too, thank you very much. She claims her energetic sovereignty, her worthiness as a person with desires of her own. As we gather a gift (or receive one), we can help the gift meet a moment well by asking: *Who does this gift revolve around, and why? Where do I want this gift's center of gravity to be located?*

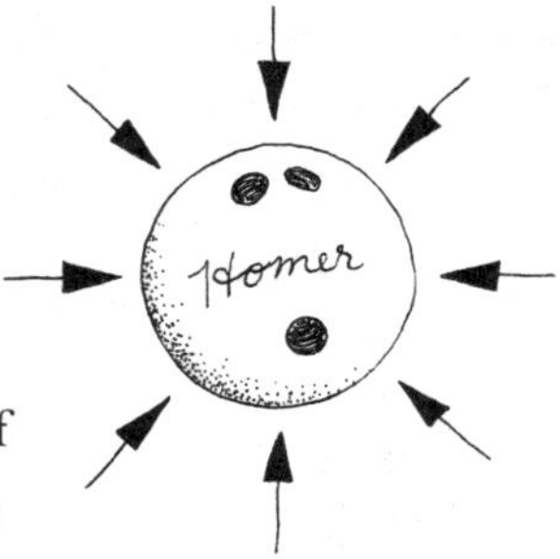

I learned a cool thing about Pluto from a friend. It makes me less sad about Pluto's demotion from being an official planet. Poor Pluto. But not really, because it turns out Pluto has a sweetie, a moon named Charon. The scientific term for their relationship is a *double planetary system* because Charon doesn't orbit Pluto quite like moons typically do. Charon has enough mass to tug on Pluto too. They are actually both attending to a point in between them as they revolve around each other, like two people doing a do-si-do. We too can do it like Pluto and Charon. We can share the center and spin around each other. It is not a matter of deciding *who* a gift should revolve around, but *who* the center of gravity should be closer to as we orbit each other. Since the primary benefit of a gift is for the recipient, it will generally be best positioned closer to them. We can set an intention from the start; we can also keep in mind that the center of gravity might evolve as our offering takes on a life of its own.

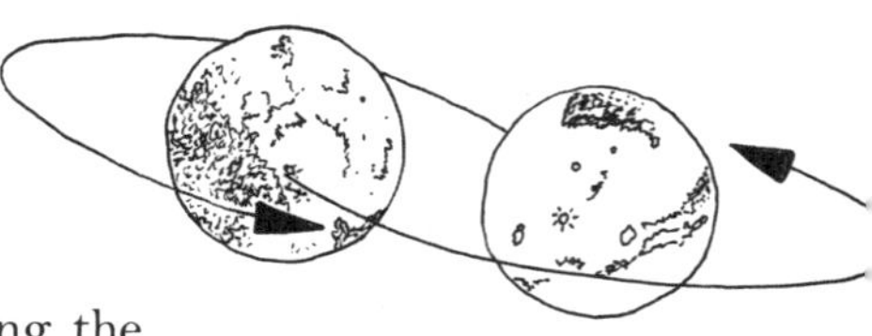

The key to good gift-giving is keeping the *relationship* in mind when composing the gift. Who are you *together*? What can *only you* give to *only them*? The words of professor of religion James P. Carse resonate: "I am not touched by an other when the distance between us is reduced to zero. I am touched only if I respond from my own center—that is, spontaneously, originally. But you do not touch me except from your own center, out of your own genius. Touching is always reciprocal."[1] In other words, let's be each other's moons.

Toddlers are some of my favorite geniuses. It is too soon for them to be anything but their authentic selves. My friend Catherine's two-year-old, Jonas, gave her a box of fancy chocolates for Mother's Day, with the help of Dad, of course. My friend described them to me as gorgeous little works of art. A dozen sweet gems tucked into crimped paper cups, each one a unique flavor and aesthetic: tarragon grapefruit with a single sliver of candied peel on top, a faceted gem molded around a single roasted hazelnut, lemon verbena with a delicate drizzle of white chocolate in a leaf pattern. Apparently, her toddler agreed about the art part. When they opened the box together to admire the chocolates, he decided they were too special to eat. Instead, he started to carry the chocolates around the house, one at a time in their little paper cups.

It became an activity: Get out the box, carefully unpack all the pieces, admire them together, carry one around for a while, carefully put it back into the box for the next time. Toddler fingerprints started to decorate the chocolate surfaces as the original sheen faded. But mother and son together came to understand that these were for savoring, not gobbling up. Until one day when Jonas was carrying one of his favorites around the house—the one with the honeycomb pattern—and out of the corner of her eye, his mom saw him suddenly pop the whole thing into his mouth! She had a good chuckle. What my friend loved about this, she told me, was that it was a moment of autonomy for him. Jonas eating the chocolate on his own was a small assertion of independence, his own unique personhood beginning to emerge. I love how my friend let her two-year-old just *do his thing*. She let the gift be *from* him, *to* her, but *for* both of them. Even though Mom was the recipient, the center of gravity staying in the middle or even a little closer to the toddler makes sense for the nature of this phase of their parent-child relationship, which is, by necessity, focused on the care of the child who is dependent. Eventually the center of gravity shifted back to Catherine. At long last, she got to eat the chocolates, fingerprints and all.

Catherine told me that she considers everything she does with her son to be an opportunity "to practice the important things of the world." This is a family that values curiosity, exploration, and joy, qualities miniaturized by the way they enjoyed the gift together. When she modeled these values with how she received her Mother's Day chocolates, her toddler responded in kind. In fact, he took the idea and ran with it, turning into a guardian of specialness.

The best position for a gift's shared center of gravity depends on the relationship, occasion, and other factors. Thinking back to Ashley's cocktail recipe for her sweetie, we can find the intended center of gravity very close to the middle of the space between giver and receiver, which is appropriate for adults falling in love. It began perhaps a nudge closer to the recipient, being based on his favorite cocktail. As the gift evolved, though, the moondance kicked in and the point in between them oscillated as Ashley had her big insight, and then so did he. A gift is kind of like a windup toy. We crank it up, release it, and then watch it go!

Self-Gifts as Self-Love

A gift can also miniaturize another near-and-dear relationship: the one we have with ourselves. Sometimes, it is good to be our own moon. Sure, people buy themselves flowers or treat themselves to a cookie, or even a vacation. But how often do people sink the same thoughtfulness into a self-gift that they would drum up for someone else they love dearly? I recall my therapist's wise words: "The most important relationship of our lives is the one we have with ourselves." And another gem from her: "*We* are the company we keep, so keep good company." So true! Yet it is so easy to forget that we companion ourselves through every moment of our lives. A good self-gift is not selfish; it is a powerful way to take care of ourselves.

Rachel here in Oakland puts this wisdom into action when she buys earrings as a gift to her inner child as part of healing her past. These aren't just any earrings; they are the most playful, colorful, flamboyant earrings I have ever seen. When she was a teenager, Rachel's general shyness and her self-consciousness about her body led her to avoid attention. Privately loving bold clothing and accessories, she would occasionally buy something she adored, but then only wear it alone in her bedroom. As Rachel got older, she grieved the fact that she had withheld her true self and missed out on much social connection while hiding in the shadows as a kid. These days, she has a rich social life. With each new pair of earrings, Rachel sends another little dose of love back in time. Her inner child being happier lets her grown-up self be so too.

I try to follow bell hooks's advice: "One of the best guides to how to be self-loving is to give ourselves the love we are often dreaming about receiving from others."[2] Every year on my birthday, I write a long greeting card to my future self, reflecting on the past year and setting intentions for the next one. Before I write it, I open and reflect upon the card I wrote on my previous birthday. *Happy birthday to me!*

Expanding Our Circles of Care

Gifts to our nearest and dearest, including ourselves, are especially poignant reminders of what is possible—how deep we can go in aligning our gifts with the richness of our closest relationships. Good gifts aren't just for people we know well, though. If our gift recipient is an acquaintance or distant family member, we can still enrich the spaces between us by giving something generic but lovely, such as a jar of jam or a candle, instead of something personal and particular, such as a book, perfume, or clothing. This increases the chances of success and lowers the chances of mismatch or even offense. You can still sink your heart into it. My aunt jars up a huge pot of olallieberry jam in her kitchen every year, picking the berries herself at a local u-pick farm and passing out the jars to all sorts of folks: friends, family, colleagues, neighbors, her children's teachers. But if you're pressed for time, or not particularly crafty, or if you need tons of gifts because you're giving them to, say, your whole pickup soccer team, just grab a bag of something fun at the market, like cute little tangerines or bite-size chocolates. (I'm partial to the ones that are foil-wrapped to look like ladybugs.) A little can go a long way.

In addition to our nearest and dearest, we can give gifts to neighbors, co-workers, strangers, organizations, ancestors, and yet-to-be-born generations. We can give to the more-than-human world: landscapes, rivers, plants, and animals. We can let other beings have mass—let them tug on our orbits, on our hearts—pulling us into the joyful do-si-do of interrelation that makes life worth living. A florist in Charlotte, North Carolina, coordinates the donation and delivery of hundreds of bouquets through the Valentine's Day Widow Outreach Project every year. A churchgoer who doesn't talk much hand-carves animals out of nectarine pits during the week and distributes them on Sundays. I once sewed a catnip toy for a boyfriend's cat I felt intimidated by. We can even gift toward extraterrestrials! Launched in the 1970s, NASA's Golden Records are essentially heavy-duty greeting cards being carried into interstellar space by *Voyager 1* and *Voyager 2*, offering photos, sounds, and songs from Earth in hopes of "first contact" in the millennia or more in front of us. (*Write back soon! XOXO!*)

Which is all to say, I invite us to cast a wide net in our gift-giving imaginations, to reach beyond the obvious to a broader spectrum of relations. It is not a question of whether we want to be in all these relationships. We *always already are.* The only question is whether we want to be conscious about the quality of the connection. I want to hold my relationships with care and attention, as if I have the fate of the whole world in my hands with each interaction. What an honor. What an opportunity. What a profound responsibility.

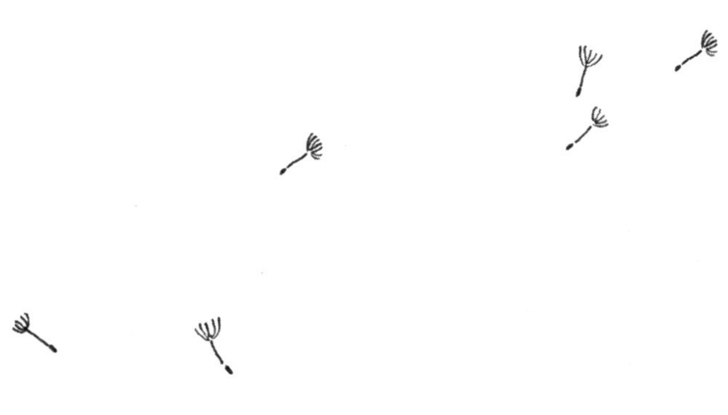

Reflect

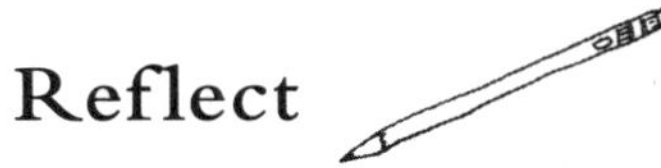

1. **Have you ever given, received, or witnessed a gift that honored both recipient and giver especially well? How was the gift something that could *only* take place in between those people?**

2. **Reflect upon a gift from your life that was worth taking seriously and another that deserved to be taken lightly. In what ways were they—or were they not—microcosms of the relationships they took place within?**

3. **Make a list of recipients you would like to honor with a gift in the next few years. Choose relationships that you want to activate and grow by way of a gift.**

4. **Design a caring gift for yourself. This gift might be directed to your inner child, your stressed self, your most private self, your best self, your future self, etc.**

3

Gift Is a Verb

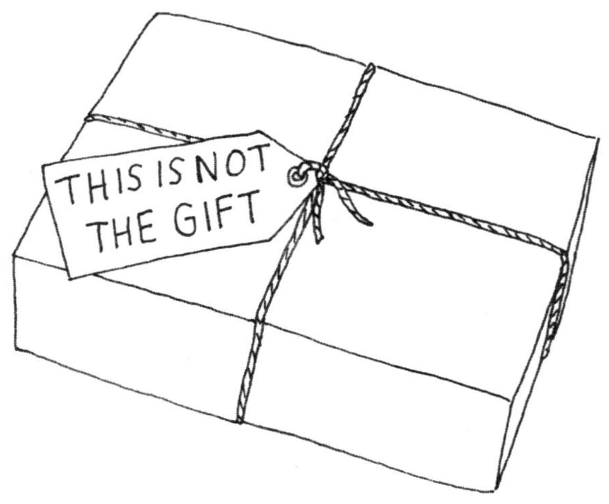

WHAT DOES MY GIFT DO?

DOES MY GIFT CARRY THE MESSAGES AND STORIES THAT I WANT IT TO?

AM I GIVING AND RECEIVING FREELY?

In the strict sense of the German word *bedingt*, we are the be-thinged, the conditioned ones.

—MARTIN HEIDEGGER, *POETRY, LANGUAGE, THOUGHT*

A Gift Is Not an Object

The idea of the gift has gotten all tangled up with the notion of the noun—the product, the object, the purchase, the possession, the box with a ribbon and a bow. A gift, though, is more *action* than object, more *process* than product, more *experience* than possession. We make a gift a *good* experience when we give from a wise heart, with real purpose.

I suggest we think of a gift primarily as a verb. To give a gift is to *do something*, and while that may involve a physical object, a gift act goes beyond the bestowal of any item. Any material aspects of a gift can be considered vessels for the flow of experience, objects-in-action. Here, I am picturing Fräulein Maria singing about her "favorite things" in *The Sound of Music*. Some of these are items one might purchase: bright copper kettles, warm woolen mittens, blue satin sashes. Others are endowments beyond possession: green meadows, raindrops on roses, wild geese that fly with the moon on their wings! I think Maria knows that flourishing is not about *having* but *doing* and *being*. Bright copper kettles lead to tea and conversation.

Warm woolen mittens allow for a walk in the snow. Not only do her favorite things lead to good times, but they comfort her in hard times. I certainly believe a brown paper package tied up with string can contain something that changes my life. Turning our attention toward what gifts of any form can *do* opens a world of possible gifts that have previously been out of imagination's range.

Prioritizing *having* can lead to a sense of so-called objects as merely passive—as things to act *upon*. An experience-based perspective helps us see that the world around us is for acting *with* and *through*. The object *as object* is a myth, and a limiting one at that. Here on Earth, it's nothing but subjects—a *communion of subjects*, in the lovely words of Thomas Berry, Catholic priest and world religions scholar. In gift-giving and in life, my hope is to keep my feet planted firmly on the ground in the company of nouns—animals, plants, minerals, artifacts, and other lively *things*—but with my eye on the *verbs*, in the ways everyone is participating.

"Doing" a Gift

When we keep *activity* in mind while choosing and designing our gifts, creative possibilities emerge. I might gift my friend a picnic with me in a park instead of (or in addition to) a beautiful picnic basket. Someone who knows me well might take me with them to the florist to get my birthday bouquet because my favorite part of a vase of flowers is getting to pick them out myself, playing with color and texture. A book can be given with a promise to read it aloud to the recipient. We can further activate any gift by building an activity—a verb—into it, such as *playing* a game, *going* to a live show, or *jumping* into a lake.

Doing a gift, as both giver and receiver, can activate many dimensions:

social, practical, kinetic, intellectual, emotional, spiritual. Sometimes, I like to go all out. Once, I got up at 4 a.m. and set out in the dark with a paper map, a box of rainbow chalk, a poem, and a plan. Spread out over a mile or so between my friend's front door and the Morcom Rose Garden here in Oakland, I drew a dozen extra-long hopscotches. Instead of numbers in the squares, I put one word in each, slowly transcribing a Mary Oliver poem titled "Dreams." Chalk arrows helped my friend find his way from the end of each colorful course (aka stanza) to the beginning of the next. I worked backward to prevent the scenario in which he discovered the hopscotch and caught up to me before I finished. But that meant I was wrapping up right in front of his house around 7 a.m., which was getting risky. I chalked "All night the dark buds of dreams open richly" and ran away! A few hours later, my friend called from the rose garden, completely blown away, feeling very special.

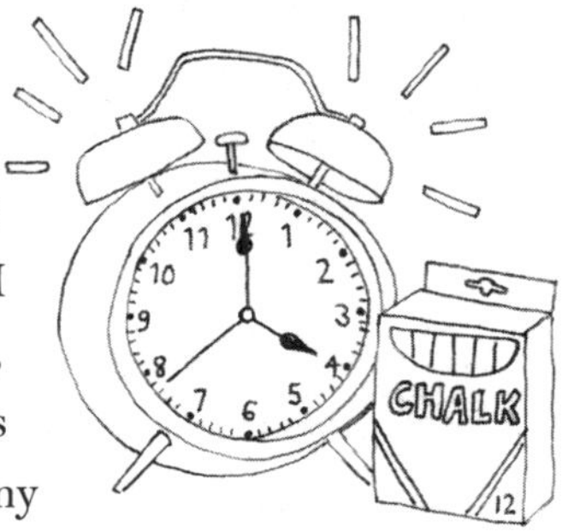

The most powerful "doing" of a gift is sometimes for the giver themselves. I remember when my friend Sarah started knitting baby sweaters and booties for her someday-children way before she was even trying to conceive. Making them at that moment in her life clarified for her the goal of becoming a mother someday and strengthened the intention that eventually led to the three babies who got to wear those sweaters. And when her children outgrew her hopeful hand-knits, Sarah kept them in play by donating them to the local "parent pantry."

I love to design elaborate gifts, like my hopscotches. Because of this natural tendency, I must sometimes remind myself that a good gift can be simple, quiet, subtle. Verbs are everywhere. Candles offer a wonderful ambiance as they flicker and warm a room. Strawberry jam promises a dozen mornings of extra-special toast. If chosen wisely, simple things can be just right. A piece of jewelry can keep someone close. Framed concert tickets can pay tribute to a shared memory. But no matter the form of the gift, I return to the verb by asking, *What can my gift do?*

Artifacts for Earthlings

The material world is alive with meaning, memory, purpose, and connection. As such, it is essential for us earthlings to keep in touch with the potential for good in our many, marvelous material cultures. Humanity's workshop is packed with creative possibilities—tools, traditions, and methods with momentum that evolved to meet their moments. We can pick up the loose ends and let the creativity of the past inform us forward. Each of us can give and receive the lively things that make sense for us. Here, I think of Robin Wall Kimmerer's Potawatomi berry bowl at the end of her book *Braiding Sweetgrass*—the wooden bowl full of forest gems with just one spoon that is ceremoniously passed around a circle of people, each berry a tiny gift from the Earth, "wrapped in red and blue" in Kimmerer's words. The bowl-in-motion is a microcosm of the way everyone is fed by the same Mother Earth, whose gifts are abundant but not bottomless, requiring reciprocity and gratitude to continue.

The offering of meaningful artifacts has been a staple of gift-giving for countless generations. These bestowals are always opportunities to envision and tinker up wonderful ways of living that are good for people and planet. When I design a gift, I draw from a personal cosmology that includes contemporary art, poetry, nature, creative reuse, and a devotion to everyday wonder. I love to pair everyday objects with meaningful rituals. So when my dear friends Justin and Ellen got married along the Navarro River under a full moon, I gave them an especially lively pair of locally made ceramic cups to mark the occasion. They were glazed in surface-of-the-moon white, and my accompanying note invited the happy couple to drink out of them on the full moon every month moving forward. As the moon waxes and wanes, the cups in their cabinet invite them to say "I do" again and again. Another family I know has a set of special napkins they received as a gift from a family friend. The napkins are embroidered with the first names of the members of their three-generation household, and an extra napkin is embroidered with "Friend." It felt so welcoming to see that word on my napkin as I sat down at their table for breakfast. The napkin keeps all of them in touch with their family value of opening their home to a larger circle.

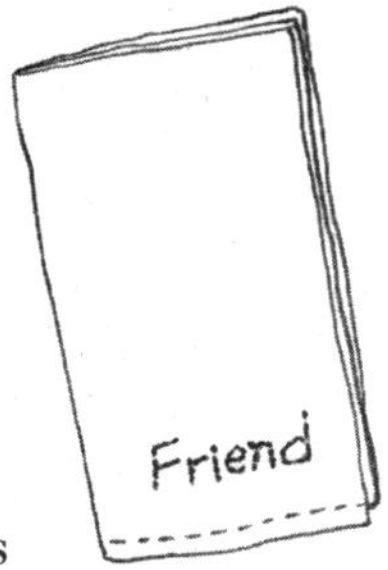

Friend

The thought of a circle growing larger brings to mind a charming conceptual artwork by Pittsburgh artist Lenka Clayton that began with a single shirt button. A gift of sorts, this object-in-action took place at a conference where Clayton coordinated an epic button swap among the attendees, a circulation of hundreds of tiny, spontaneous gifts among relative strangers. Anyone who wanted to give and receive a button would simply find the artist. She would remove a button from that person's garment, replacing it with a button that another attendee had contributed to the circle. Hundreds of people left the conference with a "new" shirt, a conversation piece that could continue to spark connection moving forward. Swifties engage in a similar web of connection when they swap homemade alphabet-bead friendship bracelets by the thousands at Taylor Swift concerts.

Remember the moment in *Indiana Jones and the Last Crusade* when Indiana tosses a handful of sand over a treacherous chasm to reveal the existence of an invisible yet perfectly walkable bridge? (If not, I highly recommend!) I think all these lovely, lively things are like that: They make the invisible visible, the truth tangible. They show us what has been here all along: deep interconnection, the invisible architecture of love through which every kind act moves.

A Gift Outlives Its Vessel

My grandparents met on the first day of junior high, courtesy of their locker assignments: No. 16 and No. 17. By senior year of high school, they were going steady and danced to "I'll Never Smile Again" at the Valentine's Day school dance. At the end of the night, my grandmother carefully folded her red, heart-shaped dance card down the middle, tore it in two, and handed half to my grandfather, saying something to the tune of "Alone, we're just half a heart, but together, the heart is whole." Just months later, my grandfather kissed his sweetheart goodbye, tucked her picture inside his pocket Bible, and went off to World War II. On the photograph, my grandmother had penned "Forget-me-not," like the flower.

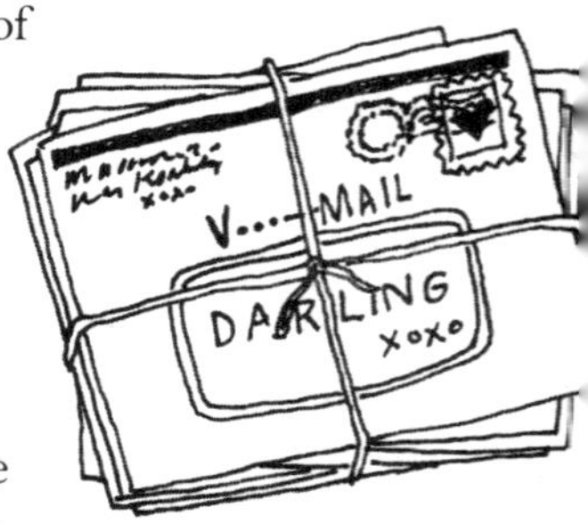

My grandmother wrote him a letter every day of the war, more than a thousand letters in all. As she wrote each one, she could not know if he was still alive. My grandfather received her letters in bundles by the dozen or more because his mailing address, a moving target, didn't get daily mail service. After reading the latest arrivals, he couldn't keep them—the lighter his pack, the better. And so he had to toss the bundles of aerogrammes into the campfire.

Before letting them go, though, my grandfather would pass them around to the other fellas in his gun crew. Not everyone had a sweetheart back home sending them tangible bits of hope, but everyone sure needed one. I imagine that even everyday details from a relative stranger must have been incredibly compelling for my grandfather's comrades, words like *grocery shopping* and *post office* stirring their hearts, providing powerful reminders of what life might be like after the war, should they make it home. Their own postwar futures beckoned. Once, the crew gathered 'round to open a box from my grandmother; inside were eighteen pairs of hand-knit socks she had made—one for each of them—to prevent frostbite.

I could only imagine how agonizing it must have been for my grandfather not to be able to keep those letters. But as my grandfather relayed this story to me, almost eighty years later, he did not appear sentimental about this. Perhaps the love letters worked more like the soldiers' chocolate or cigarette rations. Open. Enjoy what is inside. Toss the wrapper. The letters disappeared into the fire, but the love stayed with him, giving him strength and courage.

A part of me aches for there to be a dusty old box full of my grandmother's wartime letters. But an important truth about gifts is to be found in the letters' absence. The way her letters were *used up* on the battlefield shows us that the essence of a gift goes far beyond its object quality. The ephemerality of these love letters lost to history makes it clear that the true heart of this gift, and of all good gifts, is not acquisition or possession. The gift is not *used up* because it is disposable, like a paper coffee cup. Rather, it is used up because it has powered a transformation.

My grandfather survived the war. And my grandmother survived the wait. The two halves of that Valentine's Day dance card were finally reunited, and I can only imagine what an epic embrace that must have been. Her photograph was still pressed between the pages of his pocket Bible. Soon after, at their wedding, they danced to their song, Frank Sinatra crooning, "I'll never smile again, until I smile at you."

As my grandfather told me their story, I eagerly asked if he still had the photograph. I wished to hold it. Perhaps it could give me strength too. Alas, he'd lost track of it long ago. He didn't need it. He and my grandmother enjoyed the next half century together. The black-and-white image of his high school sweetheart transformed into a colorful, three-dimensional life in motion. Some gifts, the physical part anyway, get cast off like chrysalis cases. They are what gets left behind when life itself emerges.

A Gift Speaks for Itself

Regardless of whether words are part of your gift, every gift *says something.* A gift carries a story, an idea, a thought, a feeling, a question—often in wordless form.

When my friends Paul and Sam visited me from British Columbia a few years ago, they left a delightful thank-you gift for me upon their departure. During game night with them, as I popped a cheese puff into my mouth, I had mentioned that I love cheese puffs but rarely buy them. After my friends left, I found a bag of cheese puffs stashed under my pillow. Then another in a closet. And another, and another . . . It is as if the bags, as I found each one, proclaimed, "Thanks for having us" and "We had a great time" and "We'll miss you!"

The eloquence of objects was made especially apparent when a neighbor knocked on my front door and handed me a clamshell box full of dumplings, still steaming. In this case, words weren't even an option; we don't share a language. And yet, when she handed me the dumplings, I understood perfectly: "Please enjoy. I made these and am happy to share them with you." A few months before, I had assisted her in an emergency for which she had thanked me profusely at the time. As such, I sensed that the dumplings might also be saying, "Thank you again. Today, there are dumplings."

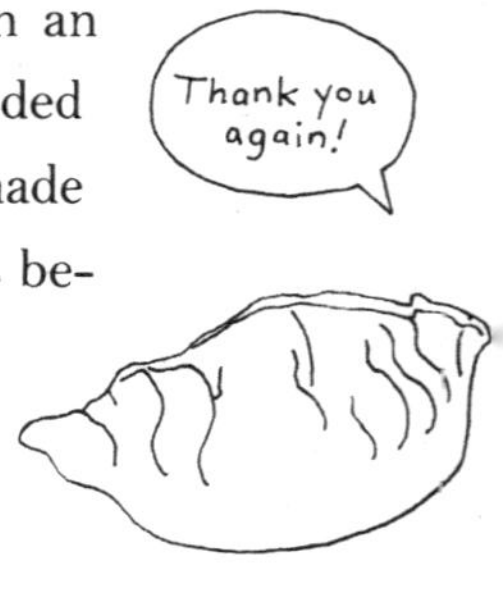

Gifts of words and experiences also carry subtext—things not said on the surface. One time after a challenging week with a boyfriend, I was looking for a way to express my commitment with more than words. He was in the habit of listening to music on YouTube, so I surprised him with a three-month premium subscription so he could listen without ads. I could tell by his face that he understood the subtext: *We're okay. We can do this. I'm still*

in. We'll still be listening together ad-free in three months. With intention and creativity, we can purposely build messages into the gifts we give. And as recipients, we can look for these messages.

By the same token, it's important to take care with whatever subtext our gift might be sending. A gift's subtext can be lovely, such as "I've been listening, and I'm trying to see the real you." But the subtext might also convey "I will be crushed if you do not like this, and as such, this gift is really all about me." Or, perhaps unconsciously, "I chose this for you because I know what is best for you." A giver might not realize their own motive. "I am giving my young son a baseball because I need my son to be good at baseball because I played in college, and I long to relive that era of my own life vicariously." The subtext might reveal a value or impose a social pressure, such as "Baby girls wear pink, not blue." I wonder how often people would change their gift idea if they could expose these types of hidden messages first and consider them before proceeding. After all, if gifts are verbs that guide relationships, we want to ensure they move us toward each other in positive ways that feel good. Unexamined intentions in gift-giving can all too easily drive us apart, so let's summon our self-awareness before we give.

True Gifts

In the pages ahead, I look at four habits that can trip us up in our gift-giving: giving gifts that mean well but don't consider impact, foisting unwanted gifts upon each other, giving with strings attached, and keeping tabs. To me, these behaviors make perfect sense in the context of a globalized industrial economy based on extraction and competition, especially when there's also an ongoing history of conquest, colonialism, and oppression. As such, gifts wrapped up in the meta-methods of competition, manipulation, fear, self-centeredness, and self-sacrifice are just par for the course. But I want to change course. I introduce some remedies here in broad strokes, and throughout the book we will continue to explore these patterns.

Purpose, on Purpose

It's the thought that counts. Yes, but it matters very much what those thoughts are and how they play out. If the point of a gift is to truly benefit someone else, then we would do well to prioritize the impact of our gift on our recipient, both by thinking it through ahead of time and by letting recipients determine whether our good intentions have landed well. Later in the book, we explore what can be done when intentions and impacts do not align. Here, I offer a preventative measure, something we can *do* to help intention align with impact. We can be sure our gift has a good, hearty *purpose,* as anchored in our imagining of what the recipient would love from us. This imaginative exercise will inevitably tug us toward the world of the recipient and help us to give something they will welcome. The point of a purpose is not to pigeonhole anyone into an outcome, but to have a reference point as we make choices about what to give and how to give it.

If someone's purpose is "cultivating closeness," a picnic will probably get them there better than a gift card or even a great book. If the purpose is "delightful escape for someone sick in bed" and you live across the country, an epic fantasy novel might be just right. If the purpose is "celebrating a friendship," then the gift would ideally reference something about the friendship that both people value. There are a thousand worthy purposes—build trust, relieve stress, express love, laugh, luxuriate, play, learn, rest, etc. As we are dreaming up our gifts, we might visualize our recipients' responses. If we know them well, this can be a good pre-check.

Giving and Receiving by Choice

Foist and *forfeit* may feel like strong words for the way most folks give gifts. Of course, people are not doing this on purpose. It is more a matter of social habit. When a gift is given, there is an assumption that the recipient will accept it; they will pretend to like it if need be and deal with it later if they don't. I wonder if there could be a mode of giving and receiving that feels less presumptuous, something to prevent undesired gifts from becoming a burden to recipients as well as the Earth. We'll explore specific strategies throughout, but here, the big-picture remedy I see is to swap in a model of *consent* for all the presumption, pressure, and awkwardness. In a gift culture of mutual consent, we would give from a posture of *proposal* and receive from a posture of *consideration.*

And so, what if we *proposed* a gift as an offering that may or may not be accepted, instead of *presuming* a recipient is somehow bound to take what was chosen for them? What if the spirit of a bestowal was less statement or command, and more question or curiosity? Instead of "This is for you," it could be "Is this for you?" For if a gift is a freewill offering, there should be just as much freewill in the receiving.

Receivers, in turn, can ask, "Is this for me?" Since ultimately what is truly for them must be determined from within, it is perfectly appropriate for them to *consider* an offering. In the consent paradigm, receivers feel free to respond authentically because their givers will accept and respect their choices. Similarly, givers can give freely because their recipients have not pressured them into it. Recipients must take care not to try to pry gifts out of people due to a sense of entitlement, anxiety, or otherwise. Neither true gifts nor true love can be wheedled out of someone. Love is always a choice, and healthy relationships honor everyone's ability to choose.

Givers can increase the chances of a yes in response to a genuine offer in lots of ways. Most of them come down to some form of *asking*—ahead of time, upon bestowal, or after. Ingrid Fetell Lee, the author of *Joyful*, told me that she wanted to give her father a bird feeder like the one she had been enjoying out her own window, but she didn't want to burden him with it if it wasn't quite right. She asked him if he wanted one before buying it for him, to be sure the installation and maintenance involved would be welcome. He said yes, and their two bird feeders led to a lively father-daughter back-and-forth of delightful photos and banter about bird sightings out their windows, connecting them across many miles. A joyful gift, indeed!

The question of whether a recipient wants a gift is actually two questions in one. To start, *Do you want this gift?* But also more generally, *Do you want to be in relationship with me?* A receiver who isn't jazzed about the gift itself but wants to say some sort of yes to the relationship—to the giver—can find creative ways to keep the spirit of the gift alive. We'll pick up this thread in chapter 11.

With (Good) Strings Attached

The next unhelpful habit is one I'm sure we're all familiar with: giving *with strings attached.* Strings of some sort are inevitable, a given. Humans need each other to survive and thrive, to do anything or be anything at all. It is the nature and quality of the strings connecting people that can become a problem. The trick is to *need* each other without *using* each other to get our needs met. Whenever the strings that bind me devolve into codependence, manipulation, or pressure against my own will and well-being, I'm miserable. I want to cut and run, to be left alone. But there are other, lovelier kinds of strings I genuinely want to be caught up in, such as the strong and stretchy threads of a mutually flourishing interdependence. Less like a line and hook, and more like string games between children's fingers, back and forth, with pleasure! I want to free myself from the harmful strings but tangle myself up in the ones that are nourishing and supportive.

I have heard unfortunate stories of parents paying for weddings and then feeling entitled to control the guest list and other details. That is not a gift; it is a purchase motivated by the parents' own desires, not those of their recipients. It's especially upsetting when such a deal is not clear up front; the couple getting married might mistake the gesture as a true gift and then succumb to the pressure of the "gift" imposing demands on them that go against their wishes for their own wedding. In another case, a nephew knew a "free" car from his uncle would come with the expectation of running errands for him for years to come. The nephew said no thank you. Seneca put it plainly, and I think the advice still stands: "Don't ruin a gift by making it into a loan."[1]

In contrast, when artist Michael Swaine wheeled his clothes-mending cart into the Tenderloin neighborhood of San Francisco, he was giving freely to his recipients—some of them unhoused, living in a rough part of the city. On the fifteenth of every month, rain or shine, for fifteen years, Swaine would set up his salvaged antique treadle sewing machine and mend people's clothes for free. He expected nothing in return. He did, however, enjoy the conversations prompted by the whole setup, which included his own quickness to be curious about others. As he mended one man's garment, the man told him, "You are the only one who listens to me." Swaine reflected to me, "This project changed who I am, these moments of amazing humanity. It was an honor for me to sit there." I imagine the artist was welcomed into the Tenderloin because his gift did not feel like charity, which oftentimes undermines a recipient's dignity via a sense that the giver has more, or is better. If we find ourselves giving or receiving in a situation involving a difference in economic status, we can invite mutual sharing and remember that everyone brings something meaningful to the encounter. Giving a gift freely doesn't mean the giver cannot also benefit from whatever happens next. The difference is in the expectation. Any benefit is pure bonus—not the repaying of a debt but a fresh offering, a new gift of its own, a result of generosity's instinct to overflow.

The spirit and skillfulness with which we weave the threads between us matter greatly. Harvard professor Robert Waldinger, the director of the longest running study of adult well-being, observes that the key to a good life is "Being engaged in things that you care about with people who you care about."[2] That sounds about right to me. Giving freely doesn't mean *no* strings; it means *good* strings, the beautiful bonds of healthy attachment and consenting connection.

It becomes a bit easier to *need* each other without *using* each other if everyone keeps in touch with their own sense of inherent self-worth as well as a sense that everyone else is also unconditionally worthy. If we do not try to outsource our own sense of worthiness to others as we give and receive—looking for them to validate our very existence—this removes a lot of pressure. For givers, a sense of worthiness provides a sturdy enough center from which to make offers—to make courageous, creative proposals for others to honestly consider. This giver can give freely because they know they are already whole, regardless of how the receiver responds to their offering. A baseline of worthiness supports emotional sovereignty for receivers too, washing away anxiety around whether other people are going to swoop in and make them feel whole.

Worthiness weaves beautiful, strong baskets from which each of us can give and receive with integrity while respecting the will and well-being of others. It also helps us see that it is not just okay to meet some of our own needs but necessary and beautiful.

Leave the Tab Open

This for that. Tit for tat. The last unhelpful mindset is *keeping tabs*, or subjecting our gift lives to the logic of market exchange. As soon as gifts are thought of as debts to be repaid, the spirit of the gift is gone. If someone is in *transaction* mode instead of *offering* mode—if the gift is *owed* rather than *bestowed*—they are robbing both giver and receiver of the positive social connections that might have otherwise been activated between them.

Keeping tabs sucks the life force out of gifts and replaces it with the weak ties of the marketplace, in which accounts are settled immediately because people don't know if they can trust each other. I suspect the impulse to settle up is a protective measure. Negative past experiences might tempt us to conclude that self-reliance is safer than connection. But when receiving a gift merely feels like a debt is being repaid or created, there's little room for generosity or gratitude. We're too busy calculating. The emotional trajectory is a closed circuit of obligation, even guilt.

To be sure, when a good gift is offered and accepted freely, there is indeed an imbalance, a sense that some sort of equilibrium has been disrupted. We can feel it, and I think we can trust our senses. Here though, where the marketplace wants us to settle up and say goodbye, a good gift wants us to stay, and to stay open—to feel the momentum of love shifting toward us and to surrender to the sense of "extra" that gifts are all about. When we intentionally leave the tab open, we keep the party going. We affirm that we want the relationship to continue and the gift to keep giving.[3] With love, we accept the loose end.

In our giving and receiving, I invite us to practice replacing *obligation* with *inspiration*. Let's act not out of "should," but "want to." If we aren't busy tracking who owes whom, or distracted by other people's expectations of us, we are more available to listen to our hearts and to give when we are genuinely moved to do so. In the delicate dance of interdependence I am reaching toward, a gift doesn't start with a desire to rid oneself of the feelings of guilt and inadequacy that debt organizes. Nor does it begin with the obligatoriness of much calendar-based gift-giving, the routine pressures to purchase gifts for occasions—birthdays, graduations, weddings, Valentine's Day—in ways that do not always dovetail with the truth of our lives. A true gift begins by paying attention to the people around us, by being thoughtful and courageous in response to the needs and desires of others, and by feeling inspired to participate in their well-being.

I like to remedy the common tendency for receivers to feel indebted by naming my freewill offering for what it is. I might say, "I had so much fun making this for you," or "I went over-the-top with my winter mailing to everyone this year; here's the one for you!" Another angle is to express gratitude for all the gestures of care my friends and family give me regularly: reliability, a ride to the airport, professional advice, a good sense of direction, a shoulder to cry on, a couch to crash on, amazing dinner parties, and hilarious game nights. When we acknowledge the broader bounty of a relationship, we affirm that our loved ones cannot possibly be in debt because they have already given us so much.

A healing salve for the emotional experience of feeling in debt can be found within: gratitude. Instead of trying to settle up with a return gift, we can take a moment to authentically absorb the offering and express gratitude to the giver. Try this: If you catch yourself feeling indebted to someone who is very generous with you, notice it, and try to tolerate whatever discomfort may come. Remember your worthiness. Seek gratitude not just for the giver, but for the whole universe of relations supporting your giver's ability to give to you so generously. If an urge to "pay it back" pops up, pump the brakes. We can remind ourselves that this is gift-giving, and it is appropriate to wait for an opportunity to reciprocate freely, creatively.

From Zero-Sum to Win-Win

Scholar of the imagination Lewis Hyde writes, "Bad faith suspects that the gift will not come back, that things won't work out, that there is a scarcity so great in the world that it will devour whatever gifts appear. In bad faith the circle is broken."[4] Scarcity encourages competition and zero-sum thinking. It would have us believe there is a finite amount of awesome in the world, so if I give you some, I will have less for it. But love is not a barrel of dry beans or a share of stock! As Mister Rogers says, "Love is like infinity: You can't have more or less infinity, and you can't compare two things to see if they're 'equally infinite.' Infinity just is, and that's the way I think love is, too."[5]

Hyde's and Rogers's words invite us to cultivate faith in the generative capacity of our care for each other. There is a deep and mutual good in the pleasure of giving and receiving. Consider a gift gathered by Mohammed. Having recently moved to Belgium from South Africa, Mohammed was eager to explore his new home. His sister's birthday was coming up. He decided to put together a "countdown" type care package for her consisting of a series of small gifts she could open—one each day—leading up to her birthday. Mohammed then set out into his new city to source small curiosities, his search often leading him off the beaten path to find eclectic wares made by local designers. One of the countdown gifts was a patterned roll of washi tape because his sister likes to hang postcards from her door. Another was a special teaspoon because his sister drinks a lot of tea. His sister got to enjoy a series of delightful gifts with personal meaning. And Mohammed's treasure hunt became a wonderful quest that helped him become more familiar with his new home. Win-win!

An elementary school music teacher in North Carolina named Deanna told me about a special gift a student offered her. At the time, he was receiving supplemental food from a school-based program for low-income families. After picking up his food kit one day, he asked Deanna if she liked ramen. She said yes, and he held out a packet of instant ramen. The teacher's heart warmed. She also knew he needed the ramen more than she did. She expressed gratitude and then said that if he liked ramen too, she wanted him to enjoy it. He kept the ramen and offered her a big hug. While the vessel of the gift—the physical object—returned to the giver, the spirit—the love inside—flowed freely. The strings between Deanna and her student soaked up both of their goodwill, and through some sort of good gift alchemy gave it back to them as more than before.

In gift-giving, I think we are on the right track when we have lost track, when we have stopped counting because we know that to give is also to receive, just as to receive is also to give. We are swept up in an ongoing dance of mutual benefit that is bigger than us. In mindfulness teacher Jon Kabat-Zinn's words, "At the deepest level, there is no giver, no gift, and no recipient . . . only the universe rearranging itself."[6] Every gift is a chance to be moved, to let the universe move through us, nudging us into fresh configurations that benefit us all.

Infinite Play

Part of the pleasure of a gift is that it takes on a life of its own. Good gifts are ever-unfurling regardless of our plans for them. Gifts continue *verbing* and *doing* into the future even after we've lost track. Along the way, a gift may evolve, transform, be rediscovered. For my thirtieth birthday, my mom gave me three antique steel bird figurines, just a half-inch tall, each holding an "envelope." One for each decade, she said. But only after my fortieth birthday did the figurines remind me of the Bob Marley song "Three

Little Birds." I finally understood the message inside those itsy (unopenable) envelopes: There's no need to worry, because "every little thing is gonna be alright." These days, the tiny trio sings it again every time they catch my eye.

A gift has a lifespan, just like living beings do. To appreciate the full extent of a gift gesture, we must stretch it out upon a timeline. A few years ago, my friend Adrienne found a way to extend an inside joke with good friends, a couple who once regifted to her a cheesy jigsaw puzzle as a joke—a custom photo of themselves, still in a thousand pieces—a gift from one of their parents. When the couple got married, Adrienne saw an opportunity to get her sweet revenge—one with a lot of love in it. She spent many hours doing the puzzle and had it framed as a wedding present, regifting it right back to the happy couple. *Gotcha! Love ya!* They all had a big laugh.

It is wise to remember that the full lifespan of any gift is simply not available at the moment of bestowal; this is why a "big hoorah" upon unwrapping a gift is nice to have, but not required—just icing on the cake. The true benefits of a shiny new volleyball for a child named Annie, for example, only emerged as she put the ball to good use in her backyard, eventually making the high school team and savoring the social life that came with the sport. A gift's bestowal is just the beginning, the planting of a seed.

I once picked up a small souvenir for a new boyfriend from a trip to Big Sur, an air freshener for his rearview mirror. Infused with essential oils, it was basically the California bohemian version of the classic pine tree. "ANTI–BAD VIBE SHIELD" was printed inside a shield shape radiating with rainbow stripes. The lovely scent lasted only a few days, but my sweetie loved the trinket and left it hanging from his mirror. A few weeks later, he told me that he had been angry with someone driving poorly on the road and, in the moment, spontaneously reached for the "vibe shield," gently tapping it to calm himself. The purpose of my gift was evolving as my sweetie stayed open to it. The air freshener was now improving his mood and protecting him while driving. Even better!

I strive to be an "infinite player" in the sense of James P. Carse: "Infinite players cannot say when their game began, nor do they care. They do not care for the reason that their game is not bounded by time. Indeed, the only purpose of the game is to prevent it from coming to an end, to keep everyone in play."[7] Months later, I was driving with this same sweetie in the passenger seat of my car, and he expressed concern that I might be following the cars in front of me too closely. Inspired by his creative repurposing of the air freshener, I dreamed up a new trinket for myself with a mighty purpose. I sawed a few inches off an old wooden ruler, drilled a hole in it, and hung it from my rearview mirror. Years later, I continue to tap it, reminding myself to leave plenty of stopping distance.

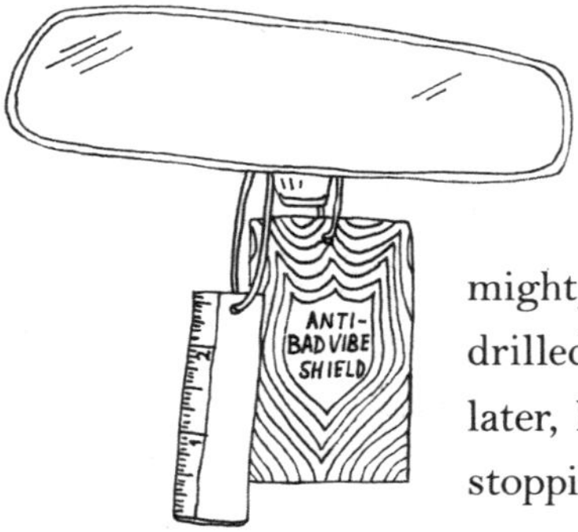

ANTI-
BAD VIBE
SHIELD

Work with Time

We can also build open-endedness into our gifts on purpose. Time is a fantastic creative collaborator, like when I crocheted a circular rag rug in three phases for my little buddy Lena, the daughter of an old college friend. Every time I visited them in Portland, Oregon, I added to the rug with scraps from a local woolen mill. Crocheting with different colors each visit resulted in a tree ring effect, a series of concentric circles. The rug grew with her, its diameter matching her height at ages four, five, and seven. Lena's family still keeps the giant crochet hook in the kitchen utensil drawer, always ready for the next round, my next visit.

Mat and Maxine, too, are playing the long game, but with a wool camping blanket. For many years, the Canadian couple has enjoyed hiking, camping, and road-tripping to national parks and other attractions all over North America. For Maxine's fiftieth birthday, Mat collected souvenir patches from all the places they had visited so far and then learned to sew (wow!) so the patches would be on the blanket at bestowal. Maxine received the gift along with the intention "To be continued . . ." The open road beckons through the blanket draped over the back of the couch in the living room between adventures. *Where next?* I love it when gifts leave wiggle room. Like the extra candle on a birthday cake, there's something to grow on.

Let's Keep in Touch

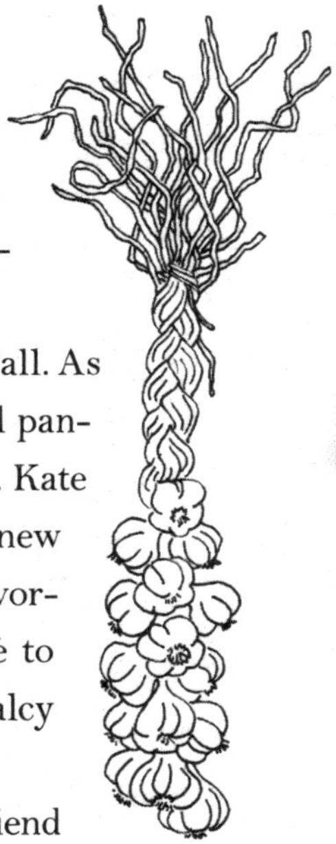

Take a look on your doorstep. The garlic fairy has visited you. Helen's phone lit up with a message from Kate. It was about a month into the coronavirus lockdown. Helen found a brown paper bag by her door, peeked into it, and discovered a wonderful surprise—a big hug from Kate in the form of a massive braid of garlic.

Just a few weeks earlier, she and Kate had traded fears, big and small. As parents living in the UK with families to feed, the threat of a global pandemic showed up as the seemingly mundane concerns of the kitchen. Kate was fixated on bouillon powder. For Helen, she wanted garlic. She knew she could pull together a tasty meal if she had fresh garlic to flavor-boost lentils or potatoes, chili or risotto. And if she could continue to make good dinners, her family could enjoy at least a hint of normalcy each night at the dinner table, finding joy in a world of unknowns.

It warmed Helen's heart to know that amid all the chaos, her friend cared about her "small" yet real concern. Out riding her bike, Kate had spotted the garlic hanging in a grocer's storefront window and immediately thought of Helen. Now hanging in Helen's kitchen, the garlic would broadcast a recurring message for many months: *I see you. I'm with you. We got this.*

But there is more. More garlic! The card that accompanied the gift said that Kate had a twin braid at her own home. Soon enough, they agreed that every time either of them minced a clove or cut a new bulb from the braid, they would check in with each other. They proceeded to text each other hundreds of little hellos, silly photos, video messages, poems about garlic, paintings of garlic, and garlic peel compositions on cutting boards. I love the way Helen and Kate stretched this gift, activating it over time by remaining receptive to its multidimensional invitations.

When Helen told me the story, she said, "I was really touched." Helen's word choice, *touched*, has wisdom in it. The garlic was the go-between, keeping them in contact within one delicious degree of separation. Each clove was another little hug, much needed and much appreciated, especially during a public health emergency requiring physical distance. Part of what was so touching to Helen about this gift, she told me, was that out of a pool of almost eight billion people worth worrying about, Kate chose to care for her. Any gesture of care in the form of a good gift is a small act of resistance to the experience of isolation endemic to our era. This is what good gifts do. They keep us in touch.

How can one person care for the whole world? What can we possibly do when our heart goes out to everyone, everywhere? I say: If you love the world, pick a buddy and hold on tight. Pick a few, actually. You are going to need them. A human life is a small collection of intimacies. If everybody can care for a handful of people, then, on the aggregate, we are caring for the whole world. The way a virus spreads is very scary—person to person to person, exponentially. This form of dispersal, though, does not belong only to terrible things. From what I can tell, love also moves in this pattern. Care radiates outward, looking for a soft place to land, to sprout, leaf, blossom, and do it all over again.

Reflect

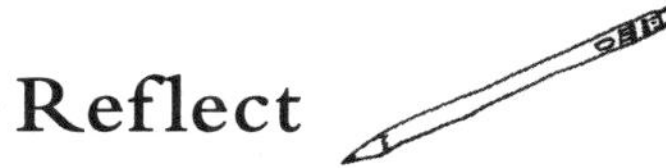

1. Consider a gift you have given or received that has emotional gravity. What message did the gift carry? What was the subtext? What did, or does, the gift *do*? What are the *verbs* it participates in?

2. Think of a gift you've received that felt like a genuine proposal—an offer to which you could respond freely, honestly. How did you respond?

3. Reflect on the spirit in which you have given and received in the past. How would you like to give and receive moving forward?

4. Dream up a gift that works with time creatively. It could have an ongoing interaction built into it like an advent calendar (slow release) or the pattern of ping-pong (back and forth), or it could be more open-ended (infinite play). Try to imagine the gift transforming and growing over time.

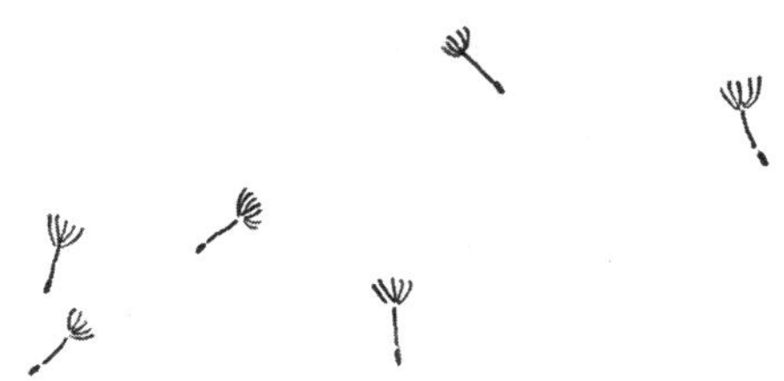

4
Not for Sale

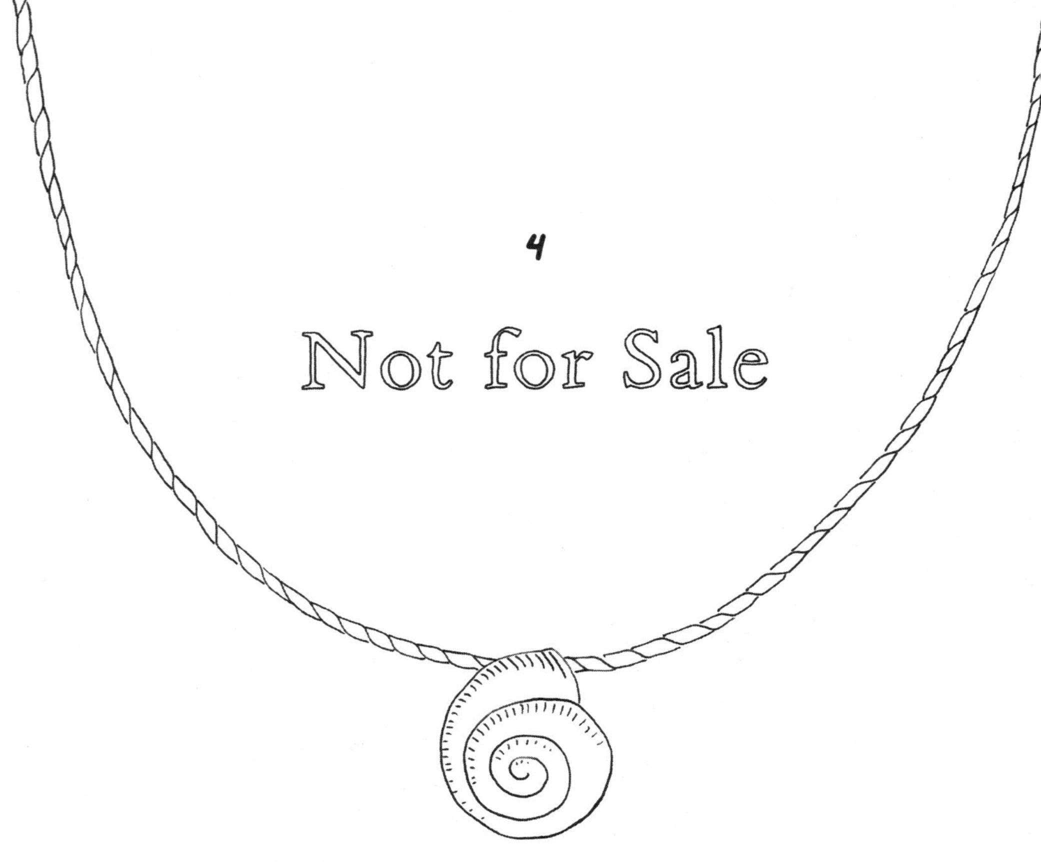

WHAT WONDERS LIE BEYOND THE SHOPPING CART?

WHERE IS THE TRUE VALUE OF MY GIFT?

*CAN A GIFT HEAL THE EARTH
INSTEAD OF HURTING IT?*

We live in all we seek. The hidden shows up in too-plain sight. It lives captive on the face of the obvious—the people, events, and things of the day—to which we as sophisticated children have long since become oblivious. What a hideout: Holiness lies spread and borne over the surface of time and stuff like color.

—ANNIE DILLARD, *FOR THE TIME BEING*

Can't Put a Price on It

Recently while hiking under a redwood canopy, I noticed something strange on the forest floor—a price tag! I had to laugh, seeing the fluorescent green sticker upon the damp humus. *Does this patch of forest floor cost $3.95? Or has planet Earth as a whole been tagged? Just the pine needle it is touching?* Soon enough, I was wondering: What if I could get a price tag maker with letters instead of numbers? I could run around stickering the world with "N.F.S.," "HELLO, FRIEND," and "WOW!"

A gift is worth so much more than its monetary cost. A gift's worth operates on a different plane entirely—in the realm of meaning, which is not limited or calculable, but abundant. We say "the thought counts" because true value is personal, interpersonal, and contextual. A deli container of chicken soup is fairly inexpensive but might mean the world to a friend home alone sick with a cold. When my high school sweetheart gave me a snail shell strung on a cord as a necklace, I swooned. A maple leaf at the height of fall colors or a simple surprise latte can change someone's whole day.

To be clear, I am not saying that all good gifts are handmade or cheap, found or free. A gold necklace for a grandmother, with one sparkling birthstone symbolizing each of her grandchildren, might be a home run gift. What the gold necklace and the snail necklace have in common is thoughtfulness, which includes thinking critically and creatively about the role of money in our gestures of care. We can call industrial capitalism's bluff even while participating in monetary exchange, reining in consumerism-run-amok and the way it eclipses the world's true offerings. Swapping in richness for riches, we can reclaim our attention and our agency at once. The amount on the price tag is far from the full story. A good gift is always priceless, at least to the recipient.

A gift can leave a recipient feeling flush because it references a shared memory or inside joke, sparks their intellect, attends to beauty, makes them feel safe, honors their past, encourages their future, celebrates their present—or for many other reasons. When I am dreaming up a gift for someone, I don't assume stores are the only places to find ingredients to activate such a rich experience for my recipient. Indeed, many of the most wonderful phenomena are too big or too small—too fleeting or too slow, too alive or too wild—to pin down, package up, and sell. "Thank God for the things that I do not own," in the words of St. Teresa of Ávila. A great gift might be borrowed instead of bought. It could merely be pointed at, wandered through, or gazed into. It might be hiding up in the night sky or a grandmother's attic.

Let's Tune In

My toddler friend Tali recently found her first penny on the sidewalk. In my world, this is right up there with losing one's first tooth. She gripped that piece of copper for almost an hour, managing to climb playground equipment without letting the coin go and walking all the way home with it. Little Tali can get excited about a penny because she's still in tune with the richness of her surroundings and everything is new to her. She is driven by her own intuitive sense of a thing's intrinsic merit. Perhaps you've seen a baby unwrap a present and be more interested in the crinkly wrapping paper and the long, shiny ribbon than the gift. I don't think it is too late for us grown-ups. We can purposely shift our attention to see our everyday surroundings with fresh eyes, reshuffling the hierarchies in our heads that lead us to treat some things—beings, places, phenomena—as more worthy of our attention than others. A dozen tulips aren't inherently better than a single dandelion plucked from a roadside, nor is the reverse true. Loosening our grip on the shopping cart frees us up to include everything beyond stores in our gift-giving repertoires. It is an issue of vocabulary. Different materials to work with provide new ways to say what we truly mean. They also let us love each other without breaking the bank or treating the Earth so terribly along the way.

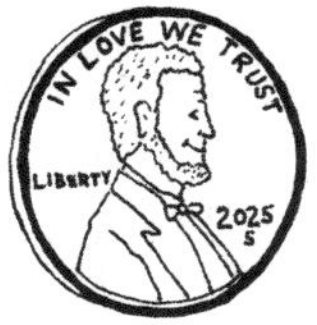

If we embrace our own trusty powers of observation and valuation—finding meaning freely and abundantly, anywhere and everywhere—we are likely to shop less. If we know we have better options, why would we waste our precious earnings on lackluster stuff that leaves so much to be desired? I like the holistic way Henry David Thoreau thinks about true cost when he says, "The cost of a thing is the amount of what I will call life which is required to be exchanged for it, immediately or in the long run."[1] Maybe this is why so many people struggle to enjoy gift-giving and find it to be an obligatory annoyance. Despite all the "choices" consumer capitalism prides itself on, it's actually slim pickings. I think most people know they and their loved ones deserve better, but they're not quite sure what better looks like or where to find it. So they toss their arms in the air and buy either something mediocre, or nothing at all. But wait! We can be anti-consumeristic without being anti-gift. We can redeem the gift as a gesture of care and make it our own without even stepping foot in a store if we don't want to. As Jenny Odell writes, "Escaping laterally toward each other, we might just find that everything we wanted is already here."[2]

And so, how might we provision our gifts thoughtfully from the great meaning-matter milieu of our lives? We can summon our inner toddler with the discernment and purpose of our grown-up self. And ignore the peanut gallery! Like Tali with her first penny, we can recognize a good thing when we find one. If we can learn to tune in, the best gift guide is always the one inside us.

Something from (Almost) Nothing

In my early twenties, I spent a year in the woods of the northern Oregon coast. The moss-covered landscape was precisely the dreamy, drippy, vibrant green I had hoped for. I rode my bicycle through the forest, hiked among the elk, and lived alone in a little wooden cabin tucked among towering trees. No internet service. No cell phone. Something even better—an old cast-iron woodstove. All winter long, I scooted my chair up close and read books in the enchanting glow of the fire, listening to the soothing tip-tap of raindrops on the cedar shingles.

Meet Gale, my neighbor down the lane. Salad greens burst from her garden. She has an outdoor shower she's rigged up with a view of the creek. Salmon spawn just outside her living room window, and she has binoculars ready for you. She won't let you leave without a sack full of wild chanterelles from her secret spot. She is magic; the first time we hugged, I swear I got fairy dust all over me.

At one point during the winter, I went away for a weekend. When I returned, it was late, dark, and freezing. I knew it would take some time for my woodstove to get going. As I drove up to my dark cabin, I lamented the fact that I was single, without a sweetie to greet me with a fire and a kiss. But when I opened the door, the place was toasty warm and cozy as ever. I was bewildered. Then it struck me: Gale. She knew I was due home that night, so she must have popped in a few hours before and built me a fire. Wow! I felt so cared for, and less alone. This "just because" gift took Gale a mere twenty minutes to make from the most ordinary materials: newspaper, firewood, a box of matches. The heartwarming prank shows how a good gift can emerge from anywhere, anytime, if we are receptive to the gift potential around us.

I once sent a friend two states away a handful of pebbles in a little cotton sack, with a note about how I was "tossing pebbles at his window," inviting him to "come out and play." It was a sweet way to say, "I miss you and wish we lived closer." When we understand that a great gift might be free or cheap, we're more likely to spot them in the wild or tinker them up. Brittni in Utah received a delightful birthday present from her boyfriend and his two children. All three of them learned how to shuffle a deck of playing cards in her honor. The boyfriend even learned a trick shuffle! When I was a kid, I would make my father IOU coupon booklets, good for things like breakfast in bed or washing the boat.

Rather than turning to stores, we can turn our attention to the countless wonders around us. I once gave the entire Dahlia Dell of Golden Gate Park to a friend, at peak bloom—an explosion of colored petals packed into whorled heads. Living flowers in a public park cannot be taken home, of course, but we can make good memories in their midst. In rural Northern California, young Ariel and her mother loved spotting hot-air balloons up in the sky on the drive to school. The higher the number, the more auspicious for the day ahead. When Ariel eventually went off to college in Massachusetts, her mom continued watching for balloons, counting them, and texting her daughter the number, sending both love and luck her way.

We can engage with the wider world of wonder as we give gifts. We just need to recognize the goodness nearby and invite it into motion with us. Dahlias or hot-air balloons. Snowflakes or blackberries. Tide pools or arroyos. Maybe it's a romantic candlelit dinner up in a neighbor kid's tree house. A Mother's Day breakfast while floating on a pond in a borrowed canoe. A playdate for a niece with a co-worker's litter of puppies. In one case, it was a whole kaleidoscope of monarch butterflies, raised by one friend and loaned to Laika, another friend, who took them to a third friend who was in hospice. The butterflies were released into her bedroom for a few hours, bringing her joy in her final days and giving her family a symbol of transformation to help them navigate the transition ahead. Gifts can be about appreciating something together. They point to a good thing, make a memorable moment, then let it go. The best gifts let us love the world and each other at once.

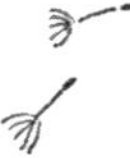

Labors of Love

Homemade, handcrafted gifts are another way to gather the abundance that is already around us, and within us, as we rise to gift occasions. They also ensure that there's a hearty helping of *you* in your outgoing gift. You might pop into stores for materials, but the point is that the gift is made via a labor of love that is impossible to price and is valuable beyond measure. Each Christmas, my pal Paul's family draws a name from a hat to determine who their gift recipient will be the following year. There are two rules: You must make the gift yourself, and you can't spend more than ten dollars on supplies. Each person gets only one present, but they spend hours unveiling them and telling their creation stories.

One year when Paul was in his twenties, his mom opened his homemade gift—two narrow bundles of dried plant matter. The gift tag said, "For us to enjoy together." Paul explained that they were cigars. He had grown the tobacco in his own backyard, planting seeds the previous spring and tending them through the summer until harvesttime. This long-term thoughtfulness astounded his mom. The cherry on top in terms of gift design was that he made her a pair: one-for-me and one-for-you. The gift sealed the deal for at least one nice long conversation between mother and son that Christmas. Isn't that what most moms really want—some quality time with their child? With the responsibility of just one gift per person, this family could focus on making extra-special items. Well done!

There are many great reasons to make gifts instead of buying them: saving money, adding a personal touch, increasing sentimental value, sharing the pleasure of special interests or skills, or just for the fun of it. Another reason is that you've got a great idea, but it is nowhere to be found among the goods and services offered by the marketplace. Daniella told me about translating an entire graphic novel from Japanese into English for her fiancé using Google Translate because the English edition wasn't available yet. She printed out the translations, cutting and pasting them into the speech bubbles of the Japanese edition.

If you dream something up that you can't make yourself, you might solicit help from friends or even commission something from a professional, like when my friends Helena and Joseph had the idea of replacing a sweet little octagonal window in his mom's bedroom with a custom stained glass one in honor of her seventieth birthday. They sketched their vision—a black-eyed Susan blossom for a mom named Susan. And since she lives in Maryland, the window also features the state flower! Helena and Joseph took their sketch to a local artisan and commissioned the glasswork. They were able to secretly swap in the new window themselves as a birthday surprise. Susan loved it.

Handmade gifts can also be quick, easy, and cheap. We can make something meaningful regardless of money or time. When a woman in Texas inherited a stash of her sister's earrings, many of them were missing their match. Her friend Heidi remade the companionless earrings into a very meaningful set of wine charms as a gift. The Shah family in New York told me about their sweet gift tradition for new babies, celebrating the newborn's birth stats across the front of a onesie with fabric paint. An engraving pen makes it easy to personalize all sorts of things—with names, dates, poems, quotations—which is a great way to add a touch of specialness to an otherwise generic object—a pencil, a spoon, a drinking glass—transforming it into something more special.

For Sale! Special!

Shopping isn't all bad. It is absolutely possible to shop with care. Many years ago, my parents gave me a wooden salad bowl for my birthday. They bought it from an artisan in Montana who turned it from a solid piece of wood, burning its wood type, "wild cherry," into the base. This was not only a great educational moment for me but also a lovely nod to the tree itself. This big, beautiful bowl is fifteen inches in diameter. I can sink my sight into the wood grain, where years of sunshine and rain alternate. If I hold the bowl sideways at the proper angle, the concentric growth rings align vertically the way they used to in the original trunk. I can fill in the gaps with my imagination, making out a vague yet real sense of the wild cherry tree this bowl used to be. But the climax of this story is a seemingly unremarkable dull-brown area running through one side of the otherwise reddish bowl. That blemishlike mark became gorgeous to me the instant my parents informed me it was the result of the tree being struck by lightning. Wow! Suddenly, what could have been seen as a flaw became a marvel that made it priceless. Sure, the bowl was once for sale. It still has exchange value. But the full story defies any price tag.

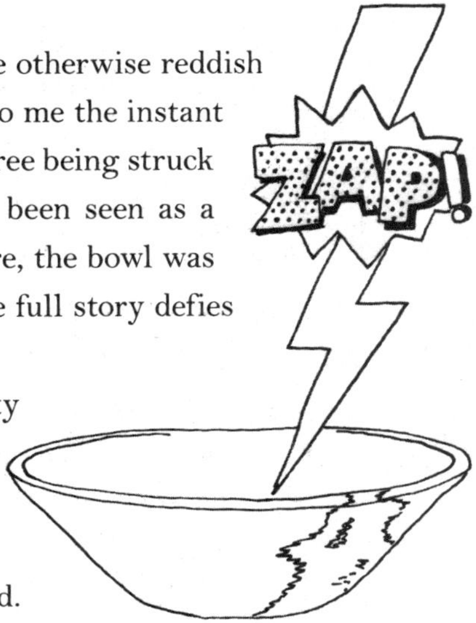

I am guessing my lightning bowl cost a pretty penny. And I like how this money moved: directly into the palm of a resourceful person who crafted an object to last for generations from a local tree that had come to a natural end. As long as I keep the bowl well oiled, I won't ever need another salad bowl. Ever. If we could get jazzed about sharing, reusing, and better distributing a small number of high-quality possessions rather than a high quantity of low-quality ones, a healthier material culture could emerge. We could make and care for lovely things that we genuinely use, while treading more gently on the Earth.

Experience gifts can also have price tags, like memberships to museums or botanical gardens, subscriptions to magazines or coffee-of-the-month clubs. There are season passes to state parks or sports games, tickets to concerts or plays, or gift cards for cooking classes, escape rooms, tarot card readings, and professional massages. Both experience and object gifts have carbon footprints to consider. The brilliance of an experience gift is that a small sum gets you access to something that's either astronomically expensive or never for sale: a Frida Kahlo painting, a breathtaking pirouette, a T-Rex skeleton, a basketball arena. Your resources are multiplied by pooling them with strangers. At the same time, you're supporting something you believe in and keeping it accessible to others.

Shopping with Dignity

I try to be as conscious as possible about the eco-footprint of my gifts. But what on earth to do about plastic? We are swimming in objects and experiences created in ways that deplete natural systems and generate waste and pollution, but it feels impractical to opt out of the whole system. Even if we handcraft our own gifts, we don't just pull them out of thin air. One Christmas, I had a lot of fun gluing googly eyes onto walnuts, adding facial expressions with a marker, and sinking them into stockings. Is that okay? Googly eyes are plastic, but they sure pack a lot of joy into a small volume of it. For me, for now, I think a few googly eyes per year is okay, but I totally get it if you draw the line somewhere else. (Maybe someday googly eyes will be made with dry black beans and sesame seeds bouncing around inside them?) I did recently decide, though, that my stash of balloons for hand-twisted balloon birthday greetings will be my last after watching a video of marine biologists extracting a balloon from the gut of a sea turtle. Balloon animals are fun, but real animals are more so.

What gets tricky is that it can often seem like the only version of something that doesn't offend the imagination is *expensive*. Since I am a knitter, I immediately think of yarn and the price difference between, say, real wool yarn and petroleum-based acrylic yarn. Even the wool yarn has its impact, traveling via plane and truck. Was the feed grain for the sheep from a farm practicing regenerative agriculture? It can be hard to determine.

Consumer behavior is just one part of the problem, and our agency is oftentimes constrained by limited information, funds, or both. I'm unwilling to assign the work of making it all better to consumers when more powerful parties are shirking their responsibility. At the same time, it is true that we can meaningfully "vote with our dollar" by directly supporting businesses that align with our values. No matter how much money we have, it matters where we put it. I think the key here is to do whatever we can from wherever we stand.

So yes, whenever we are able, let's shop responsibly, buy things we can believe in, and even skip the stores altogether. If you have the time and money to research and purchase in alignment with your own ethical system, excellent, please do. But let's also acknowledge that we need a new paradigm, not just better brands of flip-flops and crackers. Rather than losing sleep over whether the purchased aspects of my heartfelt gifts are destroying people and planet, I aim for balance and try to keep things in perspective. I suggest that we love each other *now*, in *this* world, while we still have one. We can each find our own sweet spot, again and again, a place within our means that feels dignified to us.

Treasure Hunting

If you're in the mood for a physical object gift, but nothing you can find, make, or purchase new is hitting the spot, you might end up at some of my favorite places in the universe: junk shops, thrift stores, antique fairs, estate sales, and yard sales. If you love a good treasure hunt, purchasing secondhand can be loads of fun. The carbon impact is wonderfully low too.

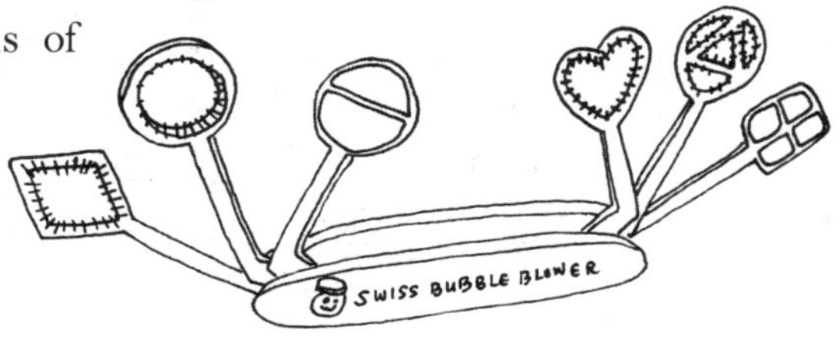

I adore the search box on eBay. When I type any keyword—such as "antique moon" or "novelty soap" or "Halley's Comet"—I get a long list of matches including many weird and wonderful things I didn't even know existed. Pro tip: Unlikely combinations of keywords compound the fun! Once, I found a vintage "Swiss bubble blower" as a gift for someone. It looks like a pocketknife, but it is made of plastic and all six of the tools that swing out are bubble wands! For me and my close friend Maya, I found a pair of matching souvenir mugs from an amusement park called Cedar Point that neither of us has ever been to. These blue and white "friendship mugs"—one lives in California and the other in Colorado—are covered in detailed illustrations of roller coasters with names like Wicked Twister, Blue Streak, and Disaster Transport. Maya and I know how to have fun, but we also know to call each other when we're feeling down, or just emotionally overwhelmed on the roller coaster of life. I smiled to myself when, the week before I sent the mug to Maya, she said to me on the phone, "Thanks for coming along on this ride with me."

Secondhand need not mean second best. I say: The more hands the better! I think of a bronze sculpture of a life-size seal on the pier in the beach town where I grew up. The seal's surface has a dull patina, but its nose is super shiny because everyone gives it a little rub as they walk by. I want to touch the seal's nose *precisely because* hundreds of thousands of people have touched it before me and will touch it after me too.

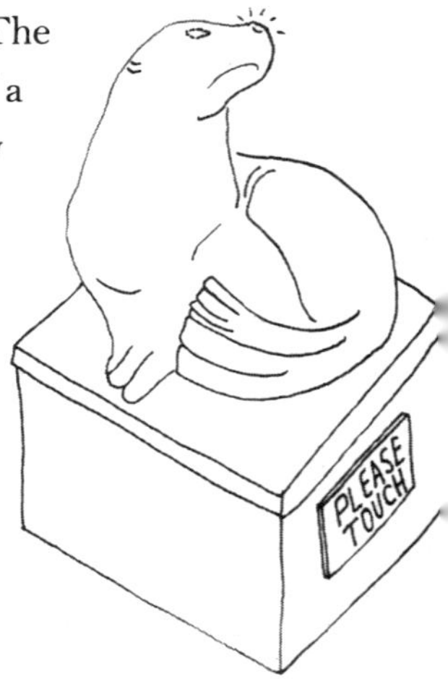

A few years ago, Anna and her husband, John, were in Bamako, the capital of Mali, and popped into an ice cream shop where their Malian friend Domo worked. When Anna and John finished their ice cream and it was time to say goodbye before flying home to Colorado, Domo surprised them by removing his handspun indigo shirt and giving it to John—a souvenir of the joy of their reunion. Anna explained to me that these indigo shirts are always on the move, constantly being regifted, and that people wear undershirts so they're in a good spot to give their shirt away whenever inspiration strikes. Months later, back in the States, John was wearing the shirt from Domo when a friend thoughtfully admired it. Something about the moment felt fitting, so John took the shirt off right then and there, and presented it as a gift. The shirt was made to make the rounds. And John wanted to keep the spirit of the gift alive. It is a beautiful, bright blue reminder that true riches are not to be found in what we privately possess, but in what we share, in our constant refreshment of the commons.

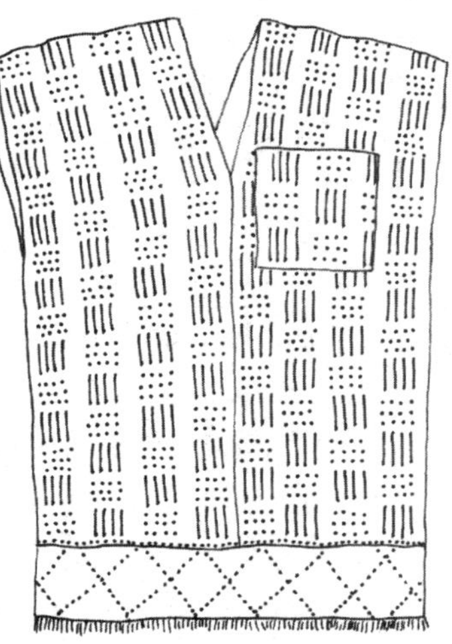

There is a reason, though, that regifts get a bad rep. Unlike when someone regifts something they own and love, sometimes people pass along things they own but never liked. I know of a set of margarita glasses that was regifted at a special occasion, without even being wrapped, to a friend who didn't even drink. Reuse is great for the planet, but it only works as a gift if the reused item is also relevant, such as when my grandmother gifted me a ceramic berry jar that had been in her kitchen for decades. The little clay blueberries on the lid speak of all the summertime berry picking we did together when I was a child.

If your secondhand gift is not relevant, it will need to be hilarious. Erik fondly remembers that when he was a child, his family had a tradition of regularly giving each other gag gifts from the quirky old junk shop in town. This practice is the same pleasure found at a "White Elephant" party, where unwanted items get shuffled around in the form of a game. It's fun and funny; I also think it has a robust critique of consumer culture built in: *What?! Can you believe this ridiculous thing exists?* To be fair, sometimes people end up with things they genuinely want that the people who brought them simply do not. When that happens, lovely! We've got a match. I remember an episode of *Seinfeld* involving the ridiculous and constant regifting of an analog label maker. Just when the game of hot potato seems like it will never end, the gift lands in the hands of someone who is happy to have it. To him, the hot potato was cool!

Let's try a creative spin on this. Do you want to come to my "Earnest Elephant" party? Here's how it works: Everyone brings something they already own, an item they love but are ready to let go of. People take turns presenting their items in show-and-tell fashion, and then the group decides which item goes home with whom. It is a great get-to-know-you activity, and basically the opposite of a White Elephant party. People bring something they love and would love to share; they go home with something they genuinely want.

But not everyone will appreciate a secondhand gift item. Some recipients may miss the relevance designed into a gift because they are distracted by the lack of a price tag or the presence of wear and tear. What then? First, you can speak up and sing the thing's praises in front of your recipient. Another approach: Fancy it up in terms of presentation. Sinking some time into gift wrapping it beautifully can communicate that the regift was purposeful. Cathy told me about a disappointing present she once received—a bike basket from her then boyfriend. On her birthday, he led her out to the garage. *Surprise!* Earlier that day, he had secretly transferred the basket from his own bicycle to hers. Except she wasn't convinced. It felt last minute, as if he had almost forgotten her birthday. Cathy genuinely wanted a bike basket and even coveted her boyfriend's, but we agreed that her "new" basket would have gone over better with her if he had, say, decorated it in a fun way—such as by gift wrapping it or putting a picnic in it, ready to roll.

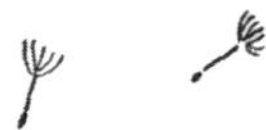

True Values

When we overidentify ourselves as consumers, shopping gets too much weight as a place to enact our genuine love for each other as well as our social and ecological responsibilities. If we can pry open a little space in between our love and our impulse to channel that love by shopping, we can enjoy some critical distance. This breathing room lets us take a different kind of inventory when making choices—getting closer to the true costs, benefits, and opportunities of various gift ideas. In this more honest accounting, we can tune in to what we really want to give (or receive) and begin to identify value on our own terms. We can be participants in wider worlds that include stores as just one of many important places to round up meaningful expressions of love.

We can make this reflective process a little easier by making a conscious habit of breaking unconscious habits. We can ask interesting questions, such as: *Am I drawn to purchase such-and-such for so-and-so from my truest, most authentic self, or is it merely because of the way I have been bombarded by ads, algorithms, and unrealistic peeks into other people's lives on social media? Is this what I really want, or just what my culture or family has conditioned me to want? Can I try an alternative and see how it feels?* The reward here is making choices around something that previously had an air of predetermination. If you sit people down and ask them what's in their heart of hearts, what really matters, they can tell you, can't they? A good gift can be a small act of resistance in response to a consumer culture's attempt to consume us, usurping our human capacity for creativity, intimacy, and generosity.

In my heart, I know finding true value separate from monetary value has the potential to be a great social equalizer, a redistribution of richness based on an abundant shared inheritance. If we can pull together marvelous gifts with any budget, no one must feel like they cannot afford to properly honor their loved ones with the gifts they deserve. I also know, though, that I can't just give anyone and everyone a seashell for their birthday or an acorn for their high school graduation and expect it to go over well. Even if I can learn to loosen the grip on my own shopping cart, I might have loved ones on my gift lists who are not interested in or available for such a project at this time. What then? In the here and now, there might be a bit of cross-paradigm gift-giving to do. We can enlist our find the sweet spots where we overlap, and summon the courage required to step into them.

In this era, the movement of material culture—the gathering, shaping, distribution, and disposal—is dominated by the marketplace. *What if* the movement were instead arranged by love and human connection? What if goodness flowed toward genuine need and opportunity for well-being? What if we set up the system around margins of care and delight, aiming for a surplus of goodness for everyone?

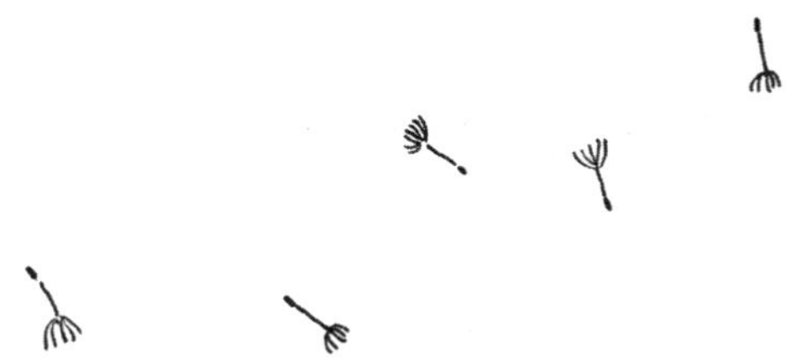

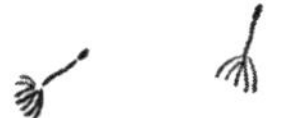

Reflect

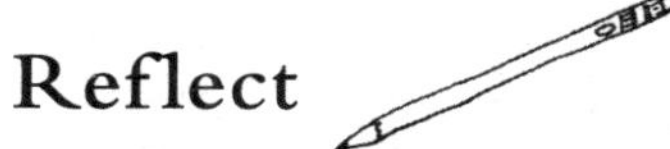

1. Consider a few gifts you've given or received and reflect upon the personal value of the gift versus the monetary value. What do you notice?

2. When a gift opportunity is approaching, visit a store you love with no intention of buying anything. Treat the store like a museum. As you browse, dream up alternatives to the store-bought items you admire—ones that are free, cheaper, homemade, found.

3. Think of three dear friends or family members, then match each one with a meaningful public place bigger and more beautiful than they could ever own—where you could take them and do something special as part of a gift. What might you do?

4. Compose and bestow a gift—a grand gesture or just a little something—that doesn't cost a dime.

5

Matter Is Marvelous

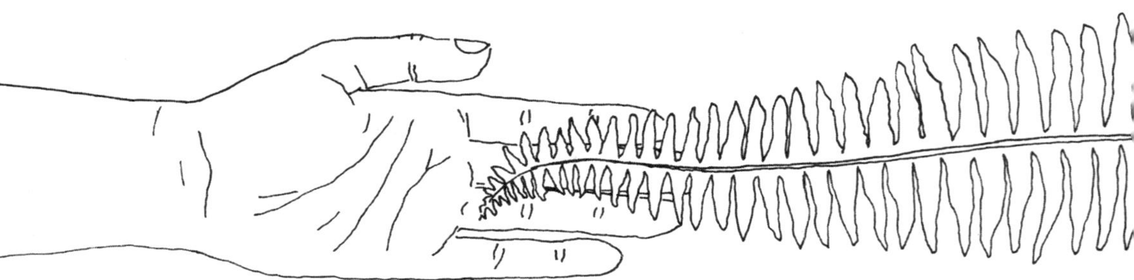

IS MY GIFT MATERIALLY ELOQUENT?

HOW IS MY GIFT AESTHETICALLY RELEVANT?

DOES MY GIFT HONOR THE EARTH?

I open the cupboard, a likely place for gifts. I think, "I greet you, jar of jam. You glass who once was sand upon the beach, washed back and forth and bathed in foam and seagull cries, but who are formed into a glass until you once again return to the sea. And you, berries, plump in your June-ness, now in my February pantry. And you, sugar, so far from your Caribbean home—thanks for making the trip."

—ROBIN WALL KIMMERER, *BRAIDING SWEETGRASS*

Our Favorite Things

Right or left? Yes or no? Another potential soul mate pops up for my consideration. For an armchair anthropologist like me, the silver lining to the slog of dating apps is a peek into the patterns of how people articulate the good life. There's a particular word my attention always snags on: *materialistic.* Once, a profile requested, with a strikingly firm tone: *Please don't be materialistic.* Obviously, the person is trying to distance themselves from the waste and vacuity of conspicuous consumerism. Excellent. Me too. And yet. Doesn't the word still somehow feel like a slight to the Earth in all its dazzling and necessary forms? Do these fellas really not want me to knit them a cute, cozy hat as things start to get serious? I think they do, as evidenced by the rest of their profile. Yes. They, like me, are in the thick of it here on Earth, in this material world. They love to cook. They hiked the Pacific Crest

Trail last year. They work at a bookstore, love their motorcycle, or tend a veggie bed. These activities are not materialistic in the pejorative sense, but they remain as earthly as soaking lentils and sautéing onions, as green and growing as the ferns along the PCT, as small as a dog-eared corner of a book made with an opposable thumb. The marvels of the material world are everywhere. I think I'll update my own profile with *Please be a materia-phile. Please love the Earth and treat it well.*

Acknowledging the material basis of our lives opens our eyes to the beauty and generosity that sustain us. It is the groundwork for practices of gratitude and reciprocity. I am reminded of a bumper sticker that I mostly agree with but also find confusing: *The best things in life aren't things.* Okay, sure, Fräulein Maria's "bright copper kettle" is not The Best Thing, but one of the best things might be friendship. And warm tea in cupped hands might encourage us to open up and speak with each other from the heart. If the teapot is also beautiful, perhaps handcrafted and imperfect, that may inspire us to be ourselves. There seems to be a fear in the culture at large that if someone cares about material things, they must be shallow and have their priorities all crooked. It doesn't have to be this way. The important question with regard to materiality is not yes-or-no, but *how so.*

The Earth Speaks

The Earth has a lot to say. It is a perpetual meaning maker, as symbols, metaphors, ideas, and feelings hitch rides on material qualities. Even when an object seems far removed from the Earth, such as a child's new plastic Lego set, the Earth is always there if you trace its sources back far enough (plastic is made from petroleum). The Earth is also present poetically, as Legos reference architectural history and hint at the ancient pyramids. Children's blocks—of plastic, wood, stone—invite dexterity, pattern play, and imagination. They build awareness of gravity, tolerance for destruction, and patience for beginning again. Any item can be approached as if it were a work of art or a natural wonder. There's no need to save our powers of aesthetic attentiveness for the rare visit to an art museum or a national park full of grand vistas. The Earth is right under our noses.

When we put together a gift, we can consciously collaborate with the eloquence of the Earth—as light as a feather, loud as a waterfall, brief as a blossom, sacred as a circle—to express the true depth of our feeling in powerful ways beyond words. This is the difference between texting my friend *Happy Birthday!* or celebrating by sneaking ten pounds of tangerines—bright orange and bursting with sweetness—into his mailbox. It is why the needlepoint pincushion my grandmother made for me is stuffed with my mother's hair—leftover locks from a decades-ago haircut. This is the traditional way—the natural oils of the hair keeping the sewing pins sharp and the sentimental source of the hair keeping the love close. To me, matter is especially marvelous when science and poetry converge and converse. This can be as simple as taking a few extra minutes at a craft fair booth to choose the wooden coffee scoop with the nicest hand feel or wood grain pattern.

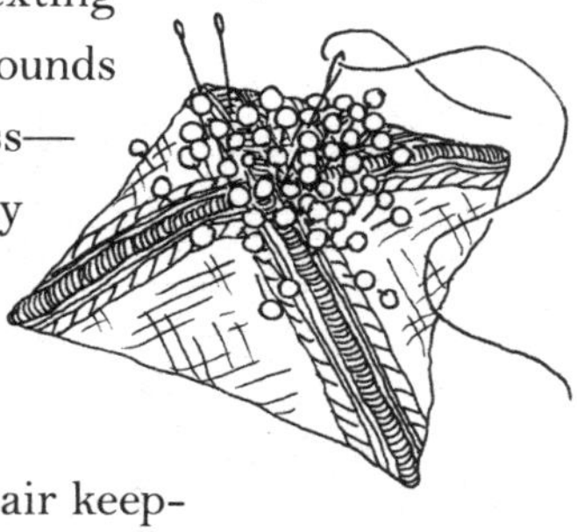

Flour, Water, Love

I am not giving up hope on dating apps yet because Laura and Harsh met on one, and they are still giddy about their new wedding rings. In the app, Laura's opening question to Harsh had been "Noodles or bread?" A courtship began and good food and their mutual love of cooking played a central role.

Harsh grew up in Los Angeles, a child of Indian immigrants. Cooking is his mother's love language, and no one who visited their house ever left hungry. Harsh soaked up the idea that food is about abundance and care. He said noodles aren't really a thing in India unless you get up north closer to Nepal and the Himalayas, so when his family was in the mood for pasta, they'd head over to Olive Garden. If you'd asked him when he a kid, Harsh would have said his favorite food was fettuccini Alfredo. After college, Harsh had an Italian roommate in San Francisco with whom he enjoyed a lot of Italian food—"It's like Olive Garden but better"—and soon after, Harsh started making pasta from scratch at home.

Laura grew up in the Bay Area with parents of Korean and Irish Catholic descent. Her mom cooked excellent Italian pasta dishes; her dad would grab a jar of Ragú at the supermarket. As a teenager, Laura made a lot of instant ramen and boxed mac and cheese for herself after school. Her mother's nickname for her was "Noodle Head." Pasta has always been her comfort food.

It was the perfect setup. When Harsh and his hand-crank pasta machine popped up in Laura's dating app feed, she swiped right. *Yes!* They met up. They cooked. They fell in love. The love stuck. They discussed their mutual desire to get engaged. Harsh wanted to propose with a special gesture, a surprise, even if Laura knew it was coming.

Harsh remembered a photo of *corzetti* pasta in a cookbook that he and Laura had once admired together. *Corzetti* is extra special because each piece, the size and shape of a silver dollar, is stamped with a design. Harsh told me that, historically in Liguria, *corzetti* were stamped with family crests. Harsh got an idea, so he signed up for a woodworking class with the intention of making a custom *corzetti* stamp.

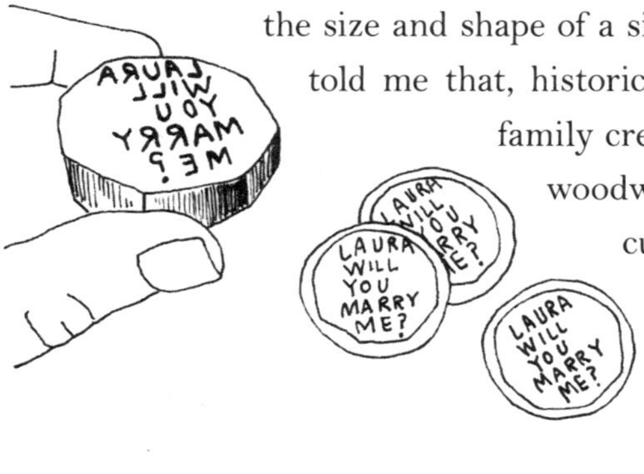

One evening a few months later, Harsh told Laura he'd like to cook dinner for her by himself. She got deliciously suspicious, so she left him alone in the kitchen. When dinner was ready, she took a seat and was greeted by a generous plate of pasta, paired with green beans and covered in homemade pesto. The circle shapes were peeking out. He had made *corzetti*! She looked closer and realized that every piece of pasta was embossed with "Laura, will you marry me?" She told him, "Yes! Of course!" Then she ate her proposal. It was a meal and a message, just for her, sealed with love. Each handstamped round of pasta was like an edible wax seal from a long line of old family love letters. It was a work of art, a good story, and nourishment for her body.

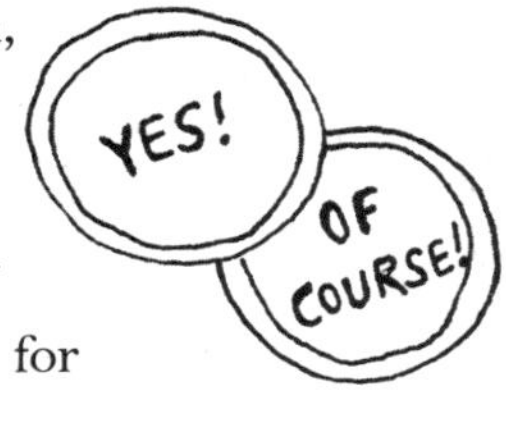

YES!

OF COURSE!

Living Responsibly

Another bumper sticker I see around town says, *Live simply, so that others may simply live.* The sticker's values of equity and responsibility resonate for me, but the word *simply* doesn't feel quite right. I do not believe the antidote to the consumerist mindset is simplicity. I do not want to become a minimalist or an ascetic. It's just not my style; have you seen how I dress?

Not only does any strategy centering the concept of *less* feel like a drag, but I think it can be a tough sell. So many people have already lost so much. If being responsible means self-restraint and sacrifice, it is going to be difficult for people to get excited about creating a better world. It's not that I don't have a moral compass; it's just that I put my faith in *eros* more than *ethics*, in *sexy* more than *should*. I want to act out of pleasure, joy, and compassion, not guilt, shame, or fear. I want to be a good global citizen because the beauty of the world moves me to.

I like to separate the word *responsibility* into two, as if it were two Legos stuck together and I'm ready to make something new. *Response* plus *ability*, or *an ability to respond.* Isn't this what has driven life on planet Earth since the beginning? Let a single cell loose on the third rock from the sun and it goes wild, a total maniac on the dance floor. One splits in two, in ten, in a thousand and more. Individual organisms survive by being creatively vulnerable to their surroundings and making the most of them. Together. Moment by moment. Add some eons and eras and epochs, let the flowers pop up and the dinosaurs do their thing for a bit while Pangaea pulls apart like my great-grandmother's dinner rolls and the Ice Age comes and goes like the longest winter ever, and here we are, everything and everyone still extravagant, abuzz with energy. For goodness' sake, even with all the extinctions humans are causing, more than eight million different species still live on Earth right now. And that's just the stuff that's alive. There are more than six hundred types of pasta in the world, half of them in Italy alone, where they have iterated into a delightful multiplicity of fun shapes with fun names like *orecchiette* (little ears) and *radiatori* (tiny radiators!) and our sweetheart, *corzetti*, which shouldn't really count as just one because *corzetti* can have any number of designs and words stamped into them, essentially pushing pasta into the realm of infinity. The energy is unstoppable, wonderful, even ridiculous! It is life on Earth. And it makes me want to get up and dance.

None of this is simple. Life is a marvel of complexity. In many ways, humans—not all of them, nor equally—have been treating this planet like a storehouse and a dump. We've been acting as if Earth is simple, plain, even boring. This posture doesn't pair well with complex living systems, nor the inner complexity of being human. Responsibility as response-ability means engaging with the lively, living planet that we've been neglecting for so long that humanity—again, not all of it, nor equally—has forgotten how fun and interesting it can be. This includes how fun and interesting *we* can be.

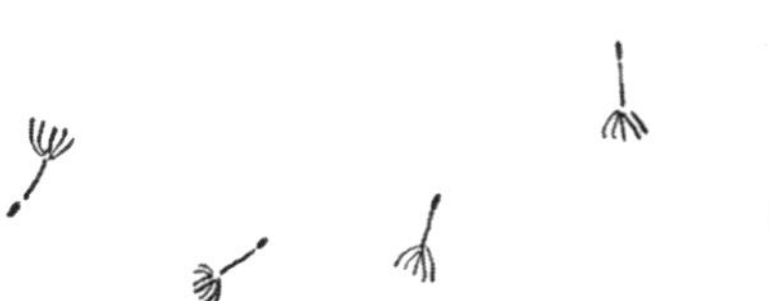

Decorative Things

Being material-savvy when choosing a gift involves considerations both poetic and practical. *Glass, metal, string.* As a surprise, Sonia in Illinois made especially meaningful stained glass star ornaments for some colleagues. She crafted each one from pieces of glass—some 170 years old!—salvaged from a huge stained glass window that had been replaced at her co-workers' church. *Calcium carbonate, the ocean.* A hiker along the Camino de Santiago—a network of pilgrimage routes in France, Portugal, and Spain—gave her friends at home shells before she left so they could think of her on her epic walking adventure while she was gone. Pilgrims usually wear shells (or tie them to their backpacks) as a symbol they are hiking the Camino. I love that this hiker gave shells before the trip, like an inverted souvenir, so her friends could "follow along" with her journey.

Paper, scissors. Karen, a schoolteacher in Newberg, Oregon, makes hand-cut paper snowflakes for her students every year, by the classful. Each one's shape holds a student's first name, radiating in repeat. After folding the paper into a tight wedge, Karen cuts out the negative space around the letters of their names. The result is dazzling, embodying the teacher's care for every student as a unique individual. The materials here are cheap and easy access—just paper! The labor is significant, but she spreads it out over the school year, and it is a labor of love.

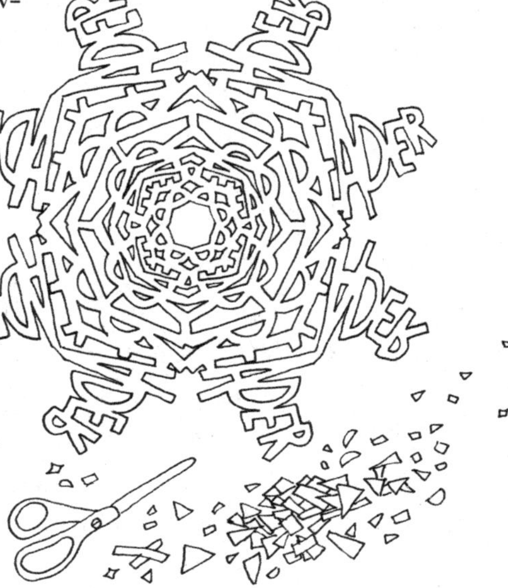

Decorative gifts intended for keeping can teach us a few things. I find that smaller items tend to make the best totems and are easier to hold on to. I can more easily find room in my home for something like a shell or a fridge magnet than something large. If I am going to give a gift that takes up a lot of room in the recipient's home, such as a framed item, I want to be confident they are going to love it. As the giver, it might be wise to check in with the recipient ahead of time about your idea, or to provide an easy way for them to decline the gift. Is the recipient a college student likely to apartment-hop for the next decade? Small gifts that are easy to relocate with might be best.

Useful Things

Some people want gifts that feel fun, superfluous, extra, and delightfully unnecessary. Others want something practical that they can use. Decorative or functional or both, a physical object meant for long-term possession is, in my mind, one of the most difficult forms of gift to do well. People often have strong preferences about what goes in their kitchens or tool chests, and they might want to choose the color, brand, style, and other features for themselves. Yes, they love coffee, but they don't want a Chemex; they prefer a French press. If you want to give someone a coffee maker, it might be prudent to do it by way of a gift card, cash, or other IOU, thereby involving your recipient in the selection. Or just ask them which one they want. This maximizes satisfaction and minimizes disappointment and waste.

Let's not underestimate the value of a practical item, especially if it is something recipients need and want but is perhaps out of budget for them or they otherwise couldn't have one. A well-delivered, practical gift arrived for me once with no gift wrap, special occasion, or fanfare. A fellow I was dating tossed a mystery piece of plumbing into our basket nonchalantly at the hardware store. Later that afternoon I realized he'd installed his purchase—a splitter—onto the main garden faucet in my yard. I now had a magical little *V* of pipe with a switch so that both drip system and hose could be attached at the same time and always ready to go. It took him only a few minutes, but he eliminated a constant source of annoyance from my week. Up until that moment, I'd had to use a wrench every time I wanted to use my hose, disconnecting the automated drip irrigation system from the faucet so that I could attach the hose in its place. And then I would struggle again to get the drip system reconnected without any leaks. The better job I did tightening it, the more annoying it would be to loosen it the next time! Then, on a random Sunday afternoon, everything changed. Wow! Who knew? He did. And now I think of him and smile when I turn on the hose with ease.

Just because an item is useful doesn't mean it can't also be beautiful, even spiritual. One woman relayed to me a poignant story of a gift she had recently given her father-in-law that was equal parts practical and profound. The beloved local doctor, father, husband, and almost-grandparent was currently in hospice, surrounded by family during his final days. Near his own portal of mortality, a vision came to him—a waking dream in which all the people whom he had loved and cared about over the course of his life came back to visit him. They lined up and gently layered a series of golden blankets upon him. He told his family about the extremely moving experience. His daughter-in-law was listening closely and got a wonder-filled gift idea. A few days later, she presented him with a gift-wrapped blanket that moved him to tears. It was golden, shimmering and soft, with a gold tassel at each corner. It was lovingly tucked around him in the days ahead, as he slowly slipped away.

Things to Wear

Gifts of clothes and jewelry can be tricky. It is all too easy to buy the wrong size, style, color, etc. Ideally, we givers feel confident in the item, the recipient has been involved in the choice before purchase, or there's an easy exit strategy or ability to exchange the item for something else. Clothes and accessories say a lot about who we are and how we want to present ourselves to the world. These are very personal, intimate items, often infused with someone's cultural heritage, gender identity, politics, or color palette preferences. Unless it is a one-size-fits-all garment, clothes have sizes and thus call attention to the shapes of bodies, and you might be risking triggering someone's body image issues. If I am not close enough to someone to know their size by heart, or to know the kind of relationship they have with their body, I am careful with clothing gifts. Unless I have a stellar reason for it, why give something so risky when there are so many other good gifts?

A garment gift, however, can be great when given with care within an appropriate, attuned relationship. I recently gave an especially meaningful one to my friend Milicent and her infant. Milicent is a huge fan of *Star Trek: Discovery* (and so am I), and so I knew she would swoon at the thought of putting her infant into a onesie featuring a "Captain Burnham" badge and "Let's Fly." And I knew we would both giggle at the rather true notion that her daughter is "in charge" of their lives for a bit. There is yet another layer of meaning. *Star Trek* has been around since the 1960s, but *Discovery* is the first of its iterations to feature a captain who is both female and Black. Part of my friend's deep desire to be a mother is to continue a lineage of strong Black women and to raise her daughter with Black joy. Since I had previously been trusted with this intention, one that is so close to my friend's heart, I hoped for the onesie to also touch on that meaning, as a way of witness. The bestowal brought my friend to tears of joy.

Living Things

Living things are another tricky but lovely category of gift. In the 1970s, a young child in Illinois named Amy loved to sing a song about an oak tree, and her grandmother Shirle knew it. When Amy was a little older, her grandmother had an oak planted in Amy's honor at the Chicago Botanic Garden. When she "gave" it to Amy by walking her over to the tree, it had a big ribbon tied around the trunk. Amy and her grandmother visited "her" tree together over the years.

Gifts of plants and other living things like puppies and lizards require their recipients to care for them over significant periods of time. Unless you're the parent of a recipient who is a child, a dog probably doesn't make a good surprise gift. A ticket to the zoo or an aquarium would be a safer bet if you want to put the kiddo in touch with animals. Plants are lovely, but they require water, pruning, fertilizer, and not everyone has a green thumb. Speaking from experience, I felt crummy when a houseplant given to me by a friend as a housewarming present died under my watch. Cacti, succulents, or other low-maintenance plants can be safer choices. A vase of cut flowers—ideally locally grown, not flown in air-conditioned planes from the other side of the globe—might be best for anyone who travels a lot or doesn't have the bandwidth or interest to care for plants. Here's a creative spin if *you* are the one with the green thumb: Plant something in your friend's honor in your own yard, such as a tomato plant, and label it with your friend's name on a wooden stake. Text them photos of it growing all summer long, and let them know when it is harvesttime.

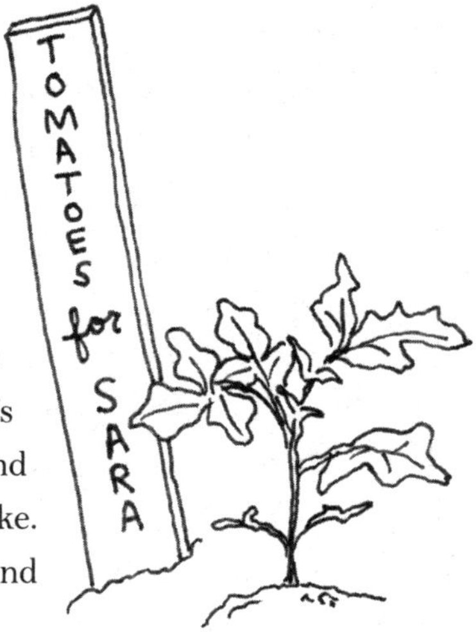

Gifts that Disappear

A curious care package once landed on my stoop, a cardboard box with air holes cut into the sides. It contained sweet onions, sent from friends in Walla Walla, Washington, who didn't want the onions to rot in the mail. Delightful! I am a big fan of gifts that are designed to disappear, such as food and drink; other consumables, such as soap, bath salts, candles, and flowers; or even greeting cards. They take up space only temporarily, require little to no maintenance, and usually don't end up in a landfill. The gift is less burdensome if the recipients don't love it or want to keep it, and there is much less pressure to display it in their home or on their body. Comestibles lower the stakes and sidestep a lot of awkwardness. This is why consumable treats make especially good gifts for people we don't know very well for whom it is difficult to choose something more durable. (Short-lived gifts are sometimes less good for people we do know well, when a relationship is aiming for forever. There is a reason why engagement rings are not made of Funyuns.) I am especially fond of gifts of food as a "thank you for having me" gesture when a houseguest hand-carries a regionally specific item from their homeplace to their host's homeplace, such as maple syrup from Vermont or the myriad Kit Kat flavors from Japan that aren't for sale here in the States: strawberry, sweet potato, chestnut.

For my friend Bijoya's fourth birthday party, I brought fruit salad. To spruce it up, I used a metal cutter in the shape of a cherry blossom, so that each bite of fruit was a little flower. Robot, of the pocketknife search party of one, put together a moonshine-making project as a gift for a friend. They began the long journey to a barrel of homegrown whiskey by planting the grains, but they do not plan on the whiskey being in peak form for many decades. Robot—a generation older—might not even still be alive when their younger friend sips the last dram, and intentionally so. Robot will still be there in spirit (and in spirits!) though—their presence lingering in the moonshine—keeping their friend company.

While we're on the subject, alcoholic beverages can make great gifts, but I suggest proceeding carefully with them. Some people are practicing sobriety. Not everyone wants booze in their household; fancy nonalcoholic drinks are festive too.

Depending on how they are produced, soaps, bath salts, lotion, perfume, cut flowers, candles, incense, and other consumables can be easier on the Earth than many other physical things because they get used up. My college boyfriend and I put on safety goggles and made a big batch of pine-scented soap as our winter solstice gift to all our friends and family. We wrapped the bars in paper labels featuring a linoleum block print of a pine sprig and a poem about bathing. Everyone got the same sweet all-purpose gift from us, but it was full of care and creativity. One and done. If the bar of soap is not for you, just pass it forward.

Experiences Are Earthly

Even if experience gifts strive to prioritize people, fun times, and making memories, materiality still plays an important role. We can design experience gifts that let the Earth speak to us through our senses—sight, hearing, taste, touch, smell, and more. A few years ago, I was unable to attend my grandfather's birthday party in person, so I hired a harpist in his town to surprise my grandfather at the party and play jazz standards and other songs by request. (And I made sure she could play "I'll Never Smile Again," my grandparents' song.) My grandfather called me on video, live from the party, absolutely delighted. In terms of materiality, part of what drew me to the idea of a harpist is that a harp is a bit of a novelty, a surprising instrument for jazz, and something that I knew would look dramatic at the party as the musician wheeled it into the backyard and started to play. My grandfather and all his friends would get to enjoy the beautiful instrument up close.

Part of the beauty of an experience gift is that it's like a bar of soap—it disappears at the end! Since it is not an object for possession, it avoids many of the burdensome issues associated with physical gifts. I do, however, always consider whether my recipient might enjoy a souvenir or other keepsake, something tangible to help the good memories stay close in the days or years ahead. When Ruth Anne treated her mom and sister to a spa day, she gave each of them a small salt heart from the spa's gift shop.

But experience gifts do come with their own list of practical considerations. If you are planning activities for other people, especially if the activity is going to be a surprise, consider your recipient's physical comfort, the duration of the activity, the weather forecast and noise level, and whether there will be crowds. Consider what might cause discomfort: amount of time on their feet, motion sickness, heat exhaustion. Should you pack sunblock, water, and snacks?

Gift Wrapping

Wrapping paper is only the beginning, but let's start with the basics. There are many great ways to wrap gifts that don't overflow one's recycling bin on garbage day. In my family, after opening a gift, we carefully remove the tape and tuck the pretty paper away for reuse. My friend Ayden's family does the same, and her mom is still wrapping gifts with paper scraps from the 1990s! My friend Jeffrey is in the habit of saving the colorful Sunday funnies from newspapers so he can wrap presents in them. I like to use the crossword page. Interesting paper ephemera are ubiquitous and fun to collect for gift wrapping. A brown grocery bag turned inside out is a blank canvas to decorate with rubber stamps or other doodles. One time I drew speech bubbles that I filled with inside jokes.

The way we wrap a gift can be a significant part of the gift itself, preparing the recipient to be ready for something special. When my friend Ali gave me an old clothes button she found on the beach, she folded a tiny origami box for it. I opened it carefully and admired the little treasure—how it had been weathered by the elements and tossed in the surf like a seashell. Gift wrapping guru Megumi Lorna Inouye has a whole book full of ideas for us: *The Soul of Gift Wrapping*. With old maps, security-pattern envelopes, calendar pages, sewing patterns, and sheet music, she wraps gifts using ingenious folding techniques that require zero tape! For Megumi, gift wrapping is an important ritual for the giver, creating the emotional space for reflection and gratitude.

Another delightful way to decorate a gift is to tie small objects onto it, such as a lollipop, a novelty pencil, or a bubble wand. Megumi loves to attach twigs, leaves, and sprigs of lavender. Pankaj, who now lives here in California, grew up in Hyderabad, in the southern region of India. He told me that, on Diwali and other holidays, marigolds are everywhere, including tucked into gift baskets to make them festive and beautiful. Any kind of flower, fresh or dried, is essentially a colorful bow tied by nature and makes for a lovely alternative to a store-bought bow. Megumi informed me that Americans send thirty-eight thousand miles of synthetic bows and ribbons to landfills every year, enough to circle the entire Earth. Gross!

Durable fabric—bandanas, tea towels, even a sock—makes great gift wrap. In Japan, people have been gift wrapping things in fabric for more than a thousand years. There are dozens of unique ways to fold and tie the beautiful, hemmed fabric pieces called *furoshiki* that can be reused again and again.

If you have a physically large present to bestow, such as a guitar or a bicycle, wrapping it might not be a practical option. Instead, consider hiding the gift somewhere nearby and giving the recipient a clue to go find it. In the case of a guitar I gave, my clue was a two-inch paper guitar that I cut out and put inside a jewelry gift box.

A gift tag can be both practical and beautiful, adding to the aesthetics of the presentation. If a gift will not be bestowed in person, a tag is an opportunity to include any contextualizing information that you'd like your recipient to read before they open the gift. (More on this in the next chapter.) All you need is a hole punch, and you can turn any fun piece of paper ephemera into a charming tag to write on.

Design Your Bestowal

For me, gift wrapping isn't just made of paper or fabric, new or reused. Gift "wrap" is the larger, marvelously material context in which the acute moment of giving takes place. To frame our gesture of care, we can consider all the usual suspects: *who, what, where, when, why,* and *how.* Marriage proposals are a great example of this. For an important gift, bestowing it creatively, even elaborately, is a big part of the whole package. Shall we present the gift in a meaningful place? With much fanfare? Would it be best to merely pull it out of our pocket on a random Thursday because it's just a "little something"? Shall there be witnesses or privacy? Background music?

We probably do not need to make our co-worker, bus driver, or dance teacher hike to the top of a mountain on a full moon to retrieve a holiday card, but for relationships that are significant enough, we might want to design a special presentation. Before she went off to college, Jessica in Seattle hid a gift under her mom's bed. Weeks later, when they were talking on the phone and missing each other, Jessica said, "Go look under your bed," and her mom was overjoyed to find a gift—a new sweater featuring fall leaves. She had been sleeping right on top of it for weeks! Elsewhere, a graduate student hid a birthday present for his girlfriend, Tania, on a shelf in their university library and gave her a Dewey Decimal number to find it. Decades later they are still together and still enjoying that memorable moment in the stacks.

For gifts that are experiential or digital, how can we make them fun to receive? Charlene's parents gift wrapped tickets to a baseball game inside a new baseball mitt for their daughter. For some kids in my life, I gave them paper IOUs to the factory tour at Jelly Belly in the form of "golden tickets" hiding inside small boxes of jelly beans. As a cute way to invite a neighbor over for a drink, I took a Sharpie to a lemon from my tree and wrote: "IOU a hot toddy on my porch." When Kelly in the Netherlands received a cute dog plushie from her partner along with a real leash and collar, it was a promise to get a real dog someday, as soon as they had a home with a yard. A few years later, they adopted Izzy Girl.

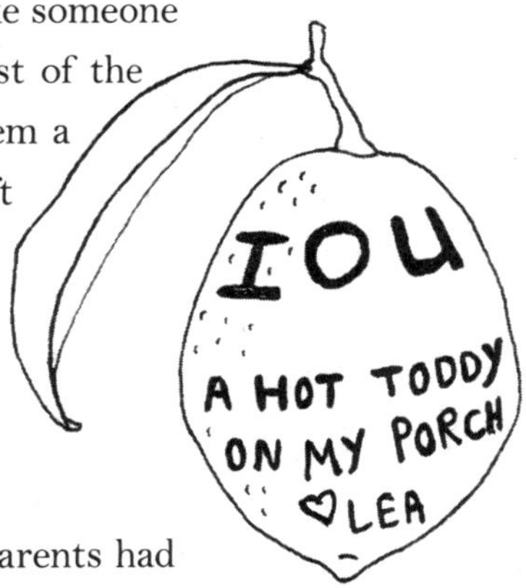

For digital gifts like ebooks, audiobooks, or custom playlists, I like to give something my recipient can touch too. I might print an image of the book cover, glue it to cardboard, and gift wrap it. If I make someone a playlist, I like to give them a handwritten list of the songs in a greeting card in addition to sending them a link to the digital playlist. Cash, gift cards, and gift certificates can be similarly made tangible. For gifts of cash to children, you can give money as two-dollar bills from the bank or fold paper bills into origami figures, which you can then tuck inside greeting cards. Two teenage brothers embarking on a special trip to New York City with their parents had been saving their own money for months at home in Toronto in case they saw something special to buy on the trip. At the airport while waiting for their flight, their parents gave them each a bag of chips. Reaching into their snacks, the boys found a surprise—a few crisp bills, extra spending money for their trip.

A Kaleidoscope of Meaning

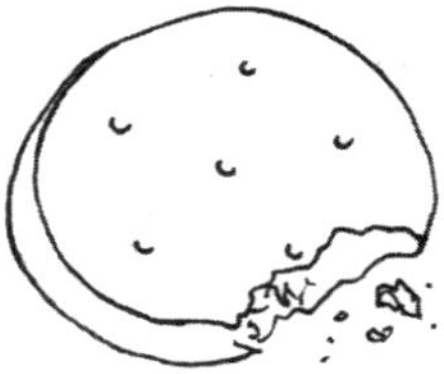

Before we close this chapter, let's bring out dessert. In your mind's eye right now, conjure up the image of your favorite cookie or other sweet treat. Now imagine it inside a large decorative metal tin lined with waxed paper, one kind among many: ginger snaps, baklava, Oreos, mil hojas, madeleines, nankhatai, vanillekipferl, animal crackers, Jammie Dodgers, s'mores, tarecos, Thin Mints, Milanos, mochi—we could go on and on.

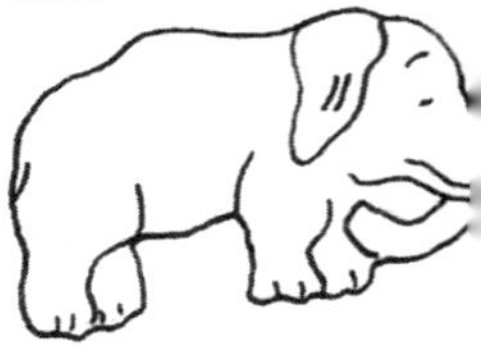

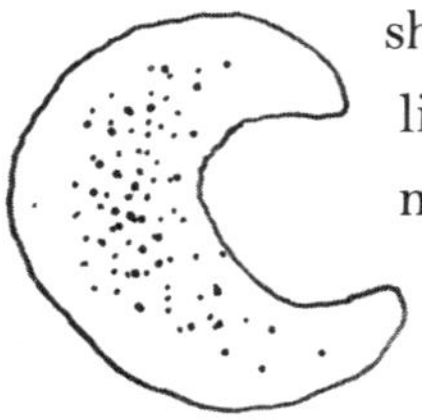

Depending on your experiences and identifications, you might find memories alongside the cookies in the tin, such as selling Girl Scout cookies or drawing rangoli designs with chalk on Diwali. If you speak Spanish, you might delight in the poetic name of the many-layered piece of mil hojas (a thousand leaves). If you are me, the animal cracker will call to mind the old Barnum's animal cracker boxes with the little cotton ribbon handles. The warm, melty s'more can strike a nostalgic chord for people who went camping as kids in the United States, but a similar note might be hit by the golden-brown tareco if your grandmother is Brazilian. The crescent shape of the hazelnut vanillekipferl looks like a moon to me, but if you live in Vienna, you'd be more likely to know it is a reference to a specific moon, the one on the flag of the Ottoman Empire. For Laura Lynn in Tennessee, the Pepperidge Farm Milano cookie is a symbol of career success and class mobility. When she was a teenager growing up in a low-income household, her family bought Hydrox cookies. Laura Lynn only got to enjoy the coveted Milano if she was lucky enough to find a bag of them in homes where she babysat. She would sneak a nibble in the pantry after the kids went to bed! These days, she buys them for herself. Her husband buys them for her too.

Humans enjoy sweet and savory nibbles all over the world, each one representing something significant and storied in its ingredients, tradition, culture, and personal history. The pull toward food is the universal human need (and pleasure!) of sustenance. The anatomy of the tongue and nose helps us receive it. Salty, sweet, bitter, sour, umami. Fragrant, fruity, woody. While what we see depends on who we are, where and whom we come from, as well as whom we spend our time with, it is also subject to our ability to be curious about what is in front of us. Matter is not just marvelous, but marvelously malleable.

If you find yourself eating an Oreo by my side and it is nighttime, I will probably sweet-talk you outside to look for the moon in the sky. If we find it, we'll twist open our Oreos and nibble away at the cream filling until the shape of the cream left on the chocolate cookie matches the current phase of the moon.

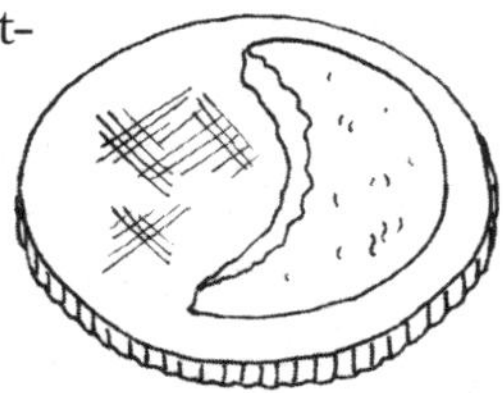

Little Worlds of Wonder

Gift-giving is an art form in the wild. In the *Wunderkammer* of everyday life, everyone is an artist, a curator, a collector. Our art supplies are anything and everything. Artistic intent matters, but we cannot pin down meaning like a bug collection. We can do our best to match material qualities and meanings to our offerings, but our recipients will take it from there. A good gift stays alive.

In the curiosity cabinet that is the whole world, everyone has a unique collection of knowns and unknowns—me, my dear ones, you, and yours. Collectively, there might not be anything new under the sun, but individually, there's plenty lying around to blow each other's minds with.

The nonverbal, full-sensory language of the Earth is always at our fingertips and under our noses. When we collaborate with the sensuous world of our existential entanglement for the sake of wonderful gifts, I think we can't help but notice the exquisite details of our Earth home. Gifts are an opportunity to affirm that materiality is meaningful, that matter matters. Animal, plant, mineral, artifact, atmosphere. Mind, body, heart, and soul. All of it, phenomenal. *Yes! Swipe right!*

Reflect

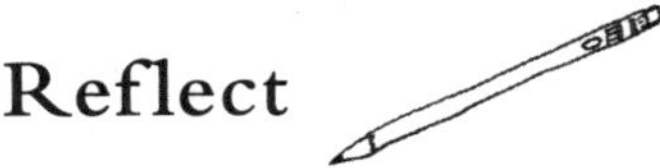

1. Look around your home for a beloved object you received as a gift. What stories does it tell? How is it materially eloquent?

2. With the next gift you give, consider both the practical constraints and the creative opportunities of its material form—decorative, useful, alive, etc. How might you highlight the marvelousness of the gift's materiality via the senses—sight, sound, scent, touch, and taste?

3. Buy or bake a batch of cookies to share with friends, family, co-workers, or neighbors. How might these cookies share a story about you, your cultural history, or your personality via their decorations, shape, ingredients, or flavor?

6

Words Are Wonderful

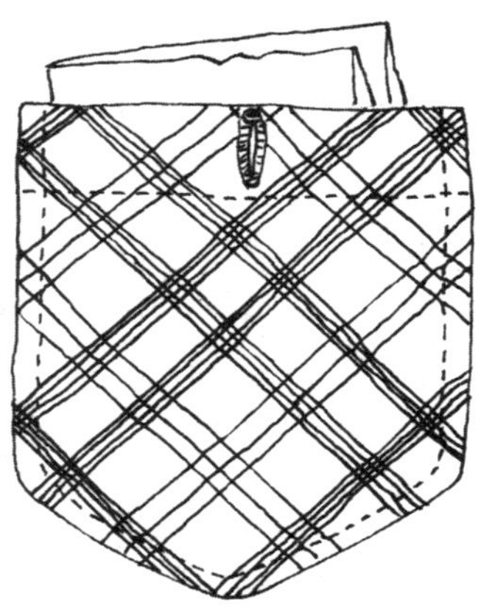

HOW CAN I FIND MY VOICE FOR A MEANINGFUL GIFT OF WORDS?

WHAT VERBAL GESTURE WILL RESONATE WITH MY RECIPIENT?

HOW CAN I CONTEXTUALIZE A GIFT WITH WORDS TO HELP MAKE MY MEANING CLEAR?

I love words so much. . . . They glitter like colored stones, they leap like silver fish, they are foam, thread, metal, dew . . . like slivers of polished wood, like coals, pickings from a shipwreck, gifts from the waves.

—PABLO NERUDA, *MEMOIRS*

Words Matter

On the edge of a cliff, at the edge of the Pacific Ocean, as the sun sank over the edge of the world, my high school crush read me a poem. A *love* poem. A love poem *he wrote, just for me.* The poem had been hiding in the chest pocket of his plaid flannel on a folded-up piece of paper. Just the two of us, held side by side by the wooden arms of a bench, I knew I was in trouble as he unfolded it and I caught a glimpse of his handwriting. Never before the recipient of such romantic affection, much less expressed so directly, I was a tiny earthquake, all nerves.

Did I thank him? Did I flee? It's all a blur, but I will never forget how it all felt. Only years later did I recognize the magnitude of the moment, the way my tectonic plates shifted that day. The gift of that poem, performed live for an audience of one, was the seed of a larger gift—an appreciation for the emotional vulnerability that makes way for the close relationships I long for. I was way out on the edge of my comfort zone, so the feeling was hardly pleasant. But I am infinitely grateful for that invitation to start practicing.

From the boy in the plaid flannel, I learned the power of words spoken in love and care. Words matter. Literally. Thankfully, we don't have to articulate ourselves to our loved ones in lines that will resonate with humanity for all of eternity. We just need to cobble together a few phrases that can reach a person we know. It could be a simple phone call, maybe even a text message. Including a poem or song by someone else that does some of the talking for you is fair game. Word choice matters, of course, but what matters most is that the sentiment the words carry is *yours.* Working with the vast array of forms and methods available to us, each of us can have a way with words. We can be the poet laureate of our own life. We are the only ones qualified for the position.

Here, let's consider direct, heart-to-heart messages first (such as a greeting card), then look at gifts in which words are combined with physical objects or experiences (such as lettering on top of a cake). We will also work with words, both written and spoken, to help set the scene for any gift form, to frame and contextualize the gift at the moment of bestowal and beyond. The more adventurous or coded the gift item, the more it can benefit from verbal contextualization.

Sealed with Love

Some people might feel that giving a gift of words alone, such as a handwritten card, is not enough. As if it's cheap or just doing the easy thing, not a significant enough token of affection. I cannot promise that it will go smoothly if we suddenly switch, cold turkey, to greeting cards in all of our gift exchange relationships. I do daydream, though, of a world in which sincere, heartfelt words are seen as a great gift form, as more than enough or maybe even the preference.

My grandmother grew up on a dairy farm in Tennessee in the 1930s. In a family surviving the Depression with many children to feed, when their birthdays rolled around, there was one main tangible item of celebration—a birthday card signed by both mother and father. After I learned this detail about my grandmother's childhood, the birthday cards she sent me every year without fail throughout my childhood took on new meaning. She often sent a physical gift as well, but now I see that it was perhaps the card that meant "birthday" and "special day" most to her. I could always sense that she took her time selecting a special card with me in mind.

When I speak with people about their epistolary lives, it's not long until a keepsake box comes out. A good letter or card can bring tears, happy and bittersweet. Marian in Los Angeles always keeps a love letter from her husband in her purse. In San Diego, Martha enjoys displaying her greeting cards in the front window of her house.

Good mail keeps us within the fold of humanity. I feel deeply seen when I see my name and address, front and center, on an envelope, in the handwriting of someone who cares about me. From the sender's side, writing and sending a letter is a valuable practice in attunement to others and self. Writing a letter prompts us to find our voice. Jotting a return address in the corner is a chance to self-see, to acknowledge one's "place in the family of things," in the words of Mary Oliver.[1] Letters remind us: *We are here. And here.* And we matter to each other.

A widow named Andrea told me how much her late husband's paper ephemera mean to her—greeting cards, sticky notes with loving messages, or just "I'm out walking the dog." They spark tears and smiles, and Andrea cherishes these more than any of the more intentional, store-bought gifts her husband gave her. "It makes me feel his presence again, his love, humor, and his marshmallow insides," she told me.

When my grandmother passed away, a small box made its way from her home to mine. I opened the lid to find dozens of handmade cards, the ones I had sent her over many years. I was touched. It was *her* keepsake box! It was a final care package from my grandmother, physical proof that we mattered to each other—and still do.

Use Your Words

If we want someone to know something, and we want to leave less up for interpretation, we might do well to heed what many parents tell their young children: *Use your words.* Words offer clarity, a crispness of communication that cuts straight to the chase. I knew just how the young man felt about me that day as I received his poem on the bench. Maybe I should have known from the wildflowers and other trinkets he had given me in previous months, but the poem spoke to me without ambiguity.

While it is relatively easy to give a physical object without having an explicit awareness of our intended meaning and purpose, a gift of words requires that we get clear on those sentiments in the first place. Writing our own words prompts us to ask ourselves what we really think and feel. What is at the heart of our well-wishing? If the process of sitting down with a pen or pencil feels uncomfortable, even more reason to stay and reflect and see what you can discover when you start putting words on the page.

The clarity of verbal communication is complemented by artfulness, the way we express a sentiment. Words arranged in uncommon ways perk up our ears. Beautiful phrases invite both giver and receiver to slow down, write and read carefully, and seek special significance. Marian, the woman with the keepsake letter in her purse, told me one of her favorite ways to say "happy birthday" in a card is "The world is a better place because you were born." When people I love are heading into a new chapter of life, I like to say, "It's going to be awesome because *you* are going to be there."

As I told you in the beginning of this book, I am the postmaster of the World's Smallest Post Service. We transcribe thousands of letters for people every year, turning their messages into "world's smallest" letters and tiny brown packages tied up with string. Since 2008, I have had the joy and honor of eavesdropping on thousands of people's letters. Here are a few of my all-time favorites, shared with the blessing of the senders.

HI MOM. THE OTHER DAY I WAS CUTTING CARROTS AND THOUGHT OF ALL THE SCHOOL LUNCHES YOU MADE FOR ME OVER THE YEARS. THAT WAS A LOT OF WORK AND I LIKELY NEVER THANKED YOU PROPERLY FOR YOUR CARE AND THOUGHTFULNESS. THANK YOU SO MUCH. LOVE, CHRIS

I CANNOT BELIEVE YOU ARE FINALLY HERE, YOU WERE ONCE JUST THE SIZE OF A BLUEBERRY. I CAN'T WAIT TO SEE YOU GET BIGGER AND BIGGER, AND TO PLAY WITH YOU EVERY DAY. LOVE, AUNTIE KARL

TO MY WIFE WHO IS MY ALL, I SEND THIS CARD SO VERY SMALL. AND THOUGH IT'S HELD BY FINGERTIPS, THE LOVE INSIDE COULD SINK 10 SHIPS.

I'M FEELING TINY AGAIN. OVERWHELMED COMPLETELY. THE LITTLEST SPECK OF LIGHT IN A UNIVERSE ADRIFT AMONG UNIVERSES. BUT THEN I REMEMBER I'M IN ORBIT WITH YOU.—A.

Good letters invite us to linger a little longer. If you're feeling stuck getting started, have no fear. Bring in the professionals. Not to speak for you, but to help you find your words. We are in some sort of heyday of fabulous greeting cards. A few tips. If you love a particular card, but the blank space inside feels too big and intimidating to fill, just cut off the front of the card and turn it into a postcard! You can also personalize the prefab text a card comes with, crossing out a word and replacing it with your own, or inserting an adjective to make it more specific to your recipient. I like to do this visually too. Recently on a thank-you card for my friend Amy, who took me to her music event in the woods, I doodled music notes into the air and instruments into the arms of a parade of insects marching across it.

If none of the greeting cards in the store feel right, browsing those cards is still a great way to get ideas. Then go home and put it all into your own words. There are also thousands of inspirational quotes online, passages from beloved books, lines from favorite songs or poems, and books about the art of letter writing. (Remember to give a shout-out to your ghostwriters.)

In 2021, a *CBS News* poll revealed that more than a third of American adults hadn't sent a personal letter in more than five years.[2] Fifteen percent had never sent one. If people aren't sending letters, that means people aren't receiving them either and the bummer is twofold. You can't make a letter come to you, but it is true that the best way to inspire good mail days in one's own mailbox is to be someone who creates them for others. *PS: Write back soon!* Or as my pen pal Polly puts it: *Please send word!*

Ruth Ann has turned her love for letter writing into a beloved weekly ritual, blocking out a half hour every Sunday evening to write one card. It is easier to get going if you keep a stash of epistolary supplies handy—stationery, pens, postage stamps. Save addresses in your phone or an address book. Beth, who used to own a greeting card shop, told me that she keeps a box full of greeting cards handy at home, filed by occasion. Ruth Ann does the same, collecting great greeting cards as she spots them in the wild, knowing eventually they will be a perfect match for an occasion and recipient. Myles and his wife have been exchanging wedding anniversary cards for more than fifteen years. When Myles finds a good source of cards, he stocks up for future anniversaries. He told me what a relief it is that their entire gift to each other is just the card, and they can focus on finding a really splendid one and writing something meaningful. Megumi told me that sometimes she elaborately gift wraps greeting cards as if they were any other present, to emphasize that they carry a lot of emotion and significance. Brilliant!

The Envelope as Canvas

Did you know that US postage stamps never expire? But the price goes up every year, so the older the stamps, the more of them you need on your envelope. In other words, the more of these tiny works of art you get to decorate your envelope with! Delightfully, it can easily take five or more antique or vintage postage stamps to add up to the current "forever" stamp value. My friend Polly calls the technique "philatelic patchwork" (*philately* is the study and collection of postage stamps and postal paraphernalia) and considers it a way to cheer up the mail system. Unused postage stamps from yesteryear can be found at antique fairs and from online vendors like eBay and Etsy. My personal favorites: the Georgia O'Keeffe *Red Poppy* stamp from 1996 (32 cents), the bright blue outer space stamp sheet from 1981 (18 cents), and the 1973 sheet of "Postal Service Employees" (8 cents), which features a delightful ten-panel tour through the postal system. I like to play with juxtapositions in the corner of a single envelope, like surrounding the 1981 Rachel Carson (early environmentalist and author of *Silent Spring*) postage stamp (17 cents) with a flurry of the 1977 butterflies (checkerspot, swallowtail, orange-tip, and dogface, 13 cents each).

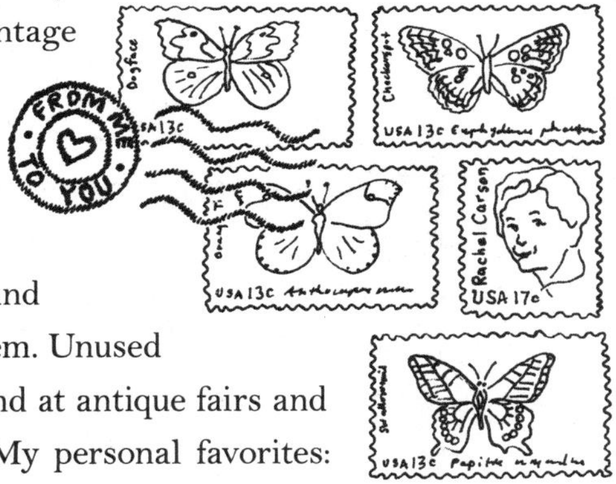

You don't have to be a greeting card connoisseur or stamp collector to give great gifts of words. That's just icing. A good stash of cards can simply be a box of identical, all-purpose notecards. It can be blank paper from your printer tray. Polly told me that one of the best letters she ever received was written on a paper plate, folded in half. It was from her father, who lived outside of town and didn't have easy access to stationery shops. I once unfolded a paper flour sack into a single giant sheet and wrote an epic letter on the blank reverse side. Polly likes to run old maps and pages from seed catalogs through her manual typewriter. The front of an animal cracker box makes a super-cute postcard. Found stationery can be charming. Make it even more so with rubber stamps, stickers, and washi tape.

Open When . . .

There are times when we might want to do something a bit grander with our words. Let's peek at a few special forms that can come in handy. The first is to invite other people to join you in sending birthday cards to a loved one you share. I suggest making it as easy as possible for people to participate. Provide the mailing address and a suggested "send by" date. This can result in a fun flurry of mail arriving right before, on, and after the birthday.

Other special forms involve series of letters. The "open when" letter bundle is an especially great setup for long-distance relationships where the intimacy is strong, but the geography is wide. On the flaps of the sealed envelopes, you can put dates, or just jot scenarios that will naturally space out the enjoyment of the letters. *Open when you are missing me. Open when you need a good laugh. Open when you're feeling creative.* "Open when" letters are also great for people heading off on long trips, servicepeople stationed abroad for extended periods of time, and kids at summer camp.

Another form involves creating an epistolary time capsule for someone, a letter dated for future opening much farther down the road. These can be especially poignant when written by new parents to their babies to read many years later. Parents can write now, while all the observations and insights are happening and fresh, but tuck the letter away until the baby is older. Grandparents can do the same, creating an heirloom of stories, wise words, and family history for their grandchildren to enjoy for decades to come, perhaps long after those grandparents are gone. I suggest putting these things into words before the moments have slipped away or the people themselves have left us. An entire series of keepsake journals (titled *Letters to My* . . . and created by yours truly) is designed for time-capsule letter writing to make the form easy and beautiful. My series includes *Letters to My Baby, Letters to My Love, Letters to My Future Self,* and many more. Each book binds together a dozen folding aerogrammes, each one with a prompt.

Letters and cards aren't just for people who live far away. Quite the contrary! My pal Adrienne started dating her wife, Katey, back in college, when the two of them would hide notes for each other around campus—taped onto classroom doors, tucked into the bark of a tree trunk. When Katey proposed many years later, inspired by their note-passing ritual, she spaced out the proposal one line at a time in a series of little notes delivered to Adrienne throughout the day. Another couple keeps two red leather-bound journals in a handcrafted wooden box with their names embossed on them in gold. Every year on their wedding anniversary, they turn to the next page and write to each other. The elegant format will keep a lifetime of love letters safe and sound, all in one place and in chronological order. Helen and Joe, a couple in Washington State, write love letters to each other *every single day.* After half a century of this, they have written over forty thousand! In their spiral notebooks, they begin each letter with a prayer, a gratitude, and the prompt "Your specialness today is . . ." Helen and Joe credit much of their long, happy marriage to their epistolary practice. They discuss their letters too. Even though they live together, they keep in touch, on purpose.

Keepsake Messages

A word lover named Sunita told me, "As I get older, I have a need for fewer things and more words." As a group gift, Sunita loves putting together keepsake memory books for the people in her circle of care, and she's good at it. Her prompts are rich and her logistics are organized. She might ask things like:

What do you love about Neena?

Do you have a special story to share?

Any birthday wishes for her?

Do you have any special photos for the book?

She also gives people a deadline, instructs folks to send her the photos via text or email, and reminds them it's a surprise. *Mum's the word!* People usually have good things to say but can greatly benefit from guidance to locate and articulate something especially meaningful. By hand with scissors and glue, or on one of the many custom photobook websites, Sunita arranges the words and photos into a scrapbook.

Sometimes the keepsake words you want most are right under your nose. Laura and her husband in Nebraska fell in love while teenagers during the early days of instant messaging with desktop computers and dial-up modems. Laura assumed the messages of their growing affection and devotion had been forever lost. Lucky for her, her husband-to-be was a computer geek. He figured out how to export the whole thing, then printed it out, and hand-bound it into a book with wooden covers. Laura, a lover of literature and the founder of the epistolary service Poetry by Post, swooned!

A keepsake "book" can also take ephemeral forms. When I chatted with Kat Vellos, friendship activator and author of *We Should Get Together: The Secret to Cultivating Better Friendships*, she suggested this yearlong birthday gift: Give a year of memories in the form of monthly messages. On the first day of each month, send your friend a text message with a shared memory that you cherish. Bonus points if you have an accompanying photograph. The memory texts create a digital archive and prompt multiple moments of re-connection along the way.

You're on the List

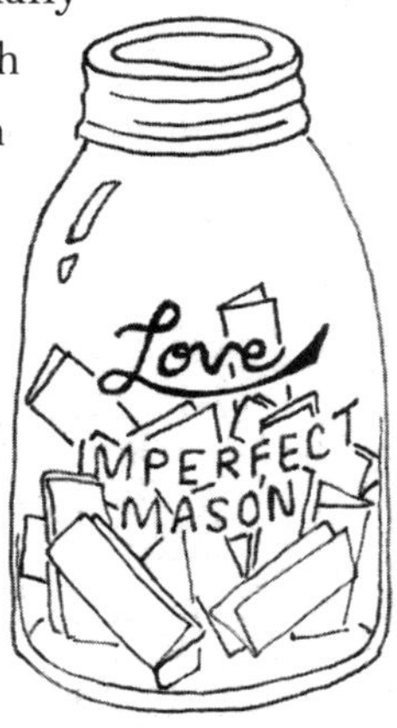

The classic list, common at work and for grocery shopping, can be used for heartfelt purposes too! I love the list as a form of communication because it ends up sounding like a poem, but it is so much easier to write. My friend Rose recently composed a list of "Seventy-Five Things I Learned from My Dad" to celebrate his seventy-fifth birthday, including: *If you talk to strangers, they're not strangers anymore. Get in the water, you'll be glad you did. The only measurement you need for garlic is a lot.* Making a list, especially a long one, encourages a specificity of expression that can reach a heart more effectively than broad, abstract statements. Marian in Los Angeles composes "One Hundred Gratitudes" lists. She doesn't want to say just, "Thanks for everything." To her Aunt Mimi, for example, she wants to say: *Thank you for afternoons on the beach and rides on the carousel. Thank you for allowing me a role in decorating your apartment. Thank you for telling me to always accept any good opportunities that come my way.* The list form lends itself to many variations, including these sweet ones in which glass canning jars full of folded-up strips of paper offer things like "Fifty Things I Love About You" or "Wise Words from Women over Fifty." The recipient can draw out a little gift of words whenever they like, thus drawing out the love over time. If gifts like this are your jam, take a look at Sherry Richert Belul's book *Say It Now: 33 Creative Ways to Say I LOVE YOU to the Most Important People in Your Life.*

Beyond the Blank Page

Personal notes are a wonderful form with a rich history, but they're just one of many ways we can work with words to communicate care. Great words are everywhere, and creative forms abound. Find one that makes you shine. Making someone a custom playlist full of relationship-relevant songs is a classic example.

I like to play the *New York Times* "Spelling Bee" game every day. Proper nouns don't get you any points, but I like to keep an eye out for my friends' names anyway. When I find the name of someone I love hiding in the hexagons, I type it out and text the friend a screenshot of the game as a little everyday gift of words. *Just thinking of you!*

We don't have to start with a blank piece of paper. My friend Jana told me about a remarkable gift she received back in high school in New York. She planted the seed for it when she told her friends that, as her birthday present, she wanted lists of words that describe her, so she could see herself through their eyes. Her best friend, Sam, went wonderfully overboard with the prompt, obtaining a dictionary and spending several weeks reading each page and highlighting every word that she felt represented Jana. Jana was blown away. Something similar could be done with a book of poems, a novel, or a magazine, highlighting words or full phrases. When I give someone a book I love, sometimes I paint watercolor borders around the passages I am most excited to share with them. This can also be done with a highlighter or simple dog-ears, or by writing notes in the margins.

Be a word collector and get creative. Does someone love to cook? Celebrate their birthday with a keepsake binder full of recipe cards solicited from loved ones. Did your high school bestie write a play for their senior project? Make them an official script booklet, like Maya in Michigan did, to commemorate the achievement. Is your son studying poetry in college? Make him a "blackout" poem or birthday greeting by crossing out words on the front page of a newspaper issued on his birthday. (The words that remain form the message.) Got a crossword lover in your life? Use an online custom puzzle generator to make a puzzle with personally meaningful words.

Spoken Words

Some gifts of words shine brightest when spoken aloud. Marian told me that she reads her "One Hundred Gratitudes" lists to her recipients in person in addition to providing them with a paper copy. Her facial expressions and tone of voice are an essential part of the gift. On our way to a picnic on a sunny day, my sweetie Oscar once suddenly declared, "I wish I could cut the sun in half, take the seeds out, and make a sun lemonade for you!" I loved the spontaneous poem so much that I asked him to say it again into a voice memo on my phone, so I could keep it forever. For birthdays, I like to text friends and family a quick selfie video of me singing "Happy Birthday" to them. This doesn't take much time but means a lot.

A song can be a lively container for a gift of words, adding the emotionality and energy of music to whatever you're hoping to communicate. Last year on Mother's Day, Angela here in the Bay Area received an email from her grown-up daughter wishing her a happy day and pointing her attention to an audio file attached to the email: Fairy_mama.wav. The song was composed and sung by her daughter, and emailed from the next state over. Two of my favorite lines are, *My mama taught me that magic is real, to look deep within and trust what I feel,* and *A fairy for a mom is the most precious gift, more enchantment and love than I could have wished.*

If you want to sing someone a song but you are not able to write or perform it yourself, consider commissioning one if your budget allows. At a tea shop I stumbled upon a flyer for a singing telegram service and did a double take. *Singing telegrams?* It turns out there are companies across the country that will send someone to a location of your choosing to serenade your loved one with a custom message. What a fun and festive way to send love when you cannot be there in person! Videos of people receiving these special deliveries reveal that both delight and horror are possible responses, so be sure that the recipient likes to be celebrated publicly. Jen Forti, the founding voice of Bellagram Telegrams in Portland, Oregon, is quick to advise that a singing telegram is not for someone who embarrasses easily. But she also reports that many recipients love it so much they are brought to tears.

If a professional singing telegram is over budget, just sing it yourself the best you can (so charming!), or do it like Lloyd in the movie *Say Anything*, holding a boom box over your head. Be a good DJ. If your loved one is across the country, text a link to a special song. Regardless of who composed it or who does the singing, choosing a song to help you communicate what is in your heart can be powerful.

Whether it is a singing telegram, a list read aloud, a wedding toast, or other spoken-word gift, many recipients will appreciate a paper copy as a keepsake. If it won't disturb the magic of the moment, a video recording is another great keepsake form.

Set in Stone, Written in Sand

Wood can be engraved. Fabric can be embroidered. Leather can be stamped. Glass can be etched. Books can carry an inscription, as can other items. I once received a pair of super-cozy pajama pants with an inscription in permanent marker on the clothes tag—just enough room for the date and "I love you." The custom words might be a more integral part of the item itself, like when Diana in Pennsylvania had a necklace made for her mother, Jayne, after her father, Bruce, passed away. Custom-made by an Etsy craftsperson, at the center of the chain was a phrase from an old love letter Bruce wrote to Jayne from Vietnam during the war. His words—*Till we meet again*—were cast in gold, an exact replica of his handwriting. If you want your words to last, consider giving them in a durable form.

Words piped across cakes with icing don't last long, but they are still meaningful. A baker once asked me if I wanted anything inscribed in icing on the top of a birthday cake I was picking up. It suddenly occurred to me that there weren't actually any rules here; the sky's the limit as long as it fits on the cake. Sure, I could have requested "Happy Birthday Erin!," but instead, I took thirty seconds to think up something more interesting. When Erin opened the bakery box, she was greeted by "Truth Seeker." Decades ago, on a solo beach walk at sunset, I spontaneously scrawled a gigantic love poem into the sand with a piece of driftwood. An hour later, my romantic interest hurried to the spot with a headlamp so he could read the poem before the incoming tide washed it away! Other creative forms for making words material: messages folded up inside homemade fortune cookies or jotted onto tea bag tags, greetings spelled out in Bananagrams tiles on a table or formed with socks across a bed or with snow in a yard.

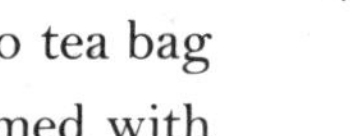

Clarify Any Gift with Words

Words are also handy in accompanying a gift, whether jotted on a gift tag or spoken aloud. Contextualizing a gift with a few words as it is opened can encourage your recipient to meet you at the meanings you have in mind.

Connie once received a bewildering Christmas present from her boyfriend, Terry. She was very much hoping—even anticipating—he would spring an engagement ring on her, but instead, he gave her a popcorn machine. That was in the 1970s. Almost half a century later, they sit, adorably, side by side on the edge of a bed and tell me that after they were married, she learned that her husband assumed every Sunday night they would have "popcorn for dinner" just as he'd done in his family for his entire childhood. She finally understood! A popcorn machine meant "I want to spend the rest of my Sunday nights with you." Thankfully, the gift gaffe didn't keep him from "popping" the question soon after, and they laugh about it today.

When we bestow a gift, we might have been scheming for days, weeks, even months or longer. It all makes perfect sense to us, but let's remember our recipient is seeing it for the first time. Words help them understand our meaning. Especially in romantic relationships, a lot of people assume that true love and soul-mate status mean their partner should be able to read their mind—to "just know." Yes, it's lovely when people can intuitively know us, but communicating clearly lays the foundation for that deeper way of knowing.

We cannot assume meaning will be shared by giver and recipient, especially in diverse societies. In the Victorian era, the "language of flowers" meant a bouquet could carry a lot of meaning and was a way to "say" things to each other that could not be spoken aloud. The message was often decoded according to a floriography dictionary, offering answers such as: *Zinnia for everlasting friendship. Orange blossoms for eternal love. Marigolds for grief. Edelweiss for courage. Clovers for good luck.* Delightful? Yes. But also confusing, as the same flower type could have multiple meanings, and the various dictionaries even disagreed about what those were.

No system of significance is universal. Native to the Americas, marigolds have been meaningful since pre-Columbian times. Today in Mexico, the marigold—*flor de muertos*—frequents Day of the Dead festivities, serving as a reminder of the brevity of life. My friend Pankaj from Hyderabad, India, says marigolds mean "celebration" to him and feature prominently at weddings. Bidisha grew up in Kolkata, the Bengal region farther north and east, and has a different marigold meaning in her heart, something more like "daily worship." There is no consensus and no need for one, not for marigolds, nor for the rest of the flowers, nor for many other things.

When I have a particular meaning in mind, I use my words to share what I see. I once presented a bouquet of *Craspedia* to a romantic interest as things were getting serious. I love these drumstick flowers, which have bright yellow spheres on top of long narrow stems. (There are two for you on the cover of this book!) To me, each one is a miniature sun. As I handed the flowers to my beloved, I drew his attention to the "suns" and said, "I want as many suns as possible with you, as many days as possible."

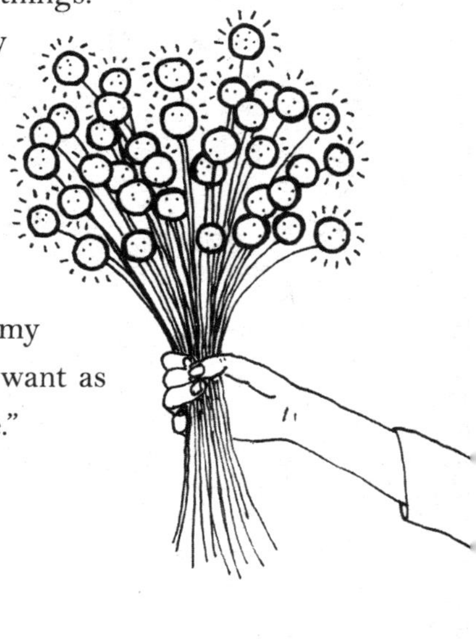

Keeping Words Alive

All people, no matter their roots, are part of a great verbal tradition—that of human language—written, spoken, whispered, sung. A gift of words in any form is an opportunity to practice verbal communications that are beautiful, generous, and kind. This world can be rough; language is used to cause harm at every scale. But words can also heal. When words resonate and feel good, it is a wonderful, powerful experience. As we take care with language in something as small as a greeting card, we are growing our capacity to do the same in other arenas, other relationships.

Words are *free.* Words are *magic.* We pull them out of thin air. We can have as many words as we can remember. The more we use them, the more we have, and we can give them away without having any fewer for it. There are so many words to choose from! And so many languages! I think we can find wonderful-enough words to communicate how we feel when we want to. We can arrange words—one by one, like a string of pearls—into beautiful gifts that mean the world.

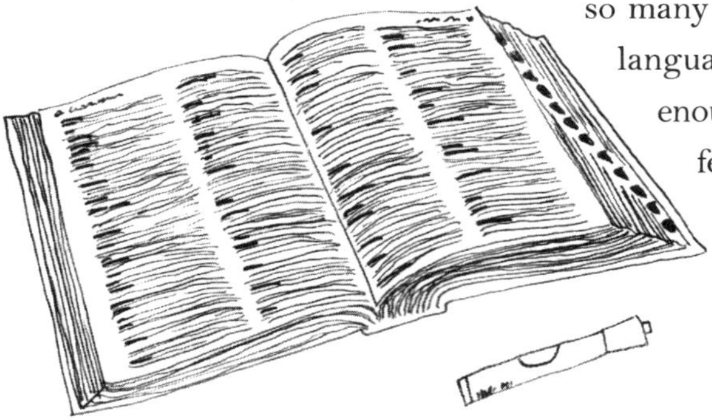

Reflect

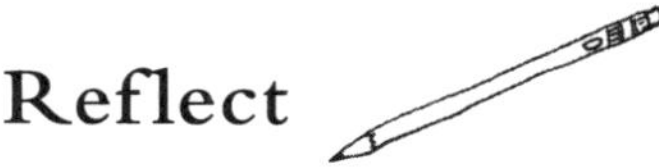

1. Does the thought of writing someone a heartfelt message feel easy or difficult, and why? Consider your nearest and dearest and whether they might love to hear from you. If words feel difficult, how might you start small? If words feel easy, how might you try a fresh format?

2. Start a journal for the sole purpose of jotting down quotations, song lyrics, lines from poems, bits of overheard conversation, etc. to have handy to incorporate into future greeting card messages. As the next occasion in your calendar approaches, put a found phrase to use.

3. Design a gift of words that goes beyond common written or printed forms. Bring your words to life by combining them with other creative and sensory forms. You might play charades until your recipient guesses your meaning. You could spell something out by rearranging a big pile of fall leaves into a couple of words, or translate your message into a secret code that your recipient must decipher.

7

People Are Precious

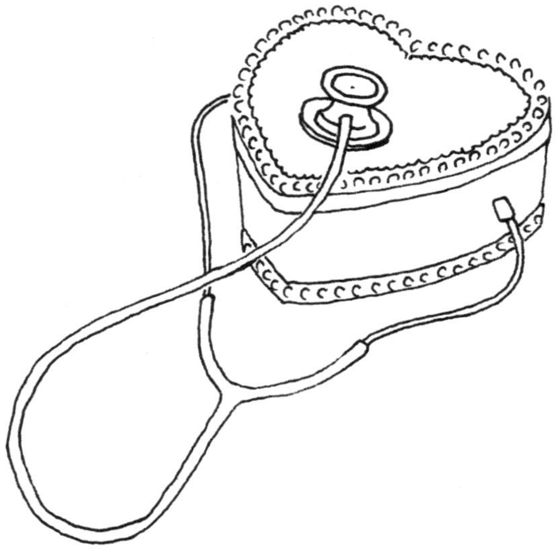

WHAT IS THE GIFT POWER OF IN-PERSON EXPERIENCES?

IS THERE AN ART TO SHOWING UP?

HOW CAN ALL GIFTS BE INFUSED WITH PRESENCE?

And the question is, when is the last time that you had a great conversation, a conversation which wasn't just two intersecting monologues . . . in which you overheard yourself saying things that you never knew you knew, that you heard yourself receiving from somebody words that absolutely found places within you that you'd thought you had lost . . . a conversation that continued to sing in your mind for weeks afterwards?

—JOHN O'DONOHUE, INTERVIEW, *ON BEING WITH KRISTA TIPPETT*

Hearts Beating Together

Dawn enters my tearoom with a gift, a heart-shaped box of cookies that she places on the table between us. Dawn is a hospice doctor, so the heart shape holds special meaning coming from her. Dawn is not at all surprised when I tell her that many of the most moving gift stories I have heard are about the alleviation of suffering. She is quick to reassure me that the presence of grief is the way we know there is love. Dawn opens the box, offers me a cookie, and I settle in for story time.

Fifteen years ago, Dawn's father, Roy, requested hospice as he approached the end of his life. In his final days, she became frantic as time ran short: *What can I do?* She wanted to do something extra special while she still could—something distinct and unique to him. Then she remembered: *mandelbrot.* A mandelbrot is an almond-based, crescent moon–shaped cookie, firm but wonderfully crumbly in the mouth. Dawn describes mandelbrot as a Jewish biscotti. It was her father's favorite cookie, and he hadn't had one in decades. Dawn explains that it isn't a kid cookie, not very sweet, but she has vivid childhood memories of her grandmother baking them and her father sitting on a chair in the kitchen awaiting his prized delight.

So Dawn pulled out a cookbook and put on her grandmother's apron. When the cookies were ready—and still warm—Dawn carried a plate of them upstairs, sat on the edge of the bed, and instructed her dad to open his mouth. With eyes still closed, his mouth opened as she gently offered a bite. His lips came down around it. The familiar crumble. And then, the "Ummmm" that his daughter hadn't heard in decades, a sound specific to *that* cookie. Her father passed away two days later, and the grief sank in. Dawn started to bake nonstop, hundreds of batches of mandelbrot for friends and family. As I listened to Dawn's story, I realized that her in-person cookie deliveries pretty much guaranteed her hundreds of hugs. How lovely. Her father's final days in this world conjured a cookie, and that cookie in turn continued to take care of his daughter for him when he no longer could, pointing her back in the direction of love, batch after batch.

Your Presence Is a Gift

Sometimes, *we* are the best gift. When I host a party, no matter the occasion, I'm hoping people can attend, not that they bring gifts. Their presence is plenty, and anything beyond that is a bonus. A guest with no physical object to bestow is not empty-handed, but openhanded, bringing hugs, high fives, hand gestures, help in the kitchen, maybe dance moves.

My dear friend Milicent once saw an opportunity to give the present of presence to our friend Vanessa. Vanessa's birthday was approaching, and Milicent knew this would be Vanessa's first birthday since her divorce, the first time in twenty years that she would be waking up alone on her birthday. A few days before, Vanessa received a call with an insightful and compassionate offer. Would she like Milicent to come over the night before her birthday and sleep on her couch, so she would have good company first thing in the morning? *Yes!* They began the birthday morning with Milicent's family tradition, playing Stevie Wonder's "Happy Birthday" and having a little dance party in the living room. Vanessa told me that Milicent's gesture was meaningful beyond measure, and that it was not something she would have thought to ask for. There are many possible variations of this wonderful gift in which we offer to accompany a loved one through a tight spot. We can go along for a stressful doctor's appointment, be on call to debrief after a job interview, even just wait in line with someone at the DMV.

Tough times, good times, or both at once—people don't just want good company, they need it. Any gift of in-person presence, for a special occasion or an ordinary day, lets us exercise our essential mammality, our inheritance as a social species. The trio of doctors who wrote *A General Theory of Love* put it eloquently: "Mammals developed a capacity we call *limbic resonance*—a symphony of mutual exchange and internal adaptation whereby two mammals become attuned to each other's inner states."[1] Not all relationships or gift opportunities warrant a gift of in-person presence, but when the moment calls for it, the benefits of the time together can nourish us to the core of our being.

When I asked a friend's mom if she had any gift stories, she immediately spoke of how important it is to make good memories with the people we love, that time together is the most precious gift. My friend's mom grew up on the Klamath River attending brush dances with her family as a member of the Yurok Tribe of California. She told me that with certain dances, the singing and dancing can go all night long. Upriver at one of these dances a few decades ago, her two-year-old nephew was sitting in her lap when a meteor shower caught them by surprise. The auntie swung her nephew around so he could wrap his legs around her waist and tilt his head back to face the sky. They savored the shooting stars together. Skip ahead to a family gathering decades later. The nephew is in his early thirties and shares that his earliest memory is one of a meteor shower. He turns to his aunt and asks her if perhaps she was there. She practically bursts with joy. We can never know quite how much we mean to each other, how deeply the good times we share nourish us and stay with us. Occasionally, we get a glimpse.

A Limbic Boost

Most nouns turn into verbs if we bring in people and add time. Gabriela in Miami decided that her niece's second birthday would be an opportune moment to pass down her own collection of mini Pound Puppies from the 1990s. At the party, she instructed her niece to close her eyes and then poured dozens of tiny stuffed animals from a bag, making it rain puppies onto her as she squealed with joy. But that was just the beginning. Over the years, Gabriela proceeded to play with the puppies *with her.* When her niece started learning the alphabet, they invented an epic game in which the tiny puppies navigate Magna-Tile worlds in search of the ABCs.

As the giver, you can fold conviviality into the gift to add to the fun, like when a child named Elleri gave her father a jigsaw puzzle with the plan to do the puzzle with him. Elleri's mom guided her to the good gift idea with a lovely prompt: *Think of things your dad likes to do, and then narrow it down to the ones that you and your dad love to do together.* In Alberta, Canada, a fourteen-year-old named Asha received two very special birthday presents—one from each of her parents, Melissa and David. Her mom and dad intuited that what their daughter needed most was space of her own. But they also saw a need for Asha to spend quality time with her parents. So from her dad,

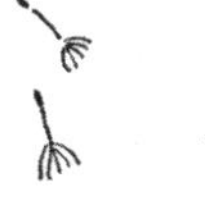

a tree house; and from her mom, a bedroom redecoration. These gifts were bestowed as activities: *From me to you, now let's do it together.* Asha and her dad designed and built the tree house; she and her mom picked out a new bedspread and wall paint. These gifts encouraged both quality time with Asha's parents, and her own growing need for independence.

Even just sitting side by side at a baseball game is a limbic boost, an opportunity to nourish each other through mutual attunement. A gift of presence can be a simple act of kindness, such as the biweekly Scrabble game between Linda (a hospice choir singer) and a 103-year-old resident she met in the hallway of a nursing home in Minnesota. When I listened to Linda recount the lovely times they shared, it was impossible to identify one of them as "giver" and the other as "receiver." Once we're in the land of limbic resonance, the benefits of deep mammalian nourishment inevitably go both ways and beyond. Such communions are energizing, and good energy keeps going.

A gift of companionship is not impossible from afar; the companion in these cases might just not be you, the gift giver. No one can replace you, but you can still give a gift that offers companionship, a balm for the widespread loneliness of this era. A round of mini golf with friends or a bread-baking workshop are gifts for your recipient to enjoy with other people. Gifts that lean toward social activities, like board games and cookbooks and even clever T-shirts, can also encourage recipients to connect with people nearby. A gift can put its recipient in touch with the more-than-human world too, such as a pair of binoculars for an aspiring birder.

When putting together a gift of presence, it is good to check to be sure such a gift is appropriate for both the relationship and the recipient. Maybe someone is depleted from long hours at work and needs downtime rather than for all their BFFs to drop in for a surprise visit. It can be tempting to think a surprise is unconditionally awesome, but some people prefer to know what's coming and even savor the anticipation. Checking in doesn't have to take the fun out of the gift; if anything, it makes it more likely to go well for all involved. But if you know your recipient relishes a surprise, by all means, go for it!

For both givers and receivers, it is important to reserve our energy for the relationships that are mutually supportive and beneficial. In the wise words of therapist and author Nedra Glover Tawwab, "When you choose your inner circle, you choose your energy."[2] We can also be choosy about *how* we share time with the people we choose. *What is the activity? How big is the group? Can I enjoy time with a relative who has different politics from me if I put good boundaries into place? Do I want an escape plan, just in case?* If you don't like or want a particular offer of in-person presence, I am here to remind you that it is in your power—at any phase—to say, "Thank you, but no." If you don't want to accept the offer as is, but you are game for part of it or want to suggest an alternative, say so and work together to find a variation that you would be happy to receive, and the giver would be happy to give.

Enriching Time

A major perk of hanging out in person is that you can incorporate full-sensory experience—interesting places, foods, clothes, textures, scents, sounds. You don't have to just talk the whole time; you can have the small adventure of a joint experience. Once you have the guest list finalized, the two most important ingredients of a great gift of time are *enrichment* and *presence.* In other words, do something interesting together, and be attentive and loving while you do it.

Every year, Auntie Rara in San Francisco dreams up an enriching, one-on-one adventure for her niece and nephew in Wisconsin. Rather than send presents throughout the year's various gift occasions, she saves up all that energy and puts it into one remarkable experience for each of them, usually in the springtime when she visits. Auntie Rara has done this since they were little, so they know the drill. And they love it. When her nephew was four years old, they visited the stalactites and stalagmites of the Cave of the Mounds. When they were older, zip-lining through a forest. Another year, riding Segways through Golden Gate Park. And others: horseback riding in a state park, a historic high tea in a Victorian house outside Milwaukee, sailing lessons. Their aunt does give each of her niblings one small Christmas gift each year, an ornament to commemorate their spring adventure—a geological specimen on a string, a little horse, a tiny sailboat.

Donna designed a simple but rich experience to do with her two grown daughters when the time came to sell their childhood home. Donna dreamed up a beautiful goodbye ritual for the house. Mother and daughters went from room to room, lighting candles, writing down memories of events and activities that took place in each room over the years, and then sharing what they wrote by reading it aloud before blowing out the candle as they left each room for the last time. Donna gathered lavender and sage, and gave it to her daughters so they could carry the scent of their childhood yard home with them.

Maybe you've heard of the "love languages" concept? Relationship educator Anne Hodder-Shipp turned a decade of observations of how people want to be loved into a pithy guide, *Speaking from the Heart: 18 Languages for Modern Love.*[3] It is a great tool for designing an experience gift—romantic or platonic—for all ages. I keep a list of her love languages from *Speaking from the Heart* in my journal.

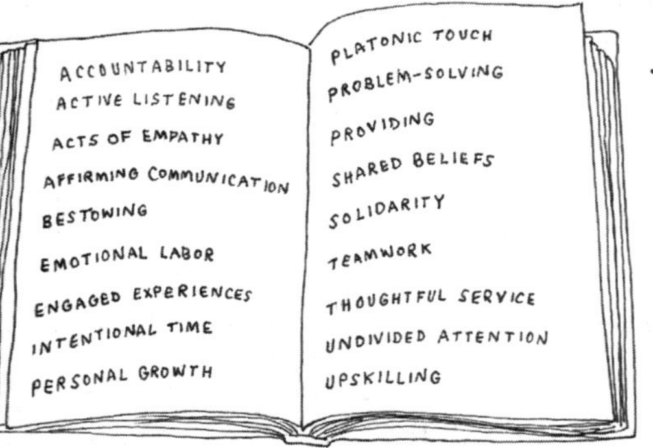

When Ashley turned fifty in Brooklyn, she decided to have fun with the fact that she had gotten that far in life without ever having had a peanut butter and jelly sandwich; she asked everyone attending her party to bring their best PB&J. In the spotlight of her birthday, Ashley tasted each one, spontaneously reviewed it, and then chose a winner. Instead of being burdened with a bunch of physical object gifts she didn't want, she solicited a fun crowd-sourced party game, guiding people toward an easy gift she would enjoy receiving. In doing so, she activated some of Hodder-Shipp's love languages, including *engaged experiences, intentional time, active listening, upskilling,* and *bestowing.*

SK invited her crush, Erin, to an unusual event—a full moon perfume party over video chat. One of them was living in New Zealand and the other in New York City, so they each drew from their respective perfume sample collections. They opened the vials, one by one, bridging the nine thousand miles between them. The scent notes rose from their skin, serving as conversation starters and story prompts. Evoking the date months later in person, SK gave Erin an exquisite French perfume—one of smoke, lavender, and violets. The crush had become a partnership. This gift was especially strong in Hodder-Shipp's languages of *undivided attention, active listening,* and *acts of empathy.*

Something for Everyone

Thoughtfully designed structures for giving and receiving let people know what to expect and how to participate. They are recipes for richness and can also be a relief to everyone involved. In *The Art of Gathering,* Priya Parker calls these "pop-up rules" and emphasizes how modern realities call for intentional structures so that diverse groups of people who do not share cultural norms can share quality time successfully.[4]

New parents Jeremy and Sarah told me they are keeping a running list of "Baby's First Experiences," in which their friends and family sign up to share enriching activities with their growing child, like "first poetry experience" and "first time popping bubble wrap." The list is an elegant way to direct their community's generosity into forms of connection that will be meaningful to them. They are letting their people know how they want to be loved while leaving plenty of room for participants to make it their own.

There is a mama-to-be blessing ceremony involving beads that has been going around. Each attendee brings a special bead to contribute and takes a turn bestowing words of encouragement and support upon the mama-to-be, who strings the beads together onto a cord as she receives the loving words. As the activity circles back to her, she has a chance to speak as well, to be seen and heard upon the precipice of childbirth.

At one ceremony I attended, there was a bead made from a tiny piece of driftwood. Its maker spoke of the wild forces outside of us that shape us as she wished the new mother courage and strength. Another bead was a big shimmering golden heart, and the speaker shared her own experience of motherhood not being the precious thing she thought it would be. In her words, it schooled her, but it also rounded her. Her wise advice was to not seek perfection, but "good enough." For the bead ceremony I facilitated, I mailed the invitees empty envelopes for their beads a month before the event. I included suggestions for where to obtain a meaningful bead, how to connect the qualities of the bead to their well-wishes, and prompts to start thinking about what they might say.

The brilliance of this ceremony is that it integrates materiality, words, and quality time. It provides an enriching structure that draws out the best in people. It is specific enough and flexible enough for people to make it their own: bead aesthetics, bead source, bead price, the meaning of their bead, how long they want to talk. The sister of the new mom, for example, might have a lot more to say than I do, and the structure allows for that. The pop-up rule of this gathering also elegantly accommodates a diversity of heritages and experiences. All the beads are valuable because they are infused with love and threaded together onto one string to keep close during birth. The facilitator of the ceremony I attended set the tone beautifully. She made an altar ahead of time and welcomed us into a sacred space infused with purpose. Everyone turned off their phones, and the mama-to-be got our full attention. Twenty-five gifts went home with the recipient, but they fit in her pocket!

Structure helps people feel comfortable interacting with dear ones and strangers alike. It is possible, however, to accidentally overdesign an experience, making something wonderful feel too constraining, too complicated, or just too long. If planning an experience gift feels exhausting, your "doing something" can be purposely "doing nothing." Time can become quality time just by grabbing an ice cream cone or catching your breath together in a meaningful place. I like to leave some wiggle room in my experience gifts. The dynamic spontaneity of people together can be plenty interesting. I'd happily let a plan get derailed for the sake of spontaneous fun.

Being Here, Now

On my bookshelf sits my well-worn copy of *Pilgrim at Tinker Creek* by Annie Dillard. One dog-ear returns me to the spot where I doodled a little tea bowl in the margin back in college: "Experiencing the present purely is being emptied and hollow; you catch grace as a man fills his cup under a waterfall."[5] If the present is a gift, then our ability to *be present* is our best hope of receiving it well. And presence is a practice, perhaps a muscle. Moment-to-moment awareness can help us stay engaged with whatever is before us. Mindfulness lets us notice and set aside the urge, for example, to grab our phone in the middle of an in-person gift of experience. We can even pregame presence before a special event or gathering by taking a moment to collect our energy and set an intention to show up fully.

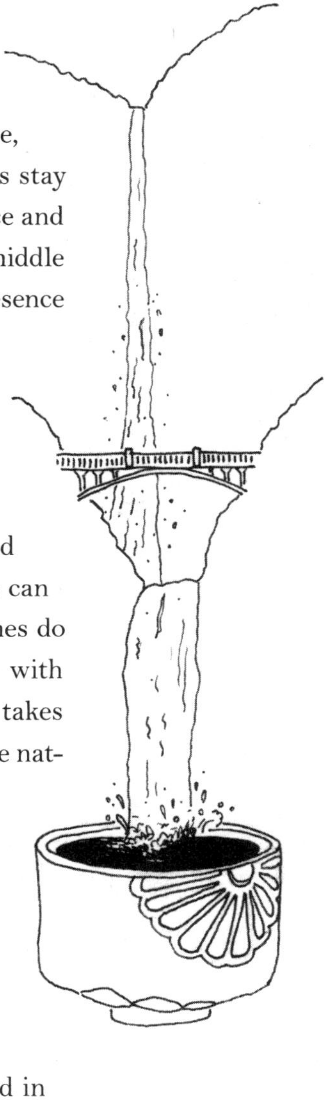

It is a cruel twist that the people we love most are the ones easiest to take for granted—family members, besties, housemates, co-parents. These are the relationships most vulnerable to the dulling forces of frequent exposure and routine. A gift of quality time to pull us beyond daily habits can refresh a relationship. There is a quick meditation I sometimes do when I want to wake up in this way while spending time with someone. I call it the Time Machine. Here's how it goes—it takes just thirty seconds and can be done with your eyes open in the natural course of whatever you are already doing.

I begin by imagining a time machine—the DeLorean from *Back to the Future*, the TARDIS from *Doctor Who*, a giant pumpkin—landing in my living room, kitchen, or wherever I may be. I disembark from my time machine a few feet away from the me that is already in the room. I've just returned from the distant future—my elder years or even centuries beyond my own death. My future self looks around in awe and walks toward my present self, then slips through my skin to merge with my body in this timeline. *This* century, *this* moment, *these* people—they become more special. I am with people dear to me, whom I haven't seen in centuries. Lucky me!

For both givers and receivers, savoring a good time after the fact helps us receive the fullest benefits. A gratitude practice completes the loop and can

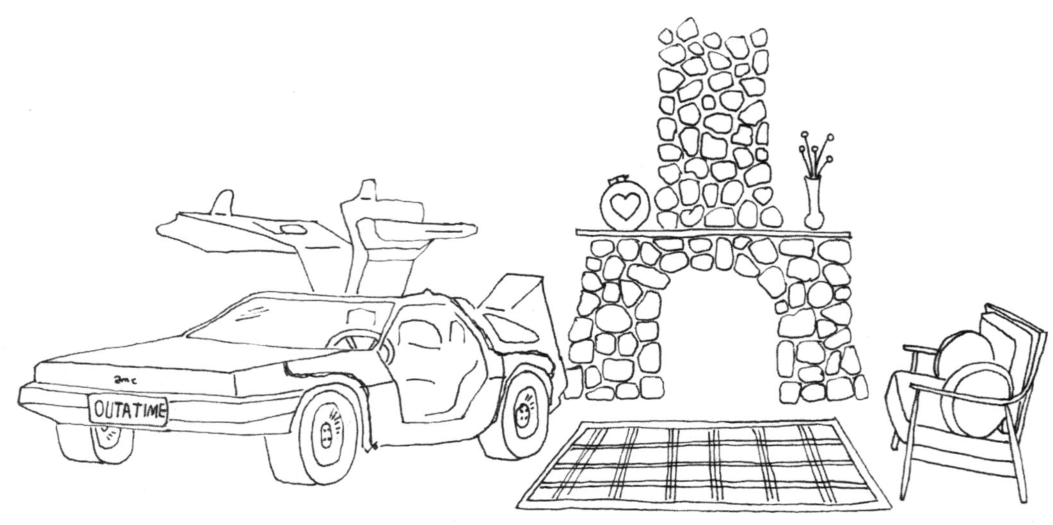

be done in many forms: in a journal, in one's imagination, via conversation or a thank-you card. My flower-collecting sweetheart Oscar and I invented a fun drawing game for this purpose. We named it Amorabilia. To play, each person privately sketches a handful of mementos after spending quality time together, then they trade papers and try to guess which moment each drawing is recalling. Something similar could be done in the form of charades.

The Faraway Nearby

Our gifts are inevitably infused with our being, with a palpable sense of presence. My grandmother knit me a bobble blanket for my high school graduation. She passed away decades ago, and yet, she is still there in every bobble; I feel her nearby. I know how much time and attention went into it. Even when she was alive, the blanket transmitted something of her spirit, the warmth of her presence, from a thousand miles away. My childhood hero, Georgia O'Keeffe, liked to write "from the faraway nearby" before signing her name at the end of a handwritten letter. Indeed, distance can both stretch and shrink in matters of the heart, in the true geography of a gift.

History is full of examples of people showing up for each other from afar, extending each other's presence in small, marvelously material ways that kept them connected, such as a photo or lock of hair when going off to war. From historian Tiya Miles I learned about beads and buttons moving between enslaved people in the United States in the eighteenth century, bridging the distances between families torn asunder. Imbued with the presence of the giver, these small mementos were "pressed into the palm of a parting loved one's hand,"[6] transforming the otherwise ordinary objects into powerful medicine that could travel many miles in a pocket.

Quality Time Begets Good Gifts

A young woman named Blu, a high school student with a remarkable quality of wisdom and poise who didn't look at her phone once during our three-hour conversation, has a gift-giving love language of sorts: books. She dreams of opening a bookstore someday, which is fitting, given that she is known for her thoughtfulness in choosing books for her inner circle. Her selections are often acutely relevant, revealing what Blu sees in her friends.

Books let us hang out inside other people's minds, including ones very different from our own. They offer quality time with their characters, with the author, and with the person who gave the book to us. A gift-wrapped book is like getting a ticket to a big adventure, maybe even a bonus lifetime. Books give us access to our own potential to change and grow. They also nurture empathy for that which we will never be.

A good book checks all three gift boxes: objects, words, experiences. I asked Blu how she chooses books for people. She said that she is able to tell when a friend is in a certain phase or season, and when they might appreciate a particular book. *How?* She spends time with them. They do things together. They talk about hard things, they listen to each other, and they are open to each other. Combine all that quality time with Blu's active reading life and the book gift ideas emerge organically because Blu is perfectly poised to know.

Heart-to-Heart

It is a treat for hearts to beat together for a bit, to give and take each other's pulses, over tea and cookies or by way of a bobble, a bead, or a book. The ticktock of a mechanical clock proceeds at regular intervals—seconds, minutes, hours. The human heartbeat, however, does not. As seen on an EKG monitor or felt within one's own chest, the length between beats is constantly changing, reflecting whatever is happening for us in the moment. A heart can change quickly, slowing down when relaxed and racing when excited or nervous. If you live to be a hundred years old, you might get three billion heartbeats in your lifetime. But each beat alone doesn't mean much. Like in a song, we need a sequence, and spaces in between. Gift-giving, especially when it involves quality time between people, can be a part of an ongoing process of nourishing a relationship, of transforming minutes into moments. While we may not be able to choose how many total heartbeats we get, I do think we have quite a bit of say in the melody they are making as they go.

Reflect

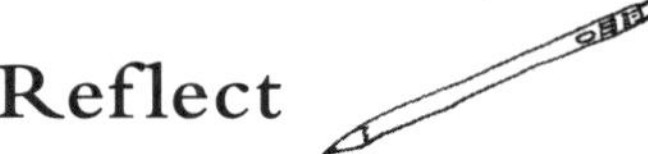

1. Design a gift for someone you love with an overarching goal of giving them "good company." As you design, include an understanding of your recipient's more-than-human forms of companionship—the landscapes, flora, fauna, artifacts, art, and architectures that spark delight, add enrichment, and encourage presence. (Reminder: It could be a book!)

2. Dream up a pop-up rule for your next birthday gathering, swapping in quality time for the default physical object gifts guests often bring. Notify your invitees or attendees.

3. Have you ever received a gift from someone that made you feel incredibly close despite their being geographically far away? How did this gift work its magic from afar? How might you close the distance between you and someone you love with a gift?

4. An experience-based gift oftentimes does not easily pack into a box with a bow, but we can increase the fun of bestowal with creative tokens such as a "golden ticket" or a baseball game ticket in a mitt. How might you present your next experience gift in a creative way?

8

Wishing Each Other Well

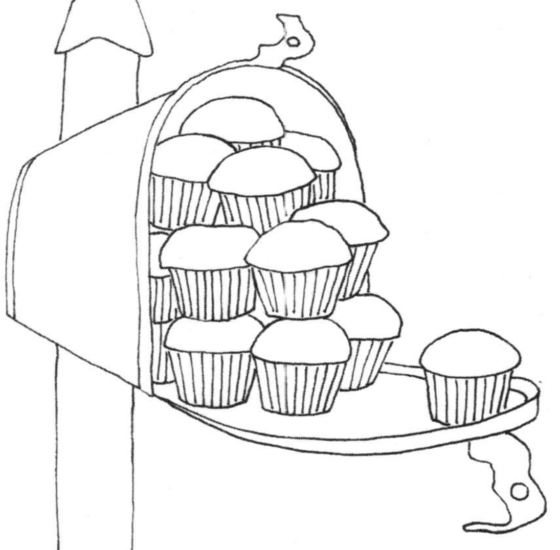

WHAT DO HUMAN BEINGS NEED, WANT, LONG FOR?

HOW CAN I CARE FOR MYSELF AS
I GIVE AND RECEIVE?

ON A PLANET IN CRISIS, IS IT EVEN
OKAY TO WANT THINGS?

Love is a vessel that contains both security and adventure.

—ESTHER PEREL, *MATING IN CAPTIVITY*

Being Well

In their heart of hearts, *what do human beings want*? What is the repertoire of wants, needs, and desires that we might gift toward? As I reflect on the gift stories I've received, it appears to me that human beings want to *heal*, to *maintain*, to *grow*, and to *wake up*. Keeping these four elements in mind can help us design our gestures of care to meet our recipients' needs upon a particular occasion or season of their lives.

Gifts That Heal

Gifts to alleviate suffering, or to *heal*, are some of the most unforgettable. Some address a serious pain point; others just make life easier or less stressful. My friend Michelle recalls a gift her mom gave her every time she had to stay home sick during elementary school—a brand-new box of crayons and coloring books. When Lisa in the Midwest learned that the only thing an ill, elderly friend would eat was the home-baked pumpkin muffins

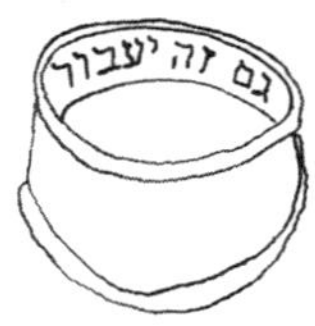

she dropped off, she kept them coming as fast as they disappeared. Another kind soul named Tamara has a finger ring engraved with "This too shall pass" in Hebrew. If one of her friends is going through something difficult, she invites them to borrow the ring until they feel better.

"Rarely, if ever, are any of us healed in isolation. Healing is an act of communion," wrote bell hooks.[1] It can be as simple as a hand gesture. I will never forget when, during a depressive episode in my twenties, one of my besties held out her hand to me when I was stuck on the couch, offering me a walk around the block. I refused for a good while, and I am forever grateful for how she waited for me to come around, keeping her hand within my reach so I could take it the moment I mustered the energy. Her outstretched hand broke the spell I was under and got me moving again. She knew exactly what I needed and put it so close to me that I could choose it for myself too.

When Annie in Los Angeles was suffering from chronic insomnia, two close friends put together a care package including a pair of cozy pajamas, a sleep mask, and lavender pillow spray. They stopped by her home at bedtime to give it to her. Annie told me that regardless of whether she slept better, she felt supported by her friends and less alone with her sleep struggles. A gift can also help heal a relationship itself, like when SP marked the end of a multiyear estrangement from her sister, IG, with the gift of matching "sister bracelets" custom inscribed with the C. S. Lewis line that IG texted to break the silence: *Courage, dear heart.*[2]

A gift that heals could also be the restoration of a lost item or another chance at an experience someone missed out on. Alexis in Los Angeles lost her whole house to the Eaton Fire. Just a few days before, she had proudly thrifted a mid-century Dutch oven, swooning over it on Instagram. After the fire, she posted a video of the charred pot in a pile of rubble and ash. A few weeks later, Alexis received a mysterious package from Northern California. When she opened it, her jaw hit the floor. It was her beloved Dutch oven!

Close enough, anyway. Bearing the same mid-century dove motif and made by Hanova of Pasadena, it was almost exactly the same, just poppy orange instead of cobalt blue. Alexis loved it. Her friends up north had seen the Instagram post and hunted down a replacement for her. Alexis told me that the significance of the dove on the side of the oven, a symbol of peace, felt more meaningful than ever. Or had it transformed into a phoenix, Alexis wondered, rising from the ashes? She lifted the lid to find a note: *You got this, Alexis.*

Gifts That Maintain

Gifts to *maintain* are all the big and small gestures of care that offer people stability, familiarity, and security. A ride to a stressful job interview or a mason jar of homemade soup as part of a "meal train" for new parents can make all the difference. A single man in Houston, Texas, once arrived home after a three-month business trip to discover a few staples—bread, milk, eggs—waiting for him in his fridge. He and some other single professionals in his neighborhood had become close after Hurricane Ike, swapping house keys, pet-sitting, giving each other rides to medical appointments, and even celebrating New Year's Eve together. One of them had stocked his fridge so he wouldn't have to make a run to the store right away. When a friend or neighbor is out of town, we can cat-sit, water their houseplants, or bring in their mail, "just because."

Gifts also maintain meaning, reminding us who we are and that we belong. Tess felt loved and accepted by her in-laws when her husband, Tyler, needlepointed her a welcome-to-the-family Christmas stocking. It matched the rest of her in-laws' stockings, fitting right in with the ones made decades earlier by Tyler's grandfather before he passed away. The stocking for Tess was part of maintaining the evolving sense of family they shared.

My friend's mom up in Yurok territory shared with me a story about a special baby basket her great-aunt wove for her from willow on the occasion of her birth. Acorn-shaped with an opening on one side, the basket is both a bed and a baby carrier that can be strapped to a parent's back. The willow plants that supplied the weaving material were harvested in the traditional, sustainable way. The willows grow wild in the Klamath watershed, where my friend's family has deep roots. As a newborn, my friend's mom had nestled into the basket weave, swaddled by blankets and leather straps. Dangling across the top was a "lifeline" of blue and white beads, which were strung onto the gut cord by her great-aunt, along with prayers, blessings, and loving well-wishes for her.

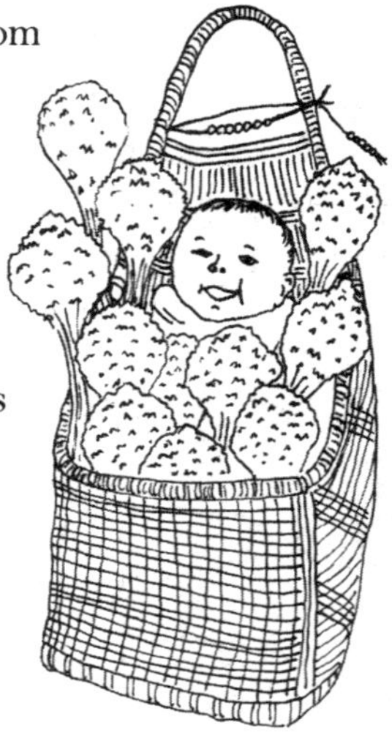

The years have been kind to this willow-root baby basket, as have its caretakers. My friend practically lived in it when she was a baby, her mom told me. And now that my friend has babies of her own, chubby little fingers admire the beaded lifeline once again, pulling the blessings forward and keeping the Yurok tradition alive.

Gifts for Growth

Gifts for *growth* encourage a sense of aliveness, offering delight, wonder, hope, play, novelty, pleasure, creativity, challenge, even healthy risk. I have a friend who gave a ropes course adventure to their family one Christmas. Family members bonded while supporting each other as they walked across tightropes suspended up in redwood trees. Lisa in Illinois put together a DIY nude figure drawing kit for her friend's fiftieth birthday to enjoy on a date night with her husband. (It included a giant red gift bow with a note, *Optional: for added comfort or play.*) As a child in the 1950s, Eileen in Colorado had fun introducing her pen pal to peanut butter by sending a jar all the way to Finland. The joy of creativity leads artist Leah Rosenberg to gift undecorated cakes to children. She delivers the cake iced white, a blank canvas, and provides colored icing. When I asked Beth (the greeting card shop owner) about her favorite gift, she was quick to say "a new friend." If you value new friends, wouldn't it be lovely to receive a birthday card containing three names and phone numbers for meetups that have been prearranged for you by a trusted mutual friend?

Gifts for growth can also go deeper, to more vulnerable territory. Empathy channeled creatively can lead us to give unexpected gifts, purposely introducing the recipient to things beyond their experience so far. Based on what we do understand about someone, we might decide to show them something new-to-them as a small adventure. Even if someone would typically opt for a day at a museum, that doesn't mean they wouldn't also love a trip to a walking labyrinth in the woods or a bonfire on the beach. Isn't this why we need each other, why it is so pleasurable to be in relation? There are tide pools to poke around in and tiny alpine strawberries to taste if you know where to look. There are corn mazes, pinball parlors, and glass elevators. There is more to love in this world than anyone could ever know or hope to see, smell, taste, hear, or touch. We can remind each other how big and beautiful the world is.

I love it when a great gift references what someone already values in addition to revealing what they might be yearning for. A musician named Tarik, Tyreek on his albums, used to work in fashion design. His personal taste led him to wear all black every day. When he eventually left the company, his coworkers threw him a goodbye party and gifted him a mustard-yellow jacket.

Bold move! They had gone out on a limb, but Tarik was glad they followed their gut and took a risk. He ended up loving it, and in time, that yellow jacket opened up a whole new world of wearing color for him.

When I read Helen Jukes's 2020 memoir, *A Honeybee Heart Has Five Openings,* I loved learning that her first bee colony had been a gift. After apprenticing for years to become a beekeeper, she was living in a house in Oxford with a back garden—finally space for a hive of her own. She hesitated. Would she be a good beekeeper? Could she keep them alive? Would they swarm, abandoning her? Helen's housemate witnessed both her desire and her nerves. The housemate organized a group gift involving an IOU for a colony of bees come springtime. Helen told me that when she opened the IOU envelope, she felt like someone had picked her up and circled her. She was deeply moved. Her other feeling was, *Oh! Now I have to really do it.* She said she might not have taken the leap toward a colony of her own without that gift; their loving nudge pushed her past her self-doubt.

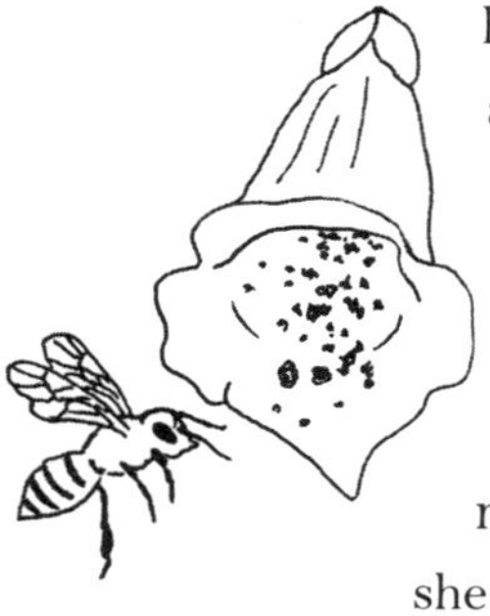

The self is an ever-unfolding mystery. It is possible to be estranged from our own deepest longings. We don't always have the self-awareness to understand what we most need and want. Even when we do, then what? Nobody else can tell me who I am, or who I should become, or how, but they might see the true me coming before I do. They might help me get out of my own way. What excites me about gifts is the idea that a loved one might see something in us, and for us, precisely because they are *not us.*

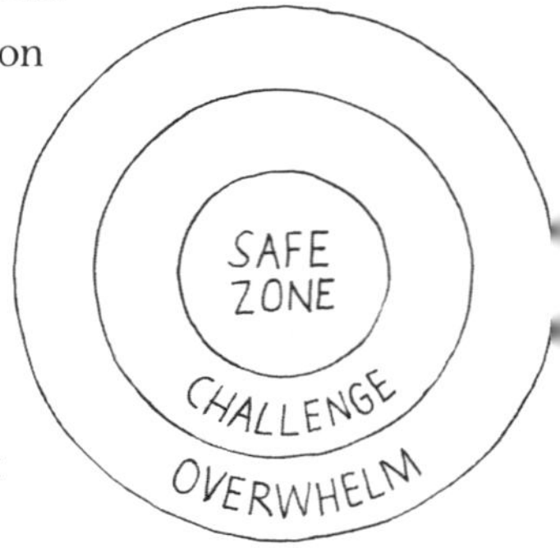

During an online workshop with self-compassion researcher Kristin Neff, she offered us a powerful diagram of three circles nested one inside another. The smallest circle in the center had "safe zone" written in it. The next circle out was labeled "challenge zone." The largest circle was the "overwhelm zone." The idea is that people learn and grow best when they are in the challenge zone. Sure, overwhelming life experiences can prompt growth, but they don't make good presents. Mihaly Csikszentmihalyi, a psychologist known for his research about flow, writes, "Enjoyment appears at the boundary between boredom and anxiety, when the challenges are just balanced with the person's capacity to act."[3] If we want to give someone a "challenging" gift but we cannot determine whether our idea is within the challenge zone or perhaps in the overwhelm zone, that might mean we do not know the recipient well enough to give them such an adventuresome gift. Or that we still have homework to do. At the same time, a little nervousness might be a good sign, an indication that a gift idea is in the challenge zone, that sweet spot where growth happens.

Gifts for growth invite us to stretch into more desirable futures and lovely possibilities—some that we might not have the courage or confidence to reach for on our own. Sometimes we need a loving nudge to become our truest, most lively selves. A nudge can even be open-ended, like when a woman turning fifty received a charming pouch of fifty pennies for her birthday, for tossing into fountains, making wishes, and dreaming up desires.

Gifts That Wake Us Up

By *wake up*, I mean the act of refreshing the ordinary such that it becomes extraordinary—by finding a new angle on it or seeing it in a new light. When something is readily accessible, it is all too easy to take it for granted. If we want to appreciate it, we must actively counteract the frame of mind conditioned by such ubiquity. When we are awake, we can get excited about—in other words, we can *desire*—the goodness we already have.

While sitting on a log one morning, my four-year-old friend Bijoya and I took our sweet time enjoying a few tangerines, but with a twist. First, I introduced her to "the Prank," which is a silly trick in which you present someone with what appears to be a tangerine, but they quickly determine that it is just a poor imposter—an empty peel spiraled back into its original spherical form. Part of the fun is that it is practically impossible to truly trick anyone with the scrappy facade. In Bijoya's case, I added an over-the-top backstory about how I had traveled the world in search of this beautiful, perfect, sweetest, juiciest tangerine *just for her.* I crossed deserts, waded rivers, climbed trees! She didn't buy it for one second, but she did burst into laughter. We went back and forth "pranking" each other with tangerines. Whenever it was my turn, she insisted I perform another dramatic backstory. I learned how much the Prank had meant to her when my birthday rolled around a few months later and she (with the help of my friend Bidisha, her mom) gifted me a pair of earrings that looked like miniature tangerine slices.

Something as simple as a tangerine in our hands can invite our inner worlds—the richness within—to come out and play. Less tangible gifts can do the same. Every month, my friend Amy gives a generous gift when she hosts an evening of community singing in the redwoods. Under the towering trees, Amy's warm welcome prepares the ground for presence. In this sacred container, she gracefully guides us through a series of songs. About halfway through, I feel like I am sparkling. I am in more direct touch with my aliveness than usual. I am all abuzz with my own desire for life as that desire is simultaneously being fulfilled. I am also reawakened to the fact that I love to sing, yet another deep desire for something that I already have—vocal cords! Amy's gift metabolizes and multiplies as I sing in the car on the way home and in the shower the next morning. It reminds me that I, too, am a container for the sacred.

When I read Walden as a college student, I underlined Thoreau's words with gusto: "It is something to be able to paint a particular picture, or to carve a statue, and so to make a few objects beautiful; but it is far more glorious to carve and paint the very atmosphere and medium through which we look. . . . To affect the quality of the day, that is the highest of arts."[4] Amen! In fact, the older I get, the clearer it is that things are only as beautiful and interesting as the attention with which I meet them, as the lens I am looking through. I am convinced that much of what we truly want is already here or nearby. We just need to notice it, savor it, protect it, and spread it around so everyone who wants some gets some.

All Together Now

Heal. Maintain. Grow. Wake up. My dear friend Sadegh once offered me a gesture of care at the intersection of all four. The occasion? A breakup. Sadegh showed up at my Tearoom of a Thousand Wonders with a paper sack of oranges and a vintage ceramic teapot crafted to look like an orange—peel texture and leaf handle. But when they lifted the lid, I saw a ceramic reamer hiding inside. Bravo! Sadegh twisted orange halves onto that little reamer while I caught them up on the breakup and they caught me up on their new apartment. The *healing* came from the good company. The *maintenance* was the nourishment of fresh orange juice. The *growth* was the pull toward the postrelationship reality that was waiting for me. The *wake-up* was the novelty teapot with the surprising reamer and the beautiful way Sadegh processed the oranges live, between us.

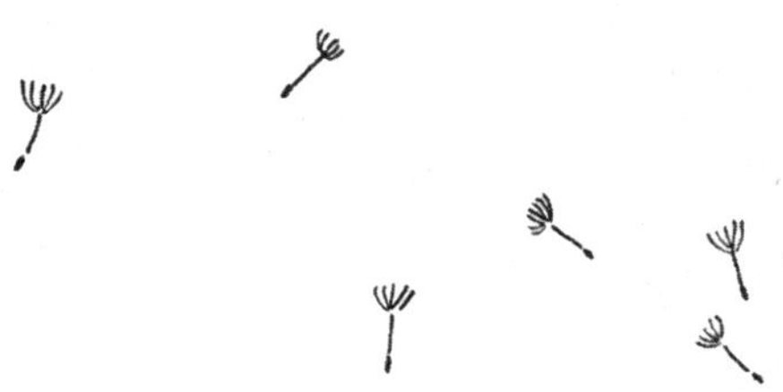

Being Seen, Being Supported

When people tell me about the most meaningful gifts they've ever received, they often talk about *feeling seen*. Feeling seen is intimately connected to feeling like we matter. It is to be acknowledged and validated, known and celebrated. It can be a very simple gesture, like when a baby named Rose suddenly pointed directly at her grandma's face from across the kitchen and declared, for the first time, "Ga-gna!" Or a little more involved, like when I honored a mathematician in my life by learning how to fold a paper craft dodecahedron for him.

I used to date a lovely man who grew up in Spokane, Washington, home of the Gonzaga Bulldogs college basketball team. When we visited his parents there during basketball season, we all watched the games together in the den on a big TV. This household also likes to play the board game Carcassonne, in which each player gets a handful of "meeples," little wooden figures of a unique color. And so, between visits, I bought some plain white meeples and painted them to look like the Gonzaga Bulldogs—adding blue and red jersey stripes, names, and numbers to the backs. Now whenever they play Carcassonne, one lucky player gets to be the home team!

In addition to being seen, people want to be *supported*. People need acts of service and material encouragements. When my car died on the Mendocino coast this past summer, the host at a bed-and-breakfast along Highway 1 took me in, bought me a bottle of motor oil in town, and let me camp out on the couch in the lobby for six hours, knitting, while I waited for the tow truck. I needed to be seen, yes, but I also needed a helping hand. How lucky to have broken down in front of such a hospitable place!

Brenda in Utah was excited about the new house she and her husband had just bought for their growing family, but she was full of dread about moving out of the old one. When she arrived home with her kids after a weeklong visit with grandparents and opened the front door of the old house, she was stunned. It was empty! She drove straight over to the new house with the kids. Everything was there! Her husband had moved one room every night after work while they were gone. The beds were made; the pictures were on the walls. Brenda told me that three neighbors stopped by in the days to come, saying they wanted to meet the person whose husband would do that for her.

I have a personalized nameplate sitting on my worktable that reads *Lea, The Support Desk.* My dear friend Erin has one of her own across town. I hand-lettered these very "official" signs on cardstock with my watercolors, then slipped them into nameplate holders from an office supply store. A tangible reminder of our intention to be there for each other, these signs prompt us to reach out, to pick up the phone and ask, "Hey, is the Support Desk available right now?" In the grand scheme of things, it can sometimes seem like none of us matter. But zoom in and look around. Grab a paper and pen. Start writing a list of names. This is the scale where people can matter because they matter *to each other.*

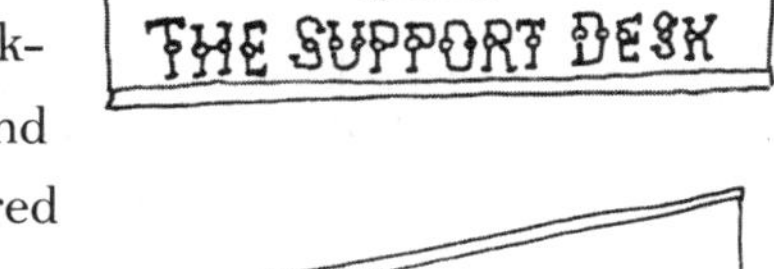

Seeing and Supporting in Hard Times

When my friend Ayden's partner, ET, was going through cancer treatment in rural Massachusetts, they both noticed how gifts for ET were also gifts for Ayden. One of their neighbors, Candace, a new acquaintance, began regularly dropping off produce and bouquets of flowers, including a practically infinite supply of backyard green beans since they were the only green vegetable ET could stomach. Candace's regular presence and intuitive understanding of how to show up came from her own experience of her dad's cancer treatment, and blossomed into a deep friendship. Other family and friends sent prepared meals, came to clean house, or to read aloud; each offering relieved Ayden from some of the weight of being the primary caregiver. When it became clear that Ayden couldn't swing the daily four-hour roundtrip drive to the hospital for ET's radiation treatment for weeks on end, neighbors and friends set up a rotation.

It is hard to fully grasp the significance of managing the ordinary for someone who temporarily cannot. To come over and wash dishes and clean toilets can immeasurably brighten a day. We can creatively tend to the details with extra sensitivity and wisdom. Whenever Candace dropped off food and flowers, she would text advance notice, such as: *Quietly dropping off more green beans in an hour or so. No need to greet me or reply unless you're looking for company today.* Her attunement to the situation was exquisite, even artful. As were the handwritten labels she put on her mason jars of homemade soup.

If we are lucky enough for people to show up for us like this, we will learn that it is possible to entrust our well-being to others, an act of much vulnerability and great reward. I wish for everyone to be embedded in such a loving community, one that lets them rest in the sense that, should they ever need it, they will be encircled in care.

Of course, hard times don't only call for acts of service and very practical gifts. This is why Candace picked all those flowers in her backyard along with the green beans. It is why one of ET's students knit a silly hat for ET's cat and sent it in the mail, adding a bit of laughter and levity to the whole situation. A healing body also needs nourishment for the mind and spirit—enrichment, entertainment, humor, beauty, compassion, hope.

A few practical tips. For the sake of the recipient as well as their caretakers, plan ahead, especially if there is uncertainty around just how challenging, time-consuming, expensive, or emotionally taxing their circumstances are going to be. Also, there are websites that can manage mutual aid logistics, from monetary gifts to sending a "song of the day." Recipients can set it up to coordinate many different forms of support, letting people care for them from near or far within any budget. Requesting greeting cards, movie recs, video messages, and the like are great low-cost options.

From Strangers to Kin

The Artist Is Present is a work by Marina Abramović that drew crowds to the Museum of Modern Art in New York in 2010. Minimal in terms of installation—just two chairs in the center of the airy atrium—it was a massive undertaking. In one chair, Abramović sat in a long gown, the dark braid of her hair resting over her left shoulder. In the other chair, a rotation of museum visitors took turns receiving the artist's attention—and offering their own. The artist sat in her chair for eight consecutive hours a day, for nearly three months. She locked eyes with more than a thousand people—silent, still, intent. It was an epic feat of focus and physical endurance. As the artist gazed into her visitors' eyes and they gazed back at her gazing at them gazing at her, on and on, many of the participants were moved to tears, including Abramović. The power of the quality of presence was palpable.

The vast majority of people who sat across from Abramović were strangers, revealing the fact that we do not need to know each other personally to see each other deeply. What does it mean, then, to meet a stranger with a gift, a significant gesture of care to see and support? While there may be exquisitely personal gifts for people we know well, there can be equally exquisite gifts for people we hardly know but with whom we share a common humanity. *Stranger* feels like the wrong word altogether. Must we be so *strange* to each other? So *estranged*?

Her first Christmas as a single mother, Charlene worried about filling her children's holiday with gifts, treats, and community. She felt alone. Then an anonymous gift arrived for her daughter. *To: Brittany.* They opened the box to find a Tickle Me Elmo, that year's most-wanted, hardest-to-get toy. Brittany was overjoyed. The gift offered her mom hope and belonging in a challenging season, an abiding sense that her community cared. Inspired by Elmo, I recently dropped off a gift at the preschool I walk by every day, a beautiful pair of fabric monarch butterfly wings for pretend play. My gift tag read: *From a friend in the neighborhood.*

Here's a creative idea, for me and for you too, if it feels like a fit. Moving forward, every time I devote resources to a gift for a child with whom I feel close, regardless of that child's financial situation, I can pair it with a gift to a child in need whom I do not personally know, perhaps prioritizing children in groups that have been financially neglected or denied opportunities. If I am unable to double my resources, I can just split whatever resources I have in half to make way for the additional gift. Another creative spin: Every year, on the birthday of someone I love who has passed away, I can give a gift in their honor to an individual or group in need, a stranger of sorts. (Psst: If you like this idea and you like to bake, check out Cake4Kids.)

If a person in a situation deserving of attention is far away geographically, seeing another's humanity might begin with literally seeing images of people in the news. We can support people we do not know personally by sharing our extra resources, if we have some, through donations to reputable aid organizations or by working for policy change as an act of service. When one part of humanity is in crisis, the parts of humanity that are safe and resourced can show up, from the faraway nearby, for those who are not.

While the needs of physical safety and survival must come first, people also want and need meaning, which is sustenance for their spirits. This is why I am drawn to contribute to the World Central Kitchen, which serves nourishing, culturally appropriate meals worldwide in response to humanitarian crises. At the time of this writing, seventy Palestinian-led community kitchens are set up in war-torn Gaza, cooking up the foods the locals know and love, and distributing them for free. For displaced Palestinians observing the sacred month of Ramadan amid the chaos of war, World Central Kitchen distributed ninety thousand special food kits, each one containing ingredients to make fifty meals from staples—such as apricot paste, canned fish, and chickpeas—as well as special items like honey, tea, coffee, and dates. One recipient, a displaced woman named Naheel in Khan Younis, reflected, "When we received the package and opened it, we were overwhelmed with joy and emotions, knowing that you had put so much thought into selecting the food items you knew we missed and needed in such difficult circumstances. It truly warms our hearts."[5]

As a guest on *Jimmy Kimmel Live!*, chef José Andrés, the founder of World Central Kitchen, turned to the audience with a call to action: "People. We need to be always next to the people in our darkest hour because we have the power to make each other better."[6] When disaster strikes, close to home or far away, I think the intensity of the situation cuts straight to the truth. The human family includes everyone. When push comes to shove, most of us do not act like *strangers*, but *familials*. The darkest hours are not "theirs" but *all of ours*.

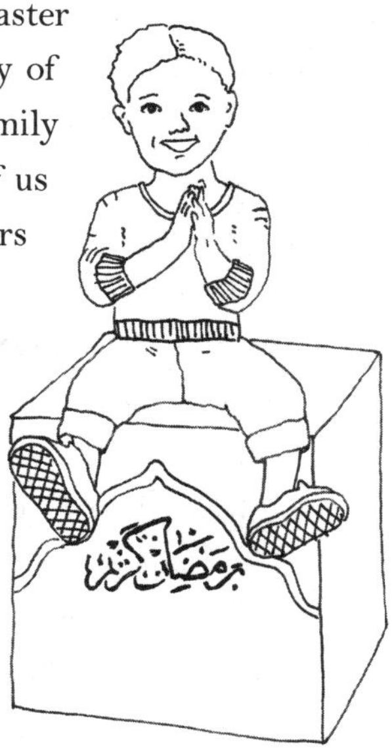

I want my gift practice to extend to serious gestures of care, even ones that blur the lines between gift, duty, and justice. If these feel important to you, you can include them in your practice too. We can stretch our imaginations across the globe and across the street. The hand that reaches out transforms a stranger into kin, reaffirming everyone's place in the circle of humanity.

Self-Love and Good Boundaries

Responsibility as response-ability inspires us to get up and do beautiful things for each other. The more we see, though, the more overwhelmed we might feel as we bear witness to the needs of the world. As such, letting one's heart go out to others must be paired with self-love.

The temptation to give beyond our means is a danger in gift-giving and everywhere else, especially when the love is strong, the stakes are high, and the social conditioning encourages it. But let's not be so generous that we don't keep enough in the larder for ourselves—energy, time, space, money, etc. Sometimes empathy can pull me so far outside of myself that I start to lose myself. But if I self-sacrifice and abandon my own well-being along the way, the gift has gone off course. In good gift-giving, we must wish ourselves well *as* we wish others well. "Boundaries are the distance at which I can love you and me simultaneously," says embodiment coach Prentis Hemphill.[7]

When we know what our own boundary is and we don't transgress it, we prevent the resentment that can come from giving more than we feel good about. A loving boundary also sustains a giver's capacity to continue being generous into the future. Just because a gift registry is set up for a wedding doesn't mean we must buy something from it. What is within our means right now might be a greeting card. The amount of credit card debt people get into while shopping for Christmas presents makes me want to scream. Can't we love each other well enough without the stress of compounding interest?

Kristen in Minnesota told me about one childhood birthday when her mom tended her own boundaries by serving Hostess cupcakes instead of her usual homemade ones. In her mom's eyes, the cupcakes from the store weren't nearly as good as the ones she could make when she wasn't busy going to nursing school. But Kristen loved Hostess cupcakes. All good!

The pressure to over give can come from outside or from within. Sometimes both. It is up to each of us to decide what sorts of relationships we want to be in, what roles we want to fill (or avoid), and what is (or is not) within our power to choose for ourselves. If I am caught up in someone else's emotions, I might feel so responsible for the way they feel—especially when it comes to what they think they need from me to feel good—that I forget myself and make hasty decisions I regret later. This, then, is the shadow side of empathy. Radical attention can be a true joy, but if I am so porous to the experience of another that I emotionally enmesh with them and get hooked, I might prioritize their well-being over my own and maybe even call it love. Staying in touch with our own self-worth can help us hold our ground, as can cultivating relationships based on mutual respect. This is, as usual, easier said than done. And it's not just a question of character. The ease with which someone can choose self-care comes back to differences in power; the resources and safety of privilege provide more freedom to choose.

My three-year-old friend and fellow penny collector, Tali, made it look easy the other day. On my way out after a dinner visit, she followed me outside and eagerly showed me the mint plant in her front yard. When she said I could take some home for tea and started to pluck leaves off the stems, I squatted down to her height and cupped my hands into a little basket shape. Tali liked the look of that empty basket and started to fill it up! Then she warmed my heart once again when she declared with clarity and confidence, in a way that would make my therapist proud, "I'm also going to save some for me." Kudos! As we pour our energy and resources into a gift for another, let's remember to also check in with ourselves by asking: *Is some of this energy actually for me?* For Tracy in Florida, one afternoon, the answer was "Yes!"

Tracy and her husband lovingly do the grocery shopping for his elderly mom. But it can be a bit of a thankless, begrudging duty because her mother-in-law takes the favor for granted. At the grocery store one day, Tracy picked up a slice of carrot cake as a treat for her mother-in-law. When she dropped off the groceries, though, she was bombarded by criticism and complaint. Tracy was fed up. Her own tank was running too low to be caring for another so generously. And so, she slipped the carrot cake out of the bag!

Once home, Tracy took the cake and a fork into her bedroom and shut the door behind her. A few minutes later, her husband came knocking. When she reluctantly cracked the door, she saw a smile and another fork. A charming scene ensued: The couple finished the carrot cake together while cozy in bed, commiserating about how challenging his mom can be. It turned out that Tracy needed the carrot cake that day. She also needed some appreciation and understanding, both of which her husband was happy to provide, especially if there was still cake.

Wishing Ourselves Well

We can bring everyone's wellness to generosity's drafting table. When my aunt makes her annual batch of olallieberry jam to share, it doubles as relaxation and stress relief for herself. When a fellow taught his friend's son how to play tennis, he maintained his own game. When Harsh learned to woodwork for his *corzetti* stamp, he was stretching a new skill. It is practically impossible to put together a gift that invites someone else to wake up to the world without waking ourselves up at the same time.

A birthday present from husband to wife during a challenging season of their lives did it all. The family was in the middle of a two-year leukemia treatment program for Misha, their three-year-old. The husband, Raphi, wasn't sure he had the energy to do something special for his wife Bekah's birthday, but it was her thirty-fifth, and Raphi had an idea too good to ignore. Raphi, Bekah, and their friends had a long-standing joke that Bekah should be president of the United States because—not a joke—she brings so much intelligence and integrity to everything she does. With thirty-five being the minimum age to be elected president, this was the year: *Bekah for President!*

Raphi reached out to their friends, recruiting them to staff a secret, faux campaign headquarters. Friends near and far, old and new, submitted testimonials and video clips of support. One whipped up a simple website, another edited the campaign video, and yet another screen-printed *Bekah Knows* T-shirts, including little ones for Misha and his sister Sybil. *Mom for President!*

Organizing the gift gave Raphi something creative and joyful to do alongside all the difficult things. Perhaps even more important, the gift gathered supportive friends around *him* while they plotted the surprise. And yes, when Bekah was directed to her campaign website and presented with a *Bekah Knows* T-shirt on her birthday, she laughed her way to tears of joy.

In opening up the process to bring together a loving gift for his wife, Raphi invited their nearest and dearest to love her too. Along the way, his creative campaign brought him into steady and often amusing contact with dear friends. His phone pinged with a first look at the campaign video while he searched, once again, for a parking spot in the hospital garage. While he was at his son's bedside, his phone pinged with GIFs and text messages like, *Hey friend, we have ten testimonials so far! And how are y'all doing this week?* Each text message or email buoyed his spirits. The gift was good for him too, and he loved serving as First Gentleman for a spell.

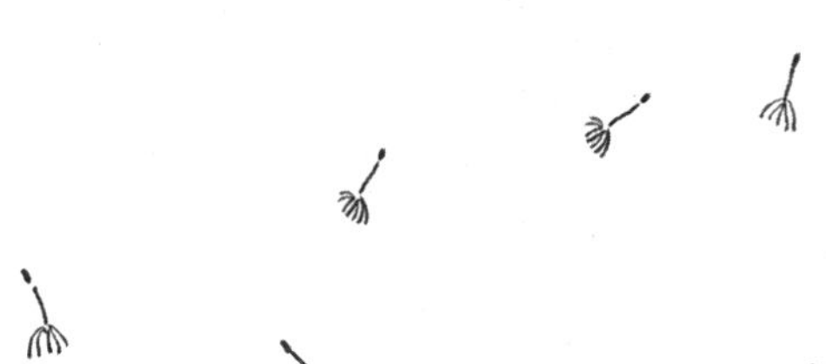

What Do We Really Want?

To *want* is not to crave, demand, hoard, or feel entitled. And to contribute to someone else's satisfaction need not squeeze us into sacrificing our own. We are not just human beings, but humans becoming. For me, to want is to pause, look around, and make a conscious assessment: *Yes, this place is awesome, and I am grateful. But this place is also a big mess, and I have a list of ideas for improvement!*

Having a body, a mind, a heart, and maybe a spirit too, requires constant maintenance and refreshment. We need clean air with every breath. We need the basics of food, water, clothing, and shelter, but sometimes I want them in fun forms—wild sourdough with a little bounce and butter, bubbly water with a squeeze of lime, a sweater knit with cables, a cozy window seat. When I attune to the desire deep within, it is a veritable cornucopia of earthly delights.

What do I really want? I want a handful of wild huckleberries, a kiss in a pumpkin patch, and the scent of creosote after a desert monsoon. I want as many supermoons and solar eclipses as I can get. I want to solve the daily mini crossword, go to a magic show, and get in line for dim sum. I want to get better at roller-skating and dancing the cumbia. I want the monarchs and native bees to be okay and the whales to continue to migrate and sing their songs whether or not I can hear them. I want the glaciers to stay put, small island nations to stay above water, oil pipelines not to run through Indigenous lands or any land at all. I want people to say "I'm sorry" and make it better. I want fewer early goodbyes. I have a lot on my list, but I believe these are reasonable requests. They are what I daydream about and chip away at. I am not entitled to any of it, but I do believe it is my birthright to reach for all of it. This is especially so since all these things boil down to non-things more like these: love, freedom, respect, beauty, belonging, joy. Yes, please and thank you all the way home.

Reflect

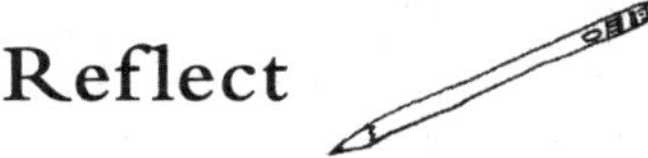

1. As a gift occasion nears, dream up a gift that offers something you observe your recipient needing and wanting most right now: to heal, to maintain, to grow, or to wake up. Try mixing and matching, for increased benefit.

2. In the context of a relationship that is safe and resilient, try giving a gift that is a loving nudge, that invites your recipient into the "challenge zone" where growth happens. Remember that you can make offers before proceeding with any of your ideas if that feels most appropriate.

3. See and support a "stranger" with a gift, someone near or far whom you don't know very well but feel confident gifting toward your common humanity.

4. At your next gift-giving opportunity, do a self-love check-in first. Are you giving within your means and honoring your own needs, well-being, and boundaries along the way?

9

The Art of Attention

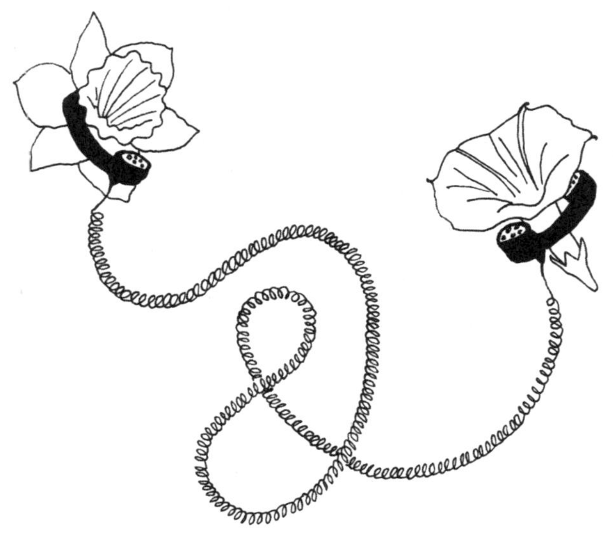

WHAT DOES MY GIFT RECIPIENT NEED, WANT, LONG FOR?

HOW CAN MY GIFT BE A GOOD LISTENER,
A COMPASSIONATE OBSERVER?

HOW CAN I KNOW IF MY GIFT WAS A SUCCESS?

Still—in a way—nobody sees a flower—really—
it is so small—we haven't time—and to see takes time,
like to have a friend takes time.

—GEORGIA O'KEEFFE, *AN AMERICAN PLACE*

People Are Particular

Our common humanity is made up of eight billion uncommon humans, each with their own life story—joys, struggles, dreams. The key to giving good gifts is to address the specific ways people *in particular* want to be seen and supported—to heal, maintain, grow, and wake up—at a particular moment or season of their life. This can be difficult to do for the same reason that it can be wonderful to do: The possibilities are practically infinite! A lava lamp? A bicycle? A pair of socks? How about a mug featuring a family photo, a Rubik's Cube, a tie-dye T-shirt, or a pastel pink poncho? There are scrapbooks, serenades, waltzes, tickets to basketball games, ice shows, ballets, and symphonies. Many people do not want any of these things. But someone, somewhere, surely wants one of them at some point. It might even make their day, or change their life. Wouldn't it be fun to make the match?

Until we become better matchmakers between our loved ones and the world of wonder in which we all live, unwanted gifts—especially objects for possession—are going to continue piling up in garages, at thrift stores, in landfills. What's a gift giver to do? And what can gift receivers do to help? The answer is both super simple and very complicated: *communicate.* Givers can *listen, observe, remember.* And recipients can *show their true selves.* We can never know another human being completely. But that is not a problem; it's the prompt. For our nearest and dearest whom we see on a regular basis, we can dream up gifts from our inside scoop on the situation, paying attention to what people say and do and trying to empathize with their experience. We can also employ more explicit methods, such as directly asking someone what they want and, from the receiving position, communicating openly about what we want.

Let's take a walk through possibilities for paying attention and touch on some of the trickier aspects of doing them well. We begin with close relationships and work our way outward to less intimate ones.

Keep an Ear Out

If we know how to listen in our everyday conversations, we can get good intel on what our loved ones want. Sometimes we can even pull a gift out of thin air, like magic! One day in my friend Dana's kitchen, she introduced me to a condiment called chili crisp. When I commented on how delicious it was, she insisted I take the rest of the jar home.

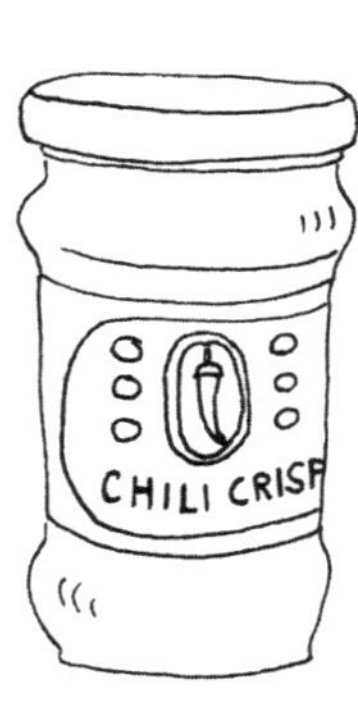

The words that lead to a gift might be subtle, off-hand comments. The gift shows we were listening. A big reader named Margaret loaned her friend Andrea a book called *The End of Your Life Book Club.* In the novel, a grown child and his mother reread favorite books together, companioning each other through the mother's terminal illness. Margaret let Andrea know she would like the book back after she was done reading it, as she had marked pages where book titles were mentioned—all real books that she wished to find and read herself at some point. A few months later when a special occasion rolled around, Andrea presented a gift—a stack of individually wrapped brown paper packages. It was the entire reading wish list that Margaret had noted.

During a humid and hot summer in Boston, a woman bemoaned how long it took the air-conditioning to cool the apartment after she got home from work. Her sweetie, Bret, a graduate student in electronics, rigged up a gift for her much like a Rube Goldberg contraption. (This was decades ago, before smartphones and apps.) He set it up so she could call her landline at home before leaving work, and when her (analog) answering machine picked up, she could type her birth date on the keypad and the sound triggered a sensor in the house to flash a sequence of lights that turned on the AC. Cool!

The Upgrade Gift

We can take note when people talk about things they want or need, but we can also notice when people talk about something they *already have*. Maybe they'd like more of it, or an upgrade. Tess had a favorite spoon—a United Airlines first-class spoon she found at a vintage shop in Brooklyn. It was the perfect weight, had a nice round bowl and a fish-scale pattern molded into the handle. She sang its praises, and her sweetie, Tyler, listened. Tyler hunted down three more matching spoons for her. "More" is one type of upgrade gift. It could also be based on "better" or "extra special." For example, if I know someone's favorite book, I could hunt down a first edition or an author-autographed copy.

If you listen carefully, you might also hear that someone wants an upgrade in the form of *less* of something. Let's call this approach "the vanishing act." I was delighted to chat with one couple who incorporates the *removal* of something burdensome into their Christmas festivities. Here's a fun twist. If it's your birthday, why not gift wrap some of your own lovely things and give them to other people in your life who will enjoy them more than you do?

Seeing the world through someone else's eyes can also reveal what a person does *not* like doing. Part of why a husband enjoyed a trip to Disney World so much was that his wife lovingly managed all of the trip logistics for him as a birthday gift. She understood how much he disliked planning. Poof! Gone. A vanishing act can also take the form of benefiting a recipient by doing labor *with* them. Near Boston, as Jane's birthday approached, she let her friends know that all she really wanted for her birthday was for everyone to come to her house to help tackle her long to-do list. Between parenting and caring for an ill partner, chores had simply stacked up to the point of overwhelm. All in one day, this pack of friends fixed a chair, swept Jane's office, organized the craft room, carried boxes up to the attic, deep-cleaned the kitchen, cleaned out her car, and hung a framed picture. Wow!

Do Your Homework

A connoisseur of, say, fountain pens, wine, crystals, or collectible Pez dispensers likely has strong opinions about the specifics of the category. If you're going to listen well enough to give something that caters to someone else's taste or collection, you must do your homework. I figured out an elegant work-around for this sort of danger a few years back when I wanted to gift wine to a friend. I wasn't in-the-know enough to choose wine for someone with her level of knowledge; however, I lived near a lovely wine bar called Ordinaire. So I asked my friend for a list of her three favorite types of wine (grape type, not winery). Then I took the list to Ordinaire, showed it to the knowledgeable fellow behind the counter, told him my budget, and asked him to choose three bottles that he thought would make a pleasant surprise. I didn't have to become a wine expert to delight my friend, just enlist the help of one.

Another approach here is to gift toward the periphery of someone's expertise or special interest—offering them something that complements it. Margaret gave her teenage son his own ice cream scoop for Hanukkah because he loves ice cream so much. As a child, Trish had a favorite teddy bear—"Peddy." She noticed her nine-year-old brother sneaking into the garage multiple times to work on something as Christmas approached. *What is he doing in there?* she wondered. On Christmas morning, he gave her a little wooden bed, just the right size for Peddy.

Reading Between the Lines

Sometimes listening and observing means paying attention to nonverbal clues. We can glean bits and pieces of who people are—and who they long to become. We can gift toward a desire that's observable even when a recipient doesn't voice it. Sometimes the gift itself can identify a desire the recipient didn't even know they had. When Maddy's friend saw him playing with her fidget spinner in her room and really enjoying it, she insisted he keep it. A decade later, he learned that he had been living with ADHD all along, and the spontaneous gift was even better for him, neurologically speaking, than they had realized.

Knowing is largely about noticing. And then remembering what we've noticed so we can reactivate it later. My friend Helena and I like the opposite flavors in a bag of jelly beans, thus making us the ideal pair to share a bag. The first time I bought some after Helena moved to Baltimore, I saved all of my rejects, which are her favorites, changed "49 flavors" on the bag to "25" with a Sharpie, and mailed them to her with an "I miss you."

It can be fruitful to put a creative spin on an enthusiasm mentioned or otherwise revealed—transforming it into something special they've perhaps never imagined. One of my favorite creative techniques is the mash-up, mixing two or more things my recipient loves into one—such as when I made a travel watercolor set in a small vintage tin for my friend Rose, who loves to paint and revels in any landscape she visits. A creative gift could also take the shape of infusing a mundane moment of a recipient's daily life with more meaning or value, such as when my friend Erin put together a "commute basket" for her uncle, filling it with car snacks and a list of podcast recommendations for him.

Reading between the lines can be especially helpful when someone we care about would enjoy something special but maybe they're not able to say so. A grandmother named Jacqueline told me about the creative way she began gift-giving for her autistic grandson. When he was a toddler, he didn't seem to enjoy receiving wrapped gifts. She did know he enjoyed music, and so, when a xylophone broke in her preschool classroom one day, she got an idea for a great gift. The next time she visited her daughter's family, she hung the loose xylophone panels in a row on a tree branch, low enough for her grandson to reach them, and then handed him the mallet. A rainbow of sound, just for him. He loved it.

A decade later, when her grandson visited her here in Oakland, Jacqueline designed another musical treat for him—a walking tour of all the wind chimes in her neighborhood. When she solicited wind chime locations from her neighbors via Nextdoor, their excitement for their wind chimes to become part of the tour warmed her heart. Map in hand, her grandson beamed as they enjoyed a big walking loop where they admired dozens of wind chimes,

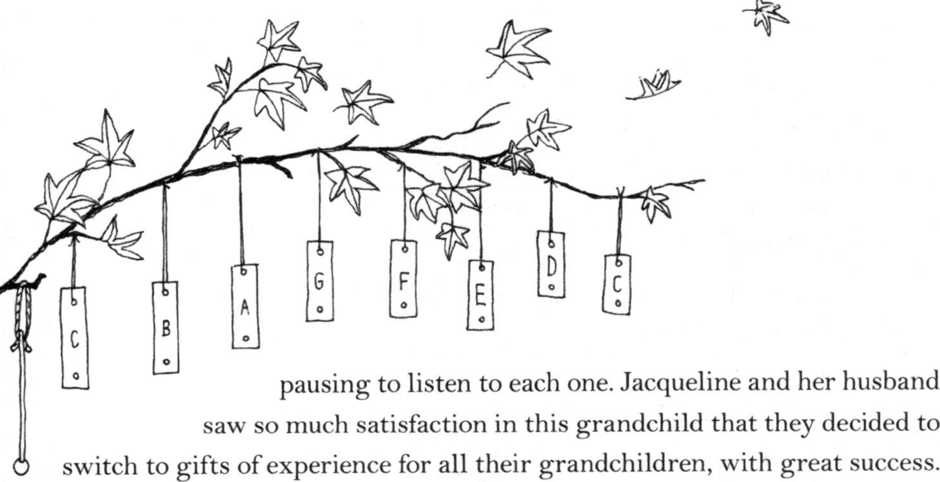

pausing to listen to each one. Jacqueline and her husband saw so much satisfaction in this grandchild that they decided to switch to gifts of experience for all their grandchildren, with great success. Next up: a rope swing!

The Dance of Empathy

When we base a gift on reading between the lines, which many good gift givers do, we must be sure we are not filling the spaces in between us with incorrect assumptions. I try to proceed with humility and curiosity. Even if it is impossible to "walk a mile in someone else's shoes," exercises of the imagination paired with honest conversations and accurate information can certainly help us get closer to understanding the experience of another. Good gifts emerge from the fertile realm of intersubjectivity, the beautiful and difficult places where our divergent human experiences overlap, converse, collide, and transform. Empathy not only brings us closer to others, to seeing and understanding the truth of someone else, but it can also bring us back to ourselves, showing us a contrast that helps us understand ourselves better too.

When I experienced my first panic attack, I was lucky to have a close friend who could appreciate what I was going through because of her own history of anxiety. That attack made me feel like I wasn't getting enough oxygen, an extremely uncomfortable sensation. At the ER, they took my vitals, said I was fine, and sent me home. But I didn't feel fine. Perhaps it was my friend seeing my worried face over video chat that sparked the compassionate, pocket-size gift that arrived a few hours later—a pulse oximeter. Whenever I needed reassurance that I was alive and well despite feeling otherwise, I could put a fingertip into the trusty plastic device and confirm for myself that my blood was getting plenty of oxygen. I was okay.

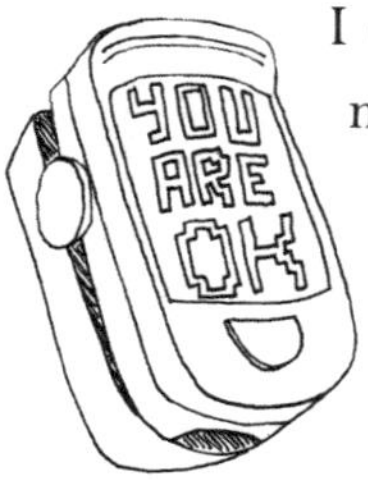

When we engage our empathic powers in caring for another, we can be most helpful if we witness their emotions without taking them on. Reaching toward another's experience does not mean abandoning our own. My friend was able to show up for me because she did not get swept up in my emotions. She held an energetic boundary between us that preserved her ability to respond wisely. To not get swept up in someone else's emotions does not mean to be emotionless. Rather, it means to ground ourselves in *our own* emotions and to share the ones appropriate for the moment, such as compassion. Many people find that concern for others leads them to dive in and start trying to "fix" things. I know I have an instinct to problem solve, so I try to remember to pause and first ask the person whether they're looking to brainstorm solutions at this time or just looking for someone to listen or keep them company. In the case of my panic attack, I wanted solutions, and ASAP!

Being on the same page is not required for empathic giving. Part of honoring another person's experience is treating their needs and wants as things of import in and of themselves. Annie in Los Angeles told me that she had wanted a perm as a child, but her parents thought a perm was silly for a seven-year-old and set the idea aside. Her aunt, though, noticed the strength of young Annie's wish. So when Annie's birthday rolled around, her aunt bought her a perm at the hair salon (with parental permission). Annie was overjoyed. It mattered not whether the aunt liked perms generally or for children, or would ever want one herself. Annie's perm has long since relaxed, but the girl who got it hasn't forgotten how her aunt's gesture encouraged her to be true to herself.

Cultivating Trustworthy Spaces

To give good gifts, the giver needs to be able to work with what is real, and the receiver needs to show enough of their true selves to offer the giver something to work with. We can encourage this by cultivating spaces in our relationships all year long that welcome our true selves, creating safe containers for authenticity and vulnerability.

One mother in the early 1980s provided one such safe container for her three-year-old son to express what he felt. Playing with a He-Man action figure one day, the young child announced to the room that he couldn't be a superhero because he was not white. Lucky for him, his mom was Yla Eason, who took his comment to heart and went shopping for a Black superhero. When there were none to be found, her visionary response was to invent, manufacture, and distribute an entirely new superhero, a Black action figure she named Sun-Man. In 2022, Sun-Man was added to Mattel's offerings. In the accompanying comic book, Sun-Man saves the day, announcing to children everywhere: *The sun shines brighter on all worlds when good people unite.*[1]

A friend of mine recently out of college received a special gift from his grandfather after mustering the courage to share with him that he is a trans man. Acceptance from his family as a whole has not come easily, but he could sense that his grandfather welcomed him—his full self—when he gifted him an antique pocket-watch chain and said, "Every gentleman needs a nice pocket watch chain." Beth in San Francisco told me that one year she gave all her family members the gift of a donation to a good cause, made in each of their honor. Beth spent significant time researching organizations whose missions aligned with her family members' values and interests, making the gifts personally meaningful. Beth, my friend's grandfather, and Yla Eason could put these good gifts together only because their family members felt free to be their true selves around them, to speak freely about things that matter to them. I like how James Baldwin puts it: "Love takes off the masks that we fear we cannot live without and know we cannot live within."[2]

It's Okay to Ask

If we want to incorporate high-quality information into a gift, but we feel like we don't have enough good data, here is a simple practice: *Just ask!* Receivers can also make requests. Lisa in the Midwest (with her locally famous pumpkin muffins and hilarious nude drawing kit) is a superstar gifter not because she reads people's minds, but because she's always on the lookout for good information and isn't afraid to ask for it. Lisa is in her forties now, but still close with a favorite professor from college who is almost ninety and slowly losing her eyesight. A few years ago, when Lisa asked her professor friend what she wanted for her birthday, she said that she could really use some recipes she could read, in a large font size. So Lisa sent her friend a whole binder of recipes that fit the bill. Even in close relationships where we already know each other well, gifts based on asking prompt us to learn more.

Now, a few caveats. Gifts that fulfill spoken desires go well only if, when asked, people answer truthfully. People might worry that a request will sound greedy, but I am more concerned that not speaking up is a symptom of not embracing our own worth.

Receivers can also ask for what they want without prompting. But remember, asking for a gift is not like ordering a beer at a bar. The heart of a request is an open-ended sharing of information with no obligation to deliver, and the person asked can respond however they see fit. If we know our loved one won't feel pressure, asking becomes easier. We can ask lightly, with sensitivity around the giver's capacity. I don't, however, recommend just dropping hints in hopes they'll catch your drift, especially if that means setting yourself up for disappointment. If we have our hearts set on something, it's best to be clear about it, or just get it for ourselves.

As my birthday approached a few years ago, I asked for what I wanted when I invited my neighbor kids to come over for blueberry pancakes before school to kick off my special day. I also knew it would be easy, and delicious, for them to give it to me. They rose to the occasion, saying yes and then some. I opened my front door at 7:30 a.m. to find two of my favorite kiddos holding up a big banner between them on my sidewalk. "Happy Birthday Lea!" was spelled out in big, hand-drawn block letters surrounded by a hundred or more colorful stickers. I asked for what I wanted, and they responded creatively, adding an element of surprise to a gift I already knew I was getting.

For some categories of gifts especially, recipients will welcome being given choice and agency. Cathy appreciated that her boyfriend gave her an IOU for a new dog and then took her to the shelter to meet all the puppies. She spent the next decade with the good company of the dog she chose that day. Depending on your situation, the same might go for artwork, cars and bicycles, clothing, trips, and other gifts involving large commitments in terms of money, time, or significance.

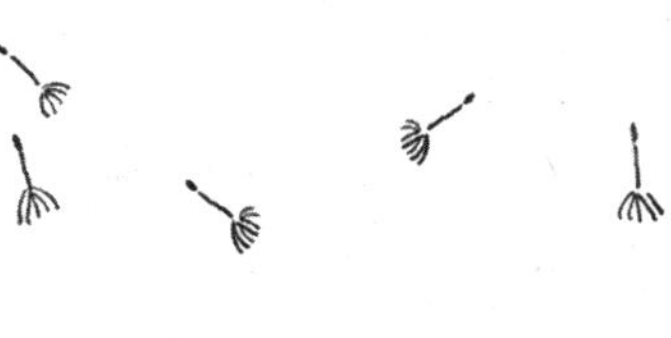

Feel It Out

Of course, asking gets us a good answer only if the person we ask *knows* what they want, which can be a surprisingly big ask! And so: *How can we get in touch with our own deepest, truest desires?* This question made me wonder: Could I work with a "feelings wheel" to tune in to a gift idea? A feelings wheel is a circular diagram of emotions—eager, relaxed, curious, confused, depleted, electric, bored, disgusted, sensitive, buoyant, hopeful, and many more. Choosing from this menu lets us be more specific when reflecting on how we feel, and this granularity matters because different emotions point to different next steps. For example, understanding that I'm not just "sad" but, say, "exhausted" or "lonely" helps me discern whether a nap or a social event would be most supportive. I ran an experiment with my friend Paul to find out whether a feelings wheel could help design a good gift.

We started by using the wheel to pinpoint how he'd been feeling lately, and went on to identify any feelings he was hoping to cultivate in his life. We then proceeded to brainstorm a gesture of care that could help meet the current needs and desires he was articulating. We generated three gift ideas, and then I let Paul choose. The result: Paul wanted to sit by a pond or a river and skip stones, like when he was a kid. Our feelings wheel experiment had surfaced some of Paul's deeper longings, allowing him to request something he didn't know he wanted and letting me give something I didn't know was in my repertoire.

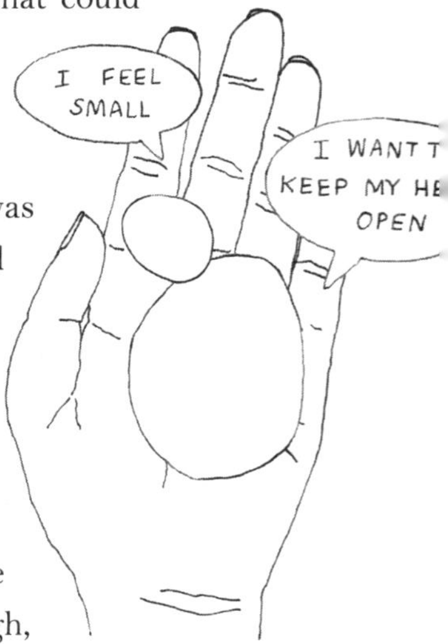

And so, the next time I was at the Navarro, I set out to collect skipping stones. Face-to-face with hundreds of thousands of river rocks, though,

I quickly realized I needed specs from Paul. He texted back immediately: *Circular, as thin as possible, and half the surface area of the palm of your hand.* I proceeded to collect almost a hundred decent skipping stones and a handful of exquisite ones. I also threw in an egg-shaped one and a cube, just for chuckles. To honor each stone, and to encourage the gift to last a long time, I gift wrapped them individually. The last time I checked with Paul, he was working his way through his epic stash, savoring each tiny present as he unwraps it and skip-skip-skips it back to the water.

Wish Lists and Beyond

Besides just asking, there are formal, social, and systematic ways to reveal one's true wants and to make requests, such as wish lists, gift registries, and the "pop-up rule" approach we discussed in a previous chapter. Some families have a habit of openly sharing wish lists, and I like the combination of the recipient getting something they want with the giver getting to choose which thing from the list to surprise them with. If you wish someone had a wish list, ask them for one and maybe they'd be happy to whip one up. Wish lists are great for distant relatives who don't know each other very well—potentially a more personal alternative to sending cash or gift cards—but they can also be great for close relations. Wish lists share information about who we are and want to become. Seeing someone's list might even spark a good idea not on the list.

Simply following someone else's wishes might seem like no fun, like ruining a surprise. But what a good trade it is in the name of relevance, satisfaction, and the prevention of waste! Besides, we can add surprise and creativity back in if that feels important. We can wrap an item from a wish list gorgeously or write a heartfelt accompanying card. We can hide a gift someone is expecting in a surprising location and provide a clue. Or otherwise bestow it in a special manner.

While we're here, let's dream up some fresh approaches to wish lists. Instead of a list with specific gifts on it, how about a list of larger categories a giver can get creative with? For example, such a wish list might read: greeting cards, experiences, secondhand items, wine, cash, picnics, novelty mugs. And how about an anti–wish list, consisting of categories of off-limits gifts? For example: no jewelry, nothing that needs maintenance or dry cleaning, no navy blue or maroon, nothing larger than my fist. Or yet another twist on the list is to switch up the person making the list and have the giver make an "offer list" instead, thereby providing the recipient a list of potential gifts to choose from. This makes it easy for a recipient to decline a gift before it's in their hands. In this form, which is essentially a multiple-choice IOU coupon, it also becomes easier to suggest a bold gift idea. An offer list can even include a fill-in-the-blank option.

Is it okay to go off registry, such as a wedding registry or a baby registry? I have done it, but only when I'm confident the receivers will prefer my idea to their own. A gift registry provides good information, though. If most of the items are very practical, useful things like diaper services or a water filter, I might be tempted to just stick to it. If it looks more like fun luxury items, I will be more likely to veer. When I can afford to, I can just do both, essentially saying: *I hear your need and I want to also give you something with more of my heart in it.* Another variation: If buying a gift from a registry feels too impersonal, just combine a registry gift with a handwritten greeting card in the real mail. And of course, if everything is too expensive, just do a card! I suggest that people setting up registries always provide low-cost and no-cost options so everyone who wants to can participate.

If you are hosting an event or getting ready to celebrate an occasion that might attract gifts, a pop-up rule along with the invitation is a great way to let people know what you are open to receiving. Guests might be relieved for the guidance. You can say, "Just bring yourself. Your presence is my present!" or "Only edible gifts please" or "If you want to buy a gift, just buy yourself a treat in honor of me and tell me what it was!" If it is your birthday, you could mention how much you love handmade cards or announce that you'd like for everyone to loan you their favorite book or donate to a good cause. One woman told her best friends that she'd love it if they would join her in volunteering at a local soup kitchen one night, and please, no gifts. I once attended a housewarming party where the host—new to the area and eager for new friends—set out a blank wall calendar and invited people to prefill it with events and activities to do together.

Paying Attention in Casual Relationships

Thus far in this chapter, we have focused on gifts for our closest relations, where it is most appropriate to pay such close attention. With colleagues, customers, neighbors, distant relatives, and others, we will not have access to many of the details that lend themselves to personalized gifts. But we can still give meaningful gifts within casual relationships. Bespoke gift designer Josh Rosenfeld at Odes Unboxed told me that he finds ways to write thoughtful greeting cards to people even if he doesn't know them well, such as a co-worker, by sharing his earliest good memory of them. He writes from the heart with whatever information is already there.

Public information provides plenty to work with. A child in Vancouver, British Columbia, who is a fan of my World's Smallest Post Service knew about my love of little things, and they made me a delightful pair of earrings—two tiny origami cranes dangling from hooks. When the band Humbird released "Song for the Seeds," it was right when I needed it. I felt so grateful that I was inspired to send the songwriter a gift via her manager—a set of musical shakers that I made from walnut shells containing various types of flower seeds, including yarrow, clover, cosmos. Each seed type makes a unique percussive sound.

If your recipient is a large group of people, the gift might need to be something more all-purpose and economical, such as the valentines received by every student and staff member from the cooking teacher at their middle school. Ms. Cook (yes, that is her real name!) makes them every year, with love. On each small piece of thick white paper, she stamps a red heart (with a stamp she carves out of a potato from the school's garden) and then handwrites the same text on each one, a different message each year: *You are loved. Love is everything. Love will find you. Choose love.* A gift for a general audience can still be wonderfully specific. A friend who used to live in South Korea told me about people there pooling resources to launch giant helium balloons carrying pairs of socks to people in need over the border in North Korea—thousands of little care packages moving between relative strangers. If I find myself in a restaurant after an afternoon on the beach, I might leave a pretty seashell—ideally a sand dollar!—with the tip.

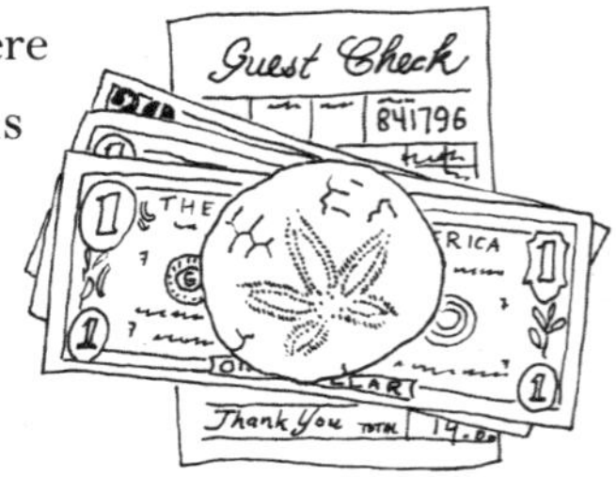

Giving Money

Let's talk about the cash gift. As someone who loves giving thoughtful gifts, I am tempted to see monetary gifts as an antisocial approach to giving that keeps people shopping and lonely. I want to brave the spaces between us, not just throw a gift card at them! But the truth is, putting money into someone else's hand is sometimes exactly what they might most want at a gift occasion, from me or anyone at all. Money not *instead* of a thoughtful gift, but *as* thoughtful gift. A creative woman in East Tennessee gave her young goddaughter a gift certificate to a local bookshop with a special instruction: *Spend half the money on yourself and the other half on gifts for other people.* Much of children's lives is determined by grown-ups, so it can be a real treat for them to go shopping, to receive the gift of choosing for themselves.

Cash can be a very efficient and elegant way of "asking" someone what they want by simply giving them full agency in the result. They don't even have to tell the giver what they spent it on, and this privacy might be a relief. Maybe what they really want is groceries, or to pay their phone bill. There is certainly no need to assume people are struggling financially, but if I do not have a strong sense of a family's situation and the invitation to their toddler's birthday party requests, say, "Target gift cards, please," I'm going to follow their lead. People with privilege and resources can be careful here, asking themselves questions like: *Do I know enough about my recipient's relationship with money to be getting involved? If they haven't explicitly invited it, can I give cash to this person without highlighting a difference in class or access that undermines their dignity? Am I being a savior or a Good Samaritan as I give money? Is the gift to benefit someone I care about, or is it more about my own ego or sense of guilt?* The people being offered such gifts can also be careful: *How does this monetary gift make me feel? Do I approve of the subtext it carries as it comes from this person? Is it most aligned with my dignity to turn it down or to take it? In what circumstances do I feel good about accepting money?*

Gifts of money, here in the United States and around the world, are not just from the financially privileged to the financially underresourced. People without much wealth are some of the most generous among us. I am aware of cash gifts moving within immigrant day laborer circles here in California, groups of friends in which any one of them might suddenly be in serious need. They take turns pooling their limited funds to help each other get by. This culture of care is also present as some of these folks regularly send portions of their paychecks to family members in need in Mexico and Central America. Part of what is complex (and potentially confusing) about distributing money is that sometimes it is a "gift" and other times it is more like familial duty or social justice. Being mindful of context can help us communicate love in appropriate ways, making sure our messages get through.

Regardless of financial need, money can make a great gift if it is given with care in an appropriate context. In Chinese culture, there is a tradition of giving *hongbao,* red envelopes with cash inside, as part of celebrating the New Year as well as other occasions. I spoke with some pals who grew up with *hongbao,* Albert in Oregon and Bryan in Singapore. Depending on the nature of the relationship, the amount of money can be quite small. Even when it is not, I learned that it's not really about the money per se; the money is moving for the sake of social ties. These red envelopes are traditionally given from married elders to younger, unmarried people in their community but sometimes pass between peers and friends as well. Cultivating social ties is the same reason I give my friendly postal carrier a small cash gift every winter. I'm not giving money because I think he needs it, or because I didn't care to put more effort and thought into the gift. It is because I don't know him well enough to choose for him, and I want him to get something he truly wants. Mostly, though, I want him to know I appreciate him.

In other contexts, a small cash gift might leave a lot to be desired. When a woman retired from being the pianist for her church, a gift card to a random chain restaurant felt terrible to her. For twenty years, she had played every Sunday morning, at evening choir practices, at every wedding and funeral, thoughtfully selecting songs and practicing. Presented to her as a gesture of thanks for decades of dedicated service, the gift card was simply too small, impersonal, and irrelevant for her to feel that the church truly appreciated her. In cases like this, the answer isn't necessarily *more money,* but *more thought.* Even an earnest effort in the simple form of a thoughtfully composed greeting card can be effective.

Attending to the "Who" and the "How"

For any gift—objects, words, experiences, cash—there is the question: *Does* that *person want* that *gift from* you? Remember the unwanted blender from earlier in the book? Interestingly, the wife did indeed want a new blender, she just didn't want it *from her husband.* In her mind, the gift of any kitchen utensil from him would carry an unwanted subtext: the idea that cooking is women's work. Her husband did not intend this subtext, but he learned to steer clear of such gifts in the future. Taking care to be relationally wise in our gifting becomes especially important when there are differences in status or power—today or historically—between givers and recipients (or the groups with which they identify).

Sometimes gifts full of love involve surprises that require secretive schemes. We can be mindful that those don't double as poor boundaries or privacy violations. For example, if planning a gift involves secretly reaching out to someone's most important relations for personal notes for a keepsake book, we should be sure it is appropriate for us to be in direct contact with those people and privy to that content. We can ask: Does my recipient not only want this keepsake book, but do they want it *from me*? When in doubt, we can get their blessing first.

Even if our recipient does indeed want a specific gift from us, there is still the question of *how* they want it. Do they love a big surprise or public reveal? My friend's middle-school-age daughter gets anxious about opening gifts in front of everyone at her birthday parties. It is especially stressful for her when two friends give her the same thing, or she opens something she already owns. I asked my friend whether it might help relieve this performance anxiety if her daughter could duck away for a moment with each friend to open their gift. Or, how about just opening the presents privately after the party? This alleviates the pressure of having to say something on the spot and allows a recipient to take their time responding, perhaps while writing thank-you notes. It also removes the potential for competition, as the kids cannot compare their gifts, or their gifts' prices, if they don't even know what the other gifts are. Since the well-being of everyone is at play, we might be wise to consider who the bystanders will be and how they, too, will feel about the gift they witness.

Fulfilling a Gift's Promise

After giving so much attention to the gift selection process, let's also tend to the *effect* of a gift given. We might want to know: *Was my gift a success? Is it in motion, staying in the air, keeping the goodness going?* Here, we can just keep paying attention in appropriate ways. Does the recipient express joy and gratitude? Did they smile, laugh, cry, get quiet? Does the gift spark a story or a good conversation? Do they wear it, hang it on a wall, talk about it, tell mutual friends about it? Do they tinker up a hilarious trophy for you, featuring you as a muscle man carrying a dollhouse tool chest? (Yes, that happened.) You could just ask, but I'd do that only if you're ready for the truth, which they may or may not share with you for various reasons, including not wanting to hurt your feelings.

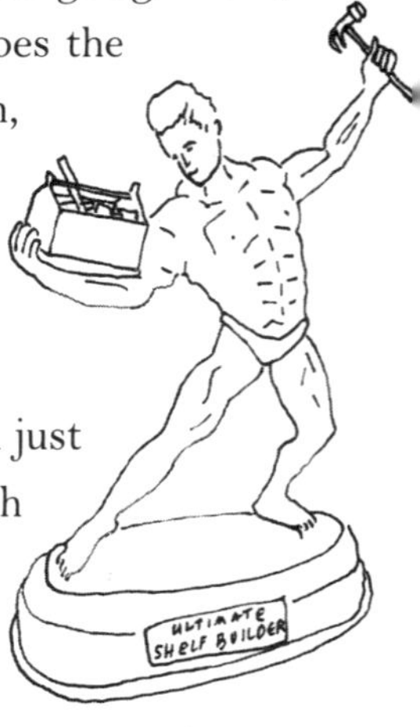

From the position of gift recipient, if we are happy with a gift and we want the giver to know, we can make an effort to express as much and receive the gift with gratitude. This is not just for the sake of the gift giver's ego; it is for the information feedback loop that will pull the relationship forward. If a gift goes well, the giver might appreciate the confirmation that their sense of you at this time, whatever the gift embodied, is more or less accurate. Even recipients, though, might not immediately know what to make of a gift. Sometimes what we're waiting on is ourselves, or our own ability to open our hearts and receive.

But truly: *Was the gift a success?* If we dig a little deeper, I think the question underneath that question is *Was the gift truly satisfying?* The satisfaction of both giver and receiver is important. *Did the recipient reveal their truth before receiving the gift? Did the giver give from their own truth?* Another question lurks underneath those: *Are giver and recipient even in touch with their own truths?* I have been mistaken about myself before; have you? I believe any final decision about authenticity cannot be anything but an inside job, so let's focus our energy on looking within. We show ourselves to other people all the time, and this can include parts of ourselves that we are not even conscious of. But we cannot show ourselves *on purpose* unless we know ourselves consciously. Self-understanding is the ongoing process and practice behind accessing the self that we are, that we want to be, and that we want other people to see in us and, in turn, respond to or gift toward.

Let's look closer at *satisfaction*. Feeling fulfilled can be a good sign that we are in tune with ourselves. If a gift given or received feels deeply nourishing to me—mind, body, heart, or spirit—it is likely to be well aligned with my values, to meet my true needs and desires. When receiving something reduces the desire for additional shiny things because we are busy savoring what we have received, that's a great sign. I see any impulse to acquire and hoard as misguided attempts to satisfy deep human needs. I wonder if the problem is not greed, but true need. Is humanity just hungry for a better way of life—one characterized by wellness, safety, liveliness, beauty, etc., of which it is genuinely not getting enough? I'm willing to give us the benefit of the doubt.

When we have the interest and energy for it, giving and receiving gifts are opportunities to dive deeper into our relationships, to exercise our humanity by seeing and supporting the truth of each other (and ourselves). Just

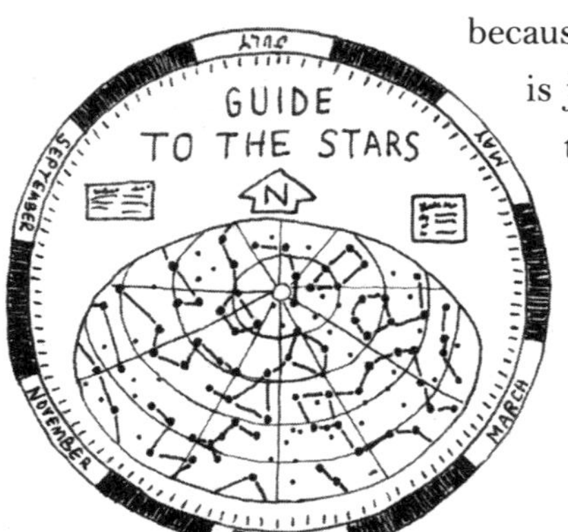

because it's not simple doesn't mean it's too hard. A gift is just a small swatch of an intricately woven relationship that is ongoing. If we pay attention, inquire, request, listen, and track the possibilities as they bubble up, good gifts—for intimates, acquaintances, and strangers alike—will organically emerge from the shifting, sparkling social constellations in which we find ourselves.

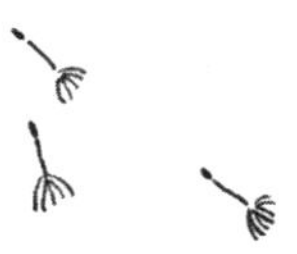

Reflect

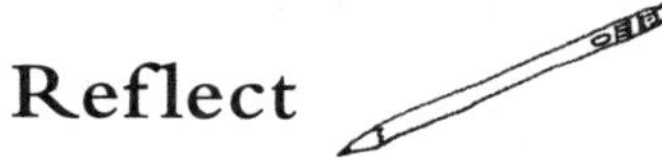

1. Have you ever given, received, or witnessed a gift that felt like it honored the recipient especially well? How did the gift make it clear that the recipient was listened to, paid attention to, seen, and supported?

2. Reflect on whether you have shown enough of your true self to your loved ones for them to gift toward the true you. With whom do you feel most welcome to be yourself? Do you invite the people around you to be real? How do you create conditions that help someone share vulnerability?

3. Is there someone in your life whose wants feel mysterious to you, who feels "hard" to gift to? How might you ask them what they want? Create a simple script and try it. Optional: Employ one of the creative methods from this chapter, such as an alternative wish list, a pop-up rule, a feelings wheel, or a mash-up.

10

Everyone Is Creative

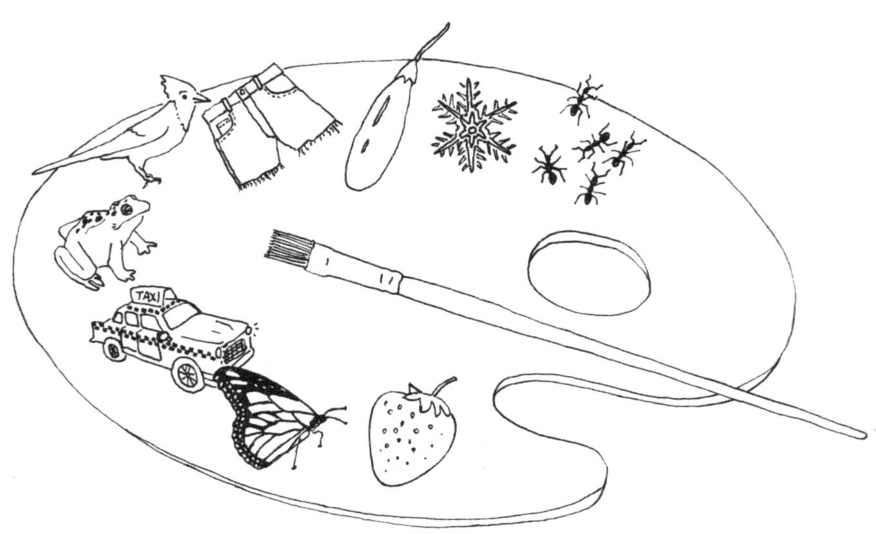

HOW CAN I BE A CREATIVE GIFT GIVER?

WHAT DO I WANT MY PERSONAL GIFT PRACTICE TO CONSIST OF?

WHERE DO GOOD GIFTS COME FROM? WHERE DO THEY GO?

So, from my point of view, which is that of a storyteller, I see your life as already artful, waiting, just waiting and ready for you to make it art.

—TONI MORRISON, WELLESLEY COLLEGE COMMENCEMENT ADDRESS, 2004

Getting Started

Every meal you've made, each idea you've pursued, all those new roads you've taken—they are evidence of a creative life at work. It is easier to see the artfulness of our lives if we drop the silly notion that art and creativity are just for professional artists, craftspeople, museums, and galleries. I prefer a more holistic sense of "art." *Art* is the process by which we are all constantly *composing and recomposing the world*, each in our own way.

Whether you consider yourself creative or not, artist or not, I believe you already have gathered most of the skills, knowledge, materials, and resources you need to give great gifts. You just need the faith that you can do it and a process you can trust.

To Thine Own Gifts Be True

When gift-giving is reduced to being each other's personal shopper, it is no wonder people can feel frustrated or underwhelmed! Nikki had long considered herself to be "bad at gifts." Meanwhile, her friend Ariel told me about how awesome it was when Nikki sent her an audio file containing a personalized birthday song, playfully written and sung by Nikki herself. It turns out Nikki may not be great at shopping, but she is great at gifts. Nikki, as we all do at times, just needed a reframe.

If we can learn to give gifts *from our own gifts*—our talents, skills, knowledge, position, personality, signature style—our gestures of care are bound to be meaningful. I imagine that you have more resources than you realize—a big bundle of goodness waiting to be activated by you. When a gift is drawn from our own internal richness combined with the richness of our relational network, it can feel like magic—like something out of nothing! Really though, we are simply enjoying the latent wealth of our lives. There is pleasure for both receiver and giver here. If you understand what makes you come alive and can offer it as part of a gift for another person, not only do you get to fill your own cup in service of another, but that spirit will carry through and the gift will be better for it.

About a decade ago, I received a huge gift from a new friend—a giant redwood tree! It was not to keep, of course. My new friend Jason on the Lost Coast deep in Northern California invited me eighty feet up into an extraordinary redwood canopy where we got to spend the night in sleeping bags on a handwoven net platform. Consider the elegant way his resources were drawn together. Jason did not own the property the tree was on, but he had access. He already owned all the necessary gear, including a climbing harness for me. He had the know-how to rig the ropes and safely belay me up there, and I already trusted him enough to let him. Gathering his own inner gifts—his geographical and ecological knowledge, physical skill, and equipment—he offered me a magical experience otherwise out of my reach. (I brought the wine and chocolate.) We awoke in the morning to yet another gift—a covey of black-capped chickadees serenading us from nearby branches.

Your hobbies and your profession both are reliable places to tap into your best resources as a gift giver. Myles in Portland, Oregon, loves to draw. As a gift for a six-year-old niece, Myles illustrated more than fifty paper lunch bags with delightful creatures: an owl, a mer-horse, a fox eating a sandwich, a dog with a book in one paw and a cup of tea in the other. At bestowal, the niece got a sneak peek at one bag and learned that there was a whole shoebox full of them her dad would use to surprise her for many mornings to come. A children's librarian named Angela takes her passion for literature and puts it to work by giving children's books to grown-ups on gift occasions. Angela has such extensive knowledge of the genre that she can give people of any age books that make them feel seen. We can keep an eye out for potential gifts while we do whatever it is we do all day, and act quickly if need be. A barista once asked me to name an animal while they made my latte. They then drew an ant for me through the foam on the surface!

If we want it to, giving from our gifts includes giving from our *potential* inner gifts. How? By giving from our own growing edge. Such a gift—one that requires us to be vulnerable, to stretch a little—can be a powerful part of love in action. Even though the thought of singing and dancing onstage terrifies me, when I recently arrived at a friend's house for her birthday party, I surprised myself by singing and dancing my way through the front door! It was an inside joke, referencing a conversation we'd had just a few days before, in which I'd wondered, "What if real life were more like a musical, and people were constantly bursting into song and dance, out of the blue?" All nerves, but driven by a mission to love my friend in this fun way, I summoned my courage on the porch, pressed play on my phone, and danced my way in, to the tune of "Best of My Love."

As usual, this isn't just about gift-giving. If humanity wants to survive and thrive in the centuries ahead, we need to dream up, revive, adjust, and generously distribute meaningful experiences that testify to the worthiness of this life. In short, we need creativity. We need active verbs in every arena, dynamic projects involving things, words, and experiences that nourish people and planet. I am confident that the opportunities to do so—big and small—are right under our noses should we look for them. Each of us has unique inner resources to call upon in this collective effort, including the tender spots inside us that call for us to heal and grow. I want to find, make, give, and receive significant things together, ones that wish all of us well. So yes, let's give good gifts. Along the way, let's also discover the unique inner gifts each of us has that we can offer the world all year long.

Gift Ecology

I have noticed that the most lovely, well-received gifts—even small or simple ones—tend to pay exquisite attention to *context*, working thoughtfully with whatever is here, whatever is happening.

When my friend Helena's husband, Joseph, had to be across the country for a few months, he dreamed up a sweet surprise to help bridge the distance between them, tucking love notes into the bundled pairs of socks in her dresser before he left town. In this way, as she got dressed without him each morning, he still wished her "good morning" and they could feel a little closer. How charming!

My heart is equally warmed by a story from a Russian household in the 1990s. The lack of access to manufactured goods right after the collapse of the Soviet Union inspired people to get crafty with everyday material culture—to make do: a TV antenna made out of forks, a lampshade from an old straw hat. In one household, a gift in the form of a wonderful prank played on a boy by his grandfather. Grandpa Oleg walks into the living room, stirring a mug of tea, no big deal. But then he clinks the side of the cup with the spoon to get his grandson's attention, lifts the spoon to his lips, and starts blowing bubbles![1] He had jigsawed a hole in the aluminum spoon, turning it into a bubble wand to delight his grandson. An artist of the everyday, he transformed the quality of the moment during a tough time.

A gift does not just come out of nowhere; it emerges from its surroundings by way of the giver. After bestowal, a gift thus constituted by context is then reabsorbed by its surroundings, via the recipient, in one way or another. A gift has real consequence. It is part of a larger system that interweaves biographical, geographical, social, cultural, racial, historical, material, psychological, spiritual, and political circumstances. To think up a good gift is perhaps less about racking one's brain and more about taking a look around. Clues are everywhere. Always already in the thick of things, we are in a prime position to participate—to compose and recompose the world through gifts. A gift begins to emerge when we notice an opportunity.

If we want to love each other well, we need to be good gift ecologists. When we interest ourselves in the wider, wilder ecology of a gift idea, we are much more likely to gift something of good fit and to receive something gracefully. When a gift goes well, the gesture either dovetails seamlessly with the good that is already here or creatively transforms what's already happening for the better. When a well-intentioned gift goes awry or falls flat, it is likely because its ecology has been ignored or misunderstood. Thankfully, the whole gift gesture doesn't hinge on getting the gift exactly "right" in terms of the gift *itself.* The larger contexts are always present too, contributing to the full experience, bolstering it, and tempering it.

European garden spiders make a good mascot for the practice of gift ecology. Native to Europe but also found in North America, *Araneus diadematus* is also known as the cross spider or crowned orbweaver. The females are born with three pairs of silk spinnerets with which they dexterously draw gossamer from their bodies into a delicate latticework spiral, strong and sticky. The spider itself draws our eye and is easiest to point to, but the spider's existence rests on a dynamic substrate that slips in and out of view, almost invisible. This web constantly captures and funnels key bits of the world to the spider, not only giving it life, but giving it its particular life. Designing or choosing a gift can benefit from a similar approach, casting our nets wide to see what our gift webs might bring in. In gift terms, each radial strand is like going out to consider a new aspect of our gift's context—the occasion, the geography, the season, the relationship history, the joys, the fears, the longings—then pulling the specific richness of those considerations back to the center, where all the radii come together. Our good gift idea is waiting for us there at the nexus where a well-fed spider is just chillin' at the heart of its radiant doily-of-the-day, nourished by its surroundings, ready for action.

When one of my besties got married in Moab, Utah, a few years ago, she asked whether I could pick up a wedding cake after I landed in Salt Lake City and take it to the campsite where the wedding would take place the following day. My answer: Happy to! And then I remembered: Moab is *hot.* I pictured a sad cake sagging as parents gave lengthy toasts. I wondered whether there could be another approach. This couple fell in love camping and climbing in the outdoors. Suddenly I was picturing s'mores. But we needed a cake.

A week later, I found myself at my dining table, playing with tall towers of graham crackers and marshmallows. Could I create a nontraditional display that still carried the tradition? After a few lackluster attempts, I discovered that tall stacks of crackers create a delightful effect if each cracker is rotated a little more than the one under it. The sharp corners of the crackers become elegant curves reminiscent of a DNA double helix. I pitched a "cake" idea to my friends, and they gave the green light.

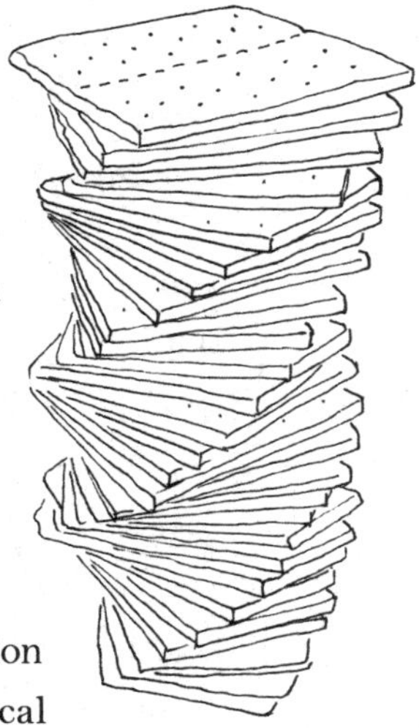

I landed in Salt Lake with a grand plan. First stop, pick up the components: graham crackers, marshmallows, and chocolate. The next day before the ceremony, as cocktail hour began, my plus-one and I stacked graham crackers and marshmallows into a tall, spiraling, multi-column composition while the bars of chocolate waited in a cooler. The whimsical "cake" structure included layers of brown paper "lace" I'd precut with a decorative craft punch, stand-ins for the chocolate until the real chocolate emerged later. The children at the wedding were the first to notice us, of course. People started to gather around and watch. Children tried to steal marshmallows. We let them.

After vows by the river, toasts at the table, and a red rock desert sunset, the newlyweds "cut" the cake by feeding each other the first two s'mores of the night. The guests then dismantled the cake on the way to the campfire. Some of the children started working the crowd, offering roasted marshmallows on sticks. In the meantime, people filled the dance floor, aka dirt floor. No disco ball above us. Just stars.

This kind of ecological thinking is relevant everywhere, not just in "nature," and it is our friend when we are dreaming up good gifts. A new grandmother named Eve drew a great gift from the richness of her own webby world. While Eve's daughter was in labor, Eve took photos of both sides of the family waiting for the baby to arrive—by the phone, on the couch, a dog gazing out the window. At one point, Eve and the other grandmother-to-be took a stroll in the garden near the hospital. They were surprised to find a rose, just one, blooming in late October. A few hours later, they learned their granddaughter had been born, and named Rose. *Welcome, little one.*

Eve tapped into her inner resources of publishing know-how and children's books from her career. She also drew upon a tenderness from her own childhood. Eve hadn't been raised to feel truly wanted in her own family, so she wanted her gift to communicate to Rose how much her family treasured her. And so, Eve designed a board book online with her photo of the garden rose on the cover and titled it *The Day You Were Born*. Each page features a family member eagerly waiting for Rose's arrival. Eve printed a book for everyone in the family. When Rose was a toddler, it became her favorite book. There was a copy waiting for her at all their houses! As such, the books wove an invisible web, linking the community of love that would raise Rose. When a gift goes well, it is like a spiderweb catching the light just right. The gift shimmers.

Collaborating with the Universe

The more attuned we are to the world of our recipient, to the context of their life, the better the chance of our gift absorbing into that world gracefully. And the more attuned we are to our own world, the more elegantly resourced our offering will be. The s'mores wedding cake and Eve's books shimmered with this kind of attunement. The cake incorporated phenomena from its context I never could have purchased or fit into my suitcase, including the landscape, the campfire, and the night sky. The cake gift drew on my own inner resources of playfulness and my eye for the unconventional. The books, too, worked within their web: childbirth, family time, the garden nearby, Eve's budget, professional experience, and even personal heartache. Some of these gifts' elements were planned for; some were surprises, like the way the cake construction became party entertainment. When we get lucky like this, I think it's rarely luck alone; a good plan invites the universe to chip in.

Marie and Laura live by the ocean in San Francisco. As Marie's thirty-second birthday approached, Laura told Marie not to go in the basement where her birthday present was waiting, too large to hide in their apartment. After Marie started to make absurd guesses as to what the gift could be, Laura told her it was an iguana since they both knew it wasn't, as wonderful as iguanas might be. The joke went back and forth for weeks as Laura went to the basement to "feed the iguana" if she needed to fetch something or do laundry. The birthday arrived and the surprise was revealed—a beautiful red bicycle! Marie was eager to go ride it on the Great Highway, which skirts the ocean. The first time she did, she was enjoying her new bike when something caught her eye, and she hit the brakes! It was a woman with something long and scaley on her shoulder. It was an *iguana*, also out enjoying the beautiful day, its iridescent scales sparkling in the sunshine.

Gift-giving calls us into risk and courage because we cannot control the whole system of relations in which our gifts participate. As frustrating as this might seem, it's actually good news. I try to resist any temptation to force an outcome because I trust that "my" gift will be a better one if I let the universe co-create it with me. I cannot think of everything, but the universe can, and does so effortlessly, in exquisite detail, at all times. Open to mystery, our gifts can hitch a ride on the richness of this self-organizing system, and so can we. This requires a loose grip in addition to a loving one. In gift-giving—and in life—I want to honor the unknown, to stay open to surprise, to make myself available for a critical mass of kismet to suddenly sweep me off my feet.

When we present a gift with the humility of a good gift ecologist—one who acknowledges that they, too, are inside the system, not outside of it—the gift sings: *I wonder if you might love this specialness I drew together with you in mind, from my current place in this sparkling web of interconnections. Might we open this mystery together, and see what happens next?*

Creativity Is a Practice

At my doctor's office last week, the nurse asked me if creativity can be learned or if it is just a gift from the universe. "Both!" I answered quickly. I think of creativity as a muscle that everyone is born with. We can keep the muscle supple and strong by using it. Yes, it may atrophy, but it will never disappear completely. I am in the habit of exercising my creative muscle; regularly showing up, experimenting, doing research, and getting feedback creates the conditions for the muses to visit me. And when they do, it feels so exhilarating that there is renewed inspiration to continue my practice. It is a self-reinforcing cycle. We can purposely cultivate specific mindsets and methods that prepare the ground for inspiration to strike again and again.

Children embody a receptiveness to the creative potential of each moment. They have a genius for transforming the most ordinary materials into vehicles of the imagination. They can't wait to show us, say, the snail house they constructed from twigs and leaves. Kids are quick to handmake a birthday card with crayons and offer it with pride. My friend Casey once received a charming "ghost detector" as a gift from her five-year-old nephew, constructed out of crumpled tin foil and a piece of string. The sculpture was inspired by their inside joke about the strange noises in Casey's apartment. She delightedly hung it in her living room. I think we grown-ups can aspire to be more like kids in our creativity—a lot less self-conscious and a lot more playful.

Creativity Toolbox

I hope the stories in this book are sparking your curiosity and creativity already. I want to add to your toolbox by offering you sixteen tried-and-true creative techniques and mindsets I turn to when I'm designing gifts or making anything at all. I hope they might serve you too.

1. Start Anywhere

A gift design might begin with a word or a phrase, a full concept or vague idea. It might begin with a material spark, a thing or process you observe through your senses that stays with you: an image, a feeling, a texture, even a scent. I try to stay open to all of it. I've designed gifts that got their start in song lyrics, landscapes, and whatever fruit is in season. Gifts can come from almost anywhere, and they might start with something already right before our eyes. I like to start early, gathering materials even before I'm fully sure where they might be leading, and letting the process take its own time as a gift occasion approaches.

2. Seek Out Inspiration

There is no need to sit there with a blank screen or sheet of paper, feeling stumped. Go get some inspiration! You don't have to start from scratch; in fact, there's no such thing. Find something to activate your mind and heart. Go to a museum, a hardware store, an antique shop. Browse a book or listen to a podcast. Tromp around in the woods. Follow your curiosity. Ask questions. Wake up your inner child.

For gifts of physical objects, words, or quality time together, we can all be constantly building our vocabulary—expanding our repertoire—just by going about our lives, awake to the world. The experience of feeling stuck is a great moment to gather more information with an empathy experiment. It was only after I printed out and closely read the lyrics to my eight-year-old friend's favorite song—"Attack of the Radioactive Hamsters from a Planet Near Mars" by "Weird Al" Yankovic—that I got the idea to knit him three little hamsters out of glow-in-the-dark yarn. *Awesome!* (He thought so too.)

3. Hack Your Assumptions

We often think of creativity as *making*, but it can also be expressed in new ways of *seeing*, beyond assumptions, beyond convention. Unexamined habits of mind and body can sometimes pull us into ruts, leaving us stuck in stale ways of thinking, seeing, and behaving. When we pause and let our awareness open, sometimes we can reveal an assumption for what it is—someone else's dream, a scrappy little notion-in-motion that grew and gained ground. Pausing can help us notice a calcified pattern that might not be serving us anymore, if it ever did. Once we can see something as *one* possibility rather than *the one and only* possibility, we can make a fresh assessment. We can ask: *What if? What else?*

My MO: At any moment I might see something in a new way, revealing an opportunity to make something more lovely, and more loving, by way of a gift. Who looks at a spoon and sees a bubble wand? Grandpa Oleg does! A box of graham crackers might not sing "wedding cake." And yet, when faced with some creative constraints, I was able to see them in a new way and put their sturdy form to an unexpected use.

We can even hack assumptions when we *receive* a gift. Michael in Georgia told me about his four-year-old grandson, Asher, receiving a novelty flashlight that cast an image of the moon on the ceiling. Soon enough, though, the child saw another possibility. Asher discovered that he could point it on the floor instead and go "dancing on the moon." *Brilliant!*

4. Practice Makes Pretty Darn Great

This is deceptively simple. Just show up, again and again. Your creative capacity will grow as you engage it and explore. Having a healthy practice includes considerations of time and space. Does a particular gift occasion, or your current personal capacity, call for a quick gift, something you can whip up in an evening? Or is it something you want to plan far in advance, sleeping on your idea and slowly developing it? For you and your life, will it work best to chip away at your gift for a half hour each day for a week, or to make it in one big session? And *where*? Design your gifts in the most creatively hospitable place to which you have access. If you're not sure where your best spot is, run some experiments. Sometimes we need to be at the desk, and sometimes we need to be in motion. I record voice memos to myself while I hike. I know I need solitude to be creative, but I've also noticed that the white noise of a busy coffee shop can help me focus. Do you get your best ideas in the shower? That's part of the creative process too. Even small environmental shifts can be powerful and set the mood for creativity, such as lighting a candle or putting your phone on silent. Grab your favorite pen and see what happens next.

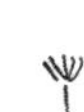

5. Trust Your Excitement

As I develop creative ideas, gift and otherwise, I trust my own excitement every step of the way, from the initial seed of an idea to the process of developing it, bestowing it, and beyond. Whenever I can, I let myself move toward ideas—colors, textures, stories, activities—that feel like they have energy in them. I trust this sense of spark and purpose to tell me I'm onto something. *Keep going!*

There is an EQ, or emotional intelligence quotient, to creativity. We can pay attention to our emotions along the way and use them to glean important information. If you are being creative along lines that are a good fit for you, I think you're going to feel energetic and lively, in flow. When I'm hot on the trail of a truly compelling gift for someone, I find myself feeling eager to put it together and bestow it. On the other hand, if I am feeling overwhelmed, it might be because I am trying to give beyond my means. Or it could mean that I've realized in my gut that a gift is somehow inappropriate for the occasion—too grand, too small, too expensive, too personal. It's important to listen to our discomfort too. Unease about an idea can mean we need to go back to the drafting table.

6. Play

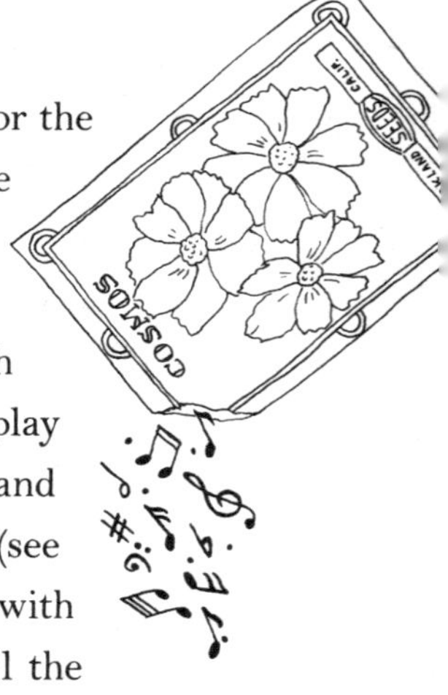

Engaging in the mode of play—agendaless exploration for the pure joy of it—is not only creative, but fun! Ironically, free play that puts process over product can also serve up wonderful results and real insights.

In many gifts that I compose, there is a phase in which I am playing with materials in the way young children play with all sorts of things from blocks to food to leaves and sand. When I made the musical shakers for Humbird (see chapter 9), I bought many kinds of seeds so I could play with them before deciding which ones to use. And I shook all the packets at the plant nursery to get an initial sense of the sounds

before deciding which ones to buy. Back in my studio, I shook them again, trying different seed sizes and quantities in the walnut shells, to see what sorts of sounds the seeds and I could make together. At some point, my executive functioning kicked in and I made some choices, creating a nice, wide spectrum of sound across the set.

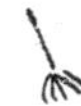

Another kind of play brings benevolent mischief to the table. A loving gag. A punny prank. A scavenger hunt with clues or other grand surprises orchestrated with precision. Rebecca once received a locked metal box for Christmas from her prankster brother while he was in the navy far from home. Nine months later, in a birthday card, he provided the key. When a pun-loving friend of mine turned twenty-two, I sewed him a tutu out of pink tulle. (Get it? "22.") Gift-giving can bring out an almost espionage-level scheming in the otherwise most mild-mannered of folks. For example, a father took his grown daughter Paula and her family to their favorite Italian spot, Nino's, where they used to go when she was a child. As always, the walls were packed with framed paintings by Nino himself, the chef-owner. At some point during the meal, a painting on the wall caught Paula's attention, and it became clear to her that she was in the painting! Her whole family was, including her husband, new baby, and two dogs. Her father had successfully orchestrated a delightful gift—commissioning the painting from Nino, making sure Paula sat within eyeshot of it, using Paula's Christmas card photo as the art reference so as not to tip her off to the grand gesture that would come with her spaghetti and meatballs. I was shocked when Paula told me her father didn't consider himself to be creative. *Bravo, Papà!*

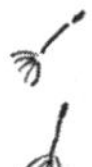

7. *Tend to Your Inner Critic*

Your inner critic might try to convince you that you weren't born to be creative. Don't fall for it. We can tend to our inner critic's chatter with mindfulness. We can notice it, thank it for its misguided attempts to protect us, and ask it to rest its weary limbs in our guest room while we swap in kinder, more fair and encouraging self-talk. This, too, is a practice, a muscle we can strengthen.

Case in point, Paula (the recipient of the painting at Nino's) is quick, like her father, to say she is not creative. But then I learned about her signature "stick figure" greeting cards that she makes from scratch by illustrating memorable moments from her relationships using very simple line drawings. These cards are so great they bring people to tears! Luckily, Paula doesn't let her own claims of not being creative keep her from creating these charming and meaningful cards. *Well done!*

8. Make It Together

If you're feeling stuck, find collaborators! The group gift is my favorite form of social gift design, letting us learn from each other and combine our skills, talents, and resources for an even greater gift. Run ideas past friends and family. Incorporate preexisting products and services into your gift. Commission elements of your idea that are outside your skill set—such as a song or a handcrafted item from an Etsy maker or a local craftsperson.

While cat-sitting for some friends, Albert and their sweetheart had a wonderful time together creating a scavenger hunt for their friends to find when they returned home. A series of clues and small puzzles, all written in the voice of the cat, led the residents through the nooks and crannies of their own home in a new way.

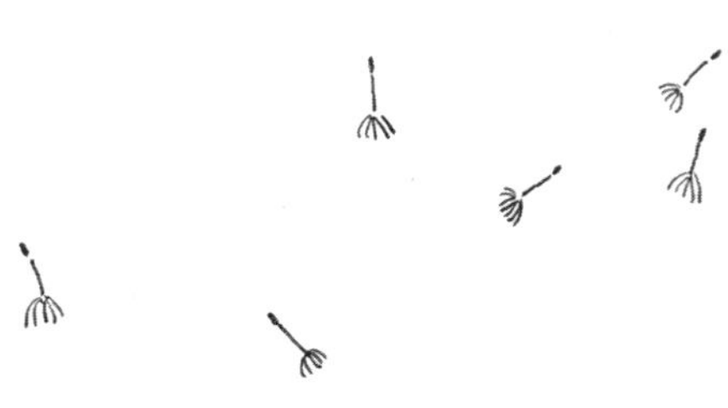

9. Dream Big

I am a strong believer in dreaming up grand gestures that are beyond my means and then whittling them down to a scope I can do. The depth and breadth of imagination that such a posture permits lets our creativity roam free, unhindered by practical concerns like money and time. As I'm working on a gift, especially if it's an elaborate one or involves lots of labor or time, I watch for opportunities to reduce scope or alter the form, in case I can't pull it off. Sometimes the scaled-down version is just as magical, often more so, but the larger vision is what sets it all in motion.

I recently decided to spell out an entire message in alphabet noodles for my friend at her baby shower, but (perhaps unsurprisingly) I was able to lay out only two-thirds of the poem on her coffee table before the festivities began, still searching for the missing letters. Time to change expectations! As part of my bestowal of the poem, I invited the mom-to-be to spell out the last third, handing her the poem and the bag of alphabet noodles. My friend was giddy with the thought of getting to finish it herself, savoring each word (and finding each letter).

Or we might reduce the scope earlier in the process. We can turn a weekend getaway into a day trip. If I'm dreaming of knitting a sweater for a new baby, I might need to switch to a hat. A thirty-six-clue scavenger hunt can be just as fun with twelve.

10. Start Small

To start small is also to say start easy, start smart, start safe. In my art studio, I am constantly mocking up scrappy prototypes and sketching in my notebook to test out ideas before investing additional resources. We can do the same with gifts. We can increase our chance of success by choosing something that doesn't feel overly ambitious but still feels sparkly and exciting. I didn't start the World's Smallest Post Service overnight. It began with one tiny letter to one dear friend. I giggled the whole time, writing as tiny as I possibly could. Pure joy. Easy peasy. A decade later, sparked by the joy that first letter brought, we were sending thousands of tiny letters and packages a year. Running small experiments and getting positive feedback can build confidence and competence as we explore our capacity to give creatively.

11. Do Research and Development

Even a little bit of research and development can go a long way when it comes to developing a gift idea. R&D includes information gathering, making prototypes, playing (#6), building skills (such as taking a workshop or watching a tutorial), soliciting feedback, and considering alternative variations (#12). When I get stuck developing a gift idea, my assumption is always that I just need more information of some sort—from a better understanding of my recipient to a better technique or craft tool. When I wrote my first tiny letter, I didn't grab just any pen in my apartment. I went to the art supply store and tested multiple pens to find the one with the finest tip.

12. Iterate

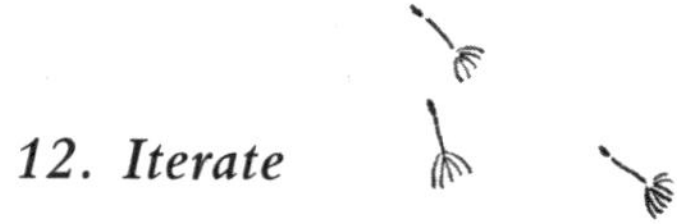

Got a good idea? Hooray! Try it out! This way. That way. And another way. Find the best version of your gift idea by developing variations on your theme with your deeper purpose in mind. Let your gift idea evolve by dreaming up successive versions of it, revisiting some of its key qualities as you go, brainstorming potential tweaks and transformations.

Remember the hopscotch poem I made at the crack of dawn, guiding my friend to the rose garden? That's too fun to do only once, don't you think? Since then, I've made another one leading some young friends of mine from their school to an ice cream parlor. In designing a kids' version, I imagined my recipients would enjoy something humorous or interactive. *Oh! How about riddles?* I obtained a book of kids' riddles and highlighted my favorites. Each hopscotch segment presented a riddle—one word per square—with a big question mark at the end. Each answer awaited at the beginning of the next hopscotch riddle a few blocks away. I decided to bestow it at the end of the school day, picking the kids up on foot and accompanying them through the whole thing. Follow the arrows! The ice cream is on me.

13. Put Together Exquisite Combinations

One of my favorite creative techniques is to combine preexisting things into something new that feels like more than the sum of its parts. Here, we get to be collector, curator, editor. A music playlist is a prime example, or perhaps a trio of spices that all go into the same special dish, recipe included. If we take it a step farther, we can make a mash-up. A simple example: A sixtieth birthday + A love of chocolate = A fellow receiving sixty chocolate bars on his sixtieth birthday!

In a mash-up, the parts interact or even transform each other, in physical form or meaning, or both. For my birthday last winter, my friend Rose cooked dinner for me at her house, where I was greeted by a gift-wrapped book of poetry and a handwritten menu announcing a multicourse meal that featured foods found in the poems. Pomelo. Dumplings. Root vegetables. Salmon. Rose's birthday was a few months later. Her mash-up inspired me to do something similar for her. My combo: a book of poems and a box of chocolates. I bought the truffles, but I transformed their meaning by pairing each one's aeshetics with a haiku. I provided an illustrated key and schemed a special presentation at the charming bookstore bar Clio's. With Rose's cocktail, the bartender handed her the box of chocolates and a clue to find the book of haikus I had planted in the poetry section. Mash-ups can involve many elements. Poems + Chocolates + Clue + Bookstore + Cocktail = Happy Birthday!

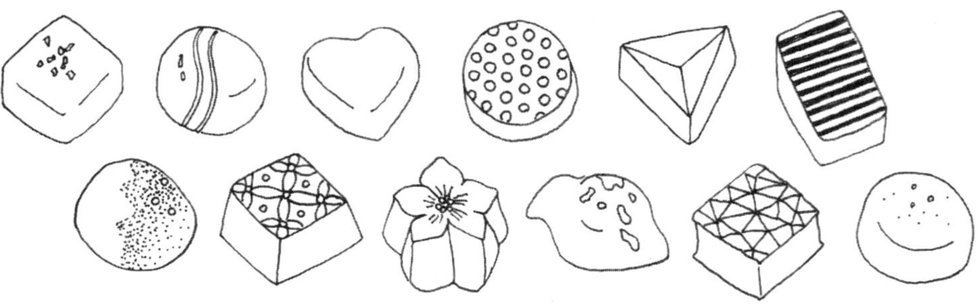

14. Don't Worry About Being Original

Being "original" by way of an innovative gift is a good idea only if it serves the deeper purpose of the gesture of care. Like a beloved folk song played over and over, a good gift deserves to be given again and again, in all sorts of different contexts. Pam and Joe in Washington State have a fun birthday tradition. If you are in their friend group, you will be surprised to notice at some point on your special day that a flock of pink plastic flamingos is in your front yard! The fact that other friends got the same treatment, and everyone got it last year too, only makes it better. It makes everyone feel that they are part of something, that they belong.

In many cases, it's not boring to repeat ourselves or play an old tune with a new spin on it, like my hopscotches. I love it when people have a signature gift that they become known for, such as great books or candied orange peels, and their community eagerly awaits receiving them.

15. Stay Nimble

Being nimble is a mindset. The ability to adapt, to wing it, to switch gears, or even to start over is essential if we want to make the highest quality compositions possible. Rigidity prevents us from homing in on the possibilities in front of us. Being nimble sets us free to respond to reality as it comes, as it changes before our eyes. It includes befriending "failure," learning to accept it as par for the course of creativity, even a good sign that experimentation is happening. Here, I like to picture a corn maze in the fall and think about the fact that a "dead end" is not nearly as terrible as it sounds. A "dead end" is just a "turnaround" or a point of redirection. It is the place where you pivot and pursue a new path forward because you have just received new information. I think creativity works like this. The more redirections that we experience, the more we can cast aside mediocre or impractical ideas, which moves us closer to a better solution. A turnaround is not actually a failure at all. It's just reality giving us a nudge, keeping us on track.

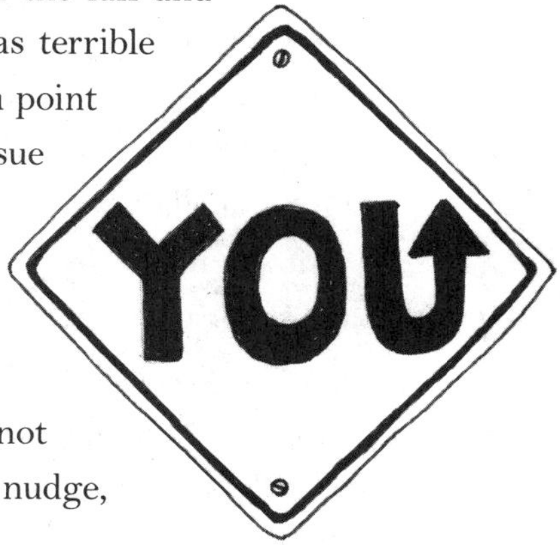

16. Be Imperfect

As the adage goes, *perfect is the enemy of the good.* In both gift-giving and life, good enough is oftentimes more than enough, plenty to get a job done well. I do not believe we can afford to let love go unexpressed because we are struggling to perfect our gestures of care. Thoughtful? Yes, please. Perfect? No need. I'm known to sometimes gift wrap half-finished hand-knits for people, so as to not miss the gift occasion. It's fine! Even humorous. I finish the gift as soon as I can.

Pairing Creativity with Thoughtfulness

When my studio intern Sadegh went off to college, I gifted them a pearl as a bon voyage gift. Rather than giving Sadegh a pearl in the common form of a piece of jewelry, though, I set a whole fresh dripping oyster on the table and handed them a knife to pry it open. The invitation was action. Their mission was to wrestle a shiny opalescent drop from the stubborn grasp of a gooey sea creature. It was perfect for an adventuresome teenager with a penchant for the surreal. Sadegh's eyes lit up, and they dove into the task with enthusiasm.

In terms of gift design, an image of Sadegh prying open an oyster with a knife certainly did not just pop into my head, out of the blue. One evening I visited a magic shop at Fisherman's Wharf in San Francisco. When I exited the shop, a pearl stall across the pier caught my eye. As a novelty for tourists, they let you pick your own oyster from a bin and then they pry it open for you, extract your pearl, and set it into a jewelry item of your choosing. Part of the excitement of this was that any given oyster could contain from one to three pearls, but the oysters were all the same price. I have never been into gambling, but if I were, this is my kind of casino! At just $15.99 for an oyster guaranteed to hold at least one pearl, it felt like a charming wager. I wondered: *Will they let me purchase an oyster, still sealed shut, so I can do the fun part myself?* Moments later, the pearl seller was handing me a pull-top can like the kind tuna comes in. How convenient! It wouldn't even smell up my bag. Feeling like I had gotten enough of my own fun out of this, I asked myself who would enjoy this as much as I do. *Sadegh.*

I, too, have been the recipient of a pearl, at my aunt's wedding when I was four years old. Right before the ceremony, she delicately lifted a small string of tiny pearls over my head, her fingertips gently clasping the necklace onto me, her flower girl, moments before we would both walk down the aisle of a cathedral in our fancy dresses. My aunt was creative in *her* way, in *her* style, and that was important because it was *from her* at *her* wedding. What mattered most was how special and loved my aunt made me feel. This was the purpose. The gift was pitch-perfect.

When it comes to gifts, something is even more important than creativity—thoughtfulness. In gift-giving, creativity is not for its own sake, but in service of a gift's purpose. The goal is not for your recipient to say, "Oh, wow, you are so creative!" but rather, "Oh, wow, this is so perfect for me!" A good gift might be complex or simple, traditional or avant-garde, practical or symbolic, rare or common, expensive or free, or anywhere in between. What matters most isn't the *what*, but the *how*, the spirit in which a gift is given and the way its benefits play out. As creative thinking-feeling-doing expands our range of possibilities, we greatly increase our ability to give and receive with integrity, to align our gifts with the fullness and depth of our love and good intention.

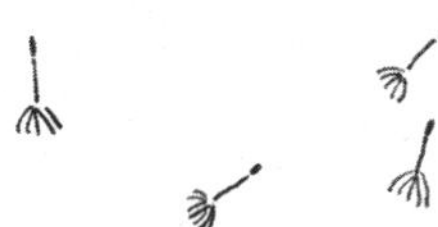

Make a New World

The process of making something is always accompanied by a subtle invitation to wake up to the fact that everything is made. It's all a *fabrication,* by which I mean that things aren't just made, but made-up. For us humans, the idea, story, or vision to make something beautiful or better appears in our imaginations first, and then—at some point, maybe, if we labor and we're lucky—in the world too. And so, if the world is constantly dreamed into being by people laboring to turn the visions in their heads and hearts into material facts, then what we imagine for ourselves matters greatly. If we can dream it up and make it, it becomes the world—the new reality, a given for whomever it touches next. We don't have to accept the status quo as inevitable because, once upon a time, someone like you or me made it. Today, again and again, we can attempt to remake it if we so desire.

I used to carry two glass marbles around in my pocket back in high school. One was the Earth, clear with solid blue continents printed on the surface; the other, a swirly rainbow. I like to think of the Earth marble as the given, the raw constraints of the world, the part we do not get to choose but are born into. The swirly rainbow, then, is what we make of it all, what we do with all that we've been given. Together, the two carry us into the future and determine what is possible. The only way to find out how much reality will afford is to make courageous proposals at the edges of the possible and see if reality says yes.

A gift is a creative act. Designing gifts for each other is a chance to acknowledge and nurture the artist inside us all. Creativity calls us to work with the world as it is in addition to the world as we wish it to become. I agree with the Afrofuturist sci-fi writer Octavia Butler: "There's no single answer that will solve all our future problems. . . . Instead there are thousands of answers—at least. You can be one of them if you choose to be."[2] As we put together remarkable gifts of good fit—thoughtfully resourced and awake to the world around us—we strengthen not just our relationships and our innate powers of creativity, but our sense of being active participants in the ongoing process of making our shared world.

Reflect

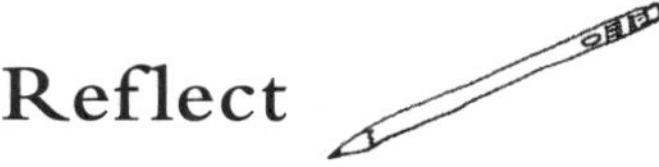

1. You are creative! Make a list of the unique resources you bring to your gifts: skills, talents, knowledge, personality traits, connections, possessions, craftiness, money, wisdom, other life experience, etc. The next time you give a gift, how might you pull these resources into play?

2. Choose a relatively mundane item that might be given as a gift: a cracker, a silver dollar, a deck of playing cards. Ask: *What else can this thing do?* From here, develop a delightful variation on how this item could be gifted. Rework its context, make a mash-up, or ask it to do something unexpected.

3. Consider a great gift you've experienced—given, received, or witnessed. How did the gift fit into its larger context or web of relations? Did the universe chip in with any delightful surprises?

11

Oops! Ouch. Now What?

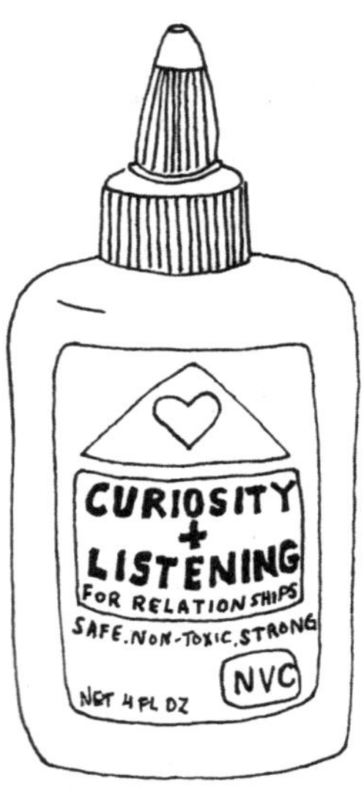

WHAT SHALL I DO WITH AN UNWANTED GIFT?

HOW CAN WE REPAIR AND HEAL WHEN A GIFT DOESN'T LAND WELL?

CAN I STAY CURIOUS AND CREATIVE IN THE FACE OF AN UPSETTING GIFT?

From time to time, sit close to the one you love,
hold his or her hand, and ask, "Darling, do I understand
you enough? Or am I making you suffer? Please tell me
so that I can learn to love you properly."

—THICH NHAT HANH, *PEACE IS EVERY STEP*

Repairing the World

At the San Francisco Museum of Modern Art a few years ago, I beheld Yoko Ono's *Mend Piece.* It was a new spin on the original 1966 version. On a table was a big pile of broken teacups and some simple materials for repair: glue, tape, cotton string, and a pair of scissors. Ono's instructions hung on the wall in a simple frame, just a few words typed in the middle of a white sheet of paper inviting us to mend the shards with wisdom and love. The rest was up to us, each of us at the table. So my friend and I sat down next to a few strangers and got to work, started to play. I thought about *kintsugi,* the Japanese art of mending broken pottery with golden lacquer. I also remembered the divine sparks and broken shards of *tikkun olam,* the Hebrew term for "repairing the world."

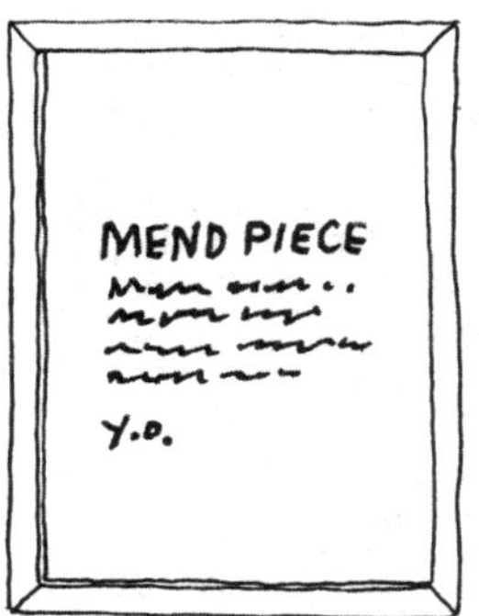

A sign invited us to display the results of our efforts, and the shelves were packed with a motley crew of makeshift forms, such as a two-handled cup pieced together with tape. Someone had turned a large, curved fragment into a tiny loom and woven a postage-stamp-size tapestry from the string. Each improvised composition on the gallery wall was a record of someone finding their way, working with what they had been given, transforming what *is* into what *can be.*

To Err Is Human

Just like a dropped dish in a kitchen, when something "breaks" or someone gets hurt, I believe it is usually an accident, or at least unintentional. Mistakes are unavoidable. Trying to never mess up is like trying to never make a typo, never trip, never get sick—impossible. The only way never to make a mistake in gift-giving is to not even try—and that's its own mistake! It is easy to make mistakes. It is human. But a mistake doesn't have to be a disaster. It can be an opening instead of a closing, a new beginning rather than an end. When something doesn't go as planned or hoped for, we might see it more like a pile of teacup shards, the raw material of reality with which we might mend the world. If to err is human, then to mend is human too.

A gift that doesn't go well—it's a familiar scenario. A sweater the recipient would never wear. Gendered toys for grandchildren that don't align with their parents' values or the children's wishes. Items that reference sensitive aspects of identity such as religion or race, but without appropriate context, sensitivity, or respect for complexity. Such situations are salvageable but require a bit of delicate handling. And we can see them as opportunities to draw closer. They can be arrows pointing both parties to an aspect of their relationship that could use more attention and care, perhaps some healing.

What if when things go "wrong" with a gift, we could practice welcoming the gift of important information? In human relationships, much goes unsaid, and it is exceedingly difficult not to fill that space with assumptions. These sneak their way into our gifts. In my mind, if a recipient bothers to tell me they don't like a gift I offer them, this likely means they consider our relationship worthy of a conversation, and that they trust me enough to take the feedback constructively, to do better next time.

I want to give you permission to get rid of any gift you don't want—to reject, to regift, to keep it moving however you see fit. I cannot, though, promise that doing so will not have uncomfortable consequences. Will the giver be offended if you give it back? Will they wallow in guilt and shame if you provide honest feedback? Will hilarity ensue? It is easy to get our signals crossed. The key is not necessarily to agree or to solve the puzzle of the misunderstanding once and for all, but to recalibrate together and stay nimble. Even if we are unable to unpack or address the full complexity of what has happened, we can show each other we are still here and committed to listening, exploring each other's points of view, and working creatively together so everyone feels okay.

To Repair Is Optional

Before we dive into how to repair a gift that doesn't go well, let's acknowledge that the recipient of such a gift is in an inevitable pickle. Here we are, feeling misunderstood or perhaps even offended, and now, must *we* be the one to break the bad news to the giver, potentially coming off as rude or ungrateful? Yikes. A recipient is well positioned to initiate a repair process because they have direct access to their experience of receiving the gift. But let's be clear. This does not obligate them to speak up or manage the whole process. Nor are recipients the only ones who can initiate the conversation. Gift givers can *ask* whether a gift has gone well, just as recipients can *inform* that it has not. These engagements are entirely optional. As recipients, we'd be wise to keep in mind, though, that if we don't speak up at some point about not liking a gift, especially if we pretend to like it, then we are unlikely to mend whatever mistake has occurred or prevent similar mistakes moving forward. And as givers, we might be wise to not assume our gift has been well received just because that seemed to be the case at bestowal.

All this begs a larger issue. Do all holes need mending, all misunderstandings need sorting, and right quick? I think not. Speaking up is not a universally good idea but is one choice among many, always made in context. Speaking up even in the safest of relationships can be difficult, and it can be more so in relationships with dynamics involving unequal power, such as between an employee and their employer. The strategies I suggest in this chapter work best in the context of relationships that are safe enough to make progress toward creative repair. Indeed, there might be times when a recipient's well-being is best served by not speaking up about an unwanted gift. If pretending to like a gift allows a gift to resolve itself smoothly and protects relationships, that could be a very skillful and appropriate response. A true gift is a freewill offering and so is a process of true repair. Not all relationships are conducive to truth and transformation, but when we trust that they are, I hope we will engage with open minds and courage. And when an unhappy recipient would prefer not to engage a giver, they can still heal and mend via other relationships and methods. Repair may be optional, but I believe healing is necessary.

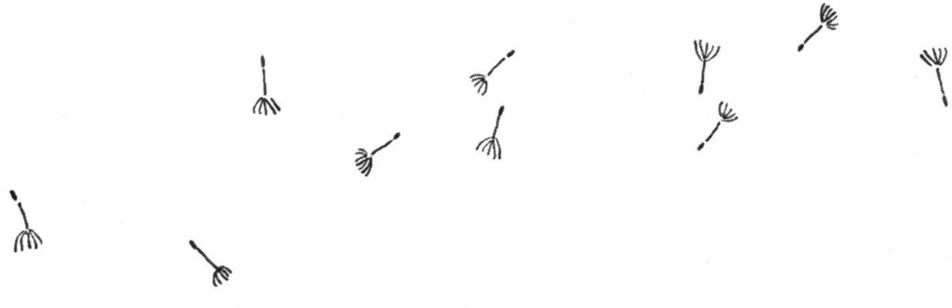

Responding Instead of Reacting

When someone attempts to care for us in the form of a gift and it doesn't go well, some sort of response is inevitable. Now what? Will we take it to heart? Tell them how we truly feel? Brush it off as a small slip? Burst into tears or just pretend to love it? Regardless of whether we end up accepting the gift, I recommend *accepting the reality* of the gesture, of what has taken place between you. There is no going back, but there is going forward, and there are choices to make about what happens next.

When a gift seems to be landing poorly, recipients and givers alike can start by asking themselves, Will I *respond* or will I merely *react*? Reactions are knee-jerk. They hijack our nervous systems and throw assumptions and unexamined emotions at a situation. The gnarly thing about *reactions* is that they can be so quick that they eclipse all possible *responses*, which are conscious and chosen. The key here is to catch a reaction before autopilot takes over, to stay in the captain's chair of our own behavior. Take a few deep breaths. Our feedback about a gift that we dislike will probably be better received if we don't give it, say, in the middle of a birthday party or on Christmas morning with everyone watching.

Yes. Breathe. A pause is powerful. Pausing gives us time to feel, and to catch reactive slips into hot-take interpretations that may or may not accurately reflect what the giver had in mind. If we take time to reflect and let the emotions of the situation flow through us first, we are likely to say something more constructive. We can try to be gracious if we feel that the well-wish was sincere, and we can do so without pretending that we like a gift we don't initially feel good about. As recipients, we can buy ourselves some time by saying, for example, that the gift has sparked our curiosity, we appreciate the giver's effort, and we want to spend some time with the offering and report back.

When we choose to respond with curiosity, we increase our options because we are calmer, more creative, and in better touch with our prefrontal cortex and all its powers of discernment and emotional regulation. As such, we make more grounded decisions. Let's look at a handful of useful directions to channel our curiosity: separating the love in a gift from the gift itself, learning to reality-check for misunderstandings, narrowing the gap between good intentions and good impact, and discerning the difference between a mean-spirited gift and one that is just lacking information. All of this will prepare us to respond well.

Look for the Love

Melissa in Alberta, Canada, told me about playing the "mitten game" with her children at Christmastime. Their advent calendar took the form of a string of mittens hanging across the living room like a decorative garland. Each mitten contained an activity or treat, including one in which family members would role-play giving and receiving gracefully by presenting random household objects to each other as "gifts." They tried to respond to a spoon or roll of toilet paper with love. They practiced making the most of it, finding something positive to say despite the awkward item. The game prepared all of them for the inevitable surprises and disappointments of Christmas present opening with extended family and friends. When done well, the mode of receiving that this game encourages is not one of acting, faking it, or just being polite. The key to "winning" this game is to assume the best, to be generous in our assumptions. We can genuinely say "thank you" for any love that we understand to be on offer regardless of how we feel about the gift item.

We don't have to love the gift to love the giver. We can say yes to the love

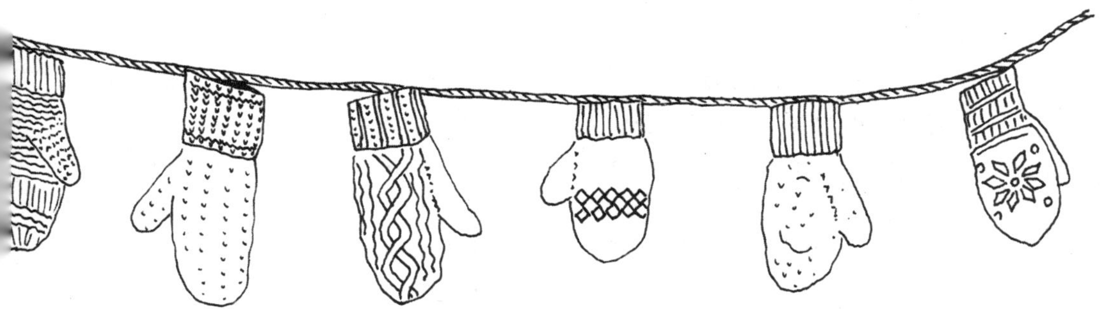

by commenting on something about the gift that we do like, appreciate, or find interesting. We can ask if there is a story behind the gift, or why the gift made the giver think of us. We can treat it as a conversation piece designed to enrich our relationship. It will be much easier to let go of an unwanted gift later if we've made an effort to soak up the love that it carried. Or, perhaps, the gift simply wasn't thoughtful or well resourced, and so, depending on the relationship, we might decide not to draw attention to that fact, and just let it go. Remember: Not all gifts are accurate microcosms!

Reality-Checking Before Responding

Even when we trust the love, and trust the giver, sometimes that is not enough to dispel our discomfort. When feelings are too hurt not to say something, though, we might thank ourselves later if we do some reality-checking before speaking. To reality-check a situation is to compare one's inner experience of a situation—the ideas, feelings, somatic sensations, interpretations, and stories we tell ourselves about reality—with the external world, which includes other people's inner worlds. Our running commentary about the world around us isn't necessarily incorrect, but it certainly can be and sometimes is. Our sense-making is swayed by our emotions, past experiences, and the tender spots inside us.

A surprise romantic private dance for two with live music. Sounds amazing, right? Not if the recipient feels too nervous to enjoy it. Sherry and her sweetie had been dating for months when he dreamed up a special evening for two at his apartment, complete with flowers, wine and cheese, and a few musician friends. Sherry loved dancing, and they had been taking swing lessons together, but what he didn't yet understand—what she hadn't yet felt comfortable sharing with him—was how self-conscious she felt about her dancing. So when Sherry saw the live band and formal dance set up *just for her,* it activated her vulnerability. She froze. They called the whole dance party off. Sherry wasn't in the challenge zone where growth happens, but in the outer zone of overwhelm.

Thankfully, they were able to use the awkward misstep as a way to better understand each other. The couple stayed together for decades, and Sherry became the confident dancer she always wanted to be, largely by dancing her way there with her sweetheart. Perhaps the real gift here is that Sherry learned that he welcomed her vulnerability, that she could trust him with her authentic self.

When we find ourselves having big emotions in response to other people, in gift-giving or otherwise, a mindful reality check can help us to distinguish between a *trigger* and a *cause.* Accountability is important. When people who love us inadvertently activate a tenderness inside us, we need to tell them so they can address it with us. That said, it is also important to be clear about just how much they are responsible for. The way a gift lands, wonderfully or terribly or anywhere in between, is rarely only about that gift. Recipients bring their own insecurities, longings, joys, and life experience to the moment. Processing a gift, especially one that doesn't go as hoped, will go much better if we can discern between a gift giver *causing* the recipient's negative reception or simply *activating* it, possibly aggravating old wounds.

Bringing Intention and Impact Together

This next angle of curiosity is especially important for givers. How can we try to eliminate the gap between *intention* and *impact*? The litmus test for success is not that we tried and had good intentions but that the gift goes over well in the mind and heart of the recipient. If they don't like it, we have missed something along the way (sometimes because they have not shown themselves truly), and we would do well to start asking questions about where things went awry. If we have laid a good foundation with this person and they feel available for it, they might offer us the gift of feedback. When a gift lands poorly, I like to consider the gift incomplete, still in process.

A gap between intention and impact is, of course, a problem only when the impact is negative, a detriment rather than a benefit. Creatively handled, such a gap can unfold beautifully, like the rearview mirror ornaments in chapter 3. If the recipient welcomes the gift and whatever impact it has on them, the gap itself is not really a problem unless there is an important message the giver wanted to impart that got lost in translation.

A woman in Florida told me that her mom had the best of intentions when she had a custom blanket made for her grandmother for Christmas, printed from a photo of her grandmother's dog who had recently passed away. On Christmas, though, the grandmother had a very strong, negative response to the blanket when she unwrapped it. She was suddenly eye to eye with her old best friend on what can already be an especially emotional day of the year, Christmas, and with everyone watching, she burst into tears. Her granddaughter told me it was clear that it was just too soon.

But here is where things take a turn for the better rather than the worse. The giver centered the experience of the recipient by apologizing, and then quickly set the blanket aside so it was not so acutely emotionally burdensome.

The intentions had been loving; the result was not as the giver had hoped. Oops! And, ouch. What happened next was remarkable, and perhaps possible only because it was preceded by such sensitivity. About a week later, the grandmother requested the blanket back. She was ready for it, had warmed up to the idea, and wanted it keeping her company at her house for years to come. In this case, the gift turned out to be a good one; the timing was just a little off, and maybe also the context of bestowal. The willingness to follow the lead of the recipient and prioritize her well-being helped the gift eventually find its way home. In the end, everyone understood each other a little better than before.

I want to draw attention to the giver's graceful behavior. Notice what she did *not* do—get defensive. She humbly accepted and respected her recipient's feelings about the blanket. Elsewhere, another family was in a similar scenario, but the giver got so publicly upset about his recipient disliking his gift that everyone in the room immediately started caring for the giver (good intentions) while abandoning the recipient (negative impact) who had been offended by the gift and what it meant to her. Everyone, of course, needs care and attention, and everyone can get it from appropriate sources at appropriate moments. Good intentions are a great start, but if we truly wish someone well, we will stay the course and keep listening so we can learn how to love them on their terms, not just ours.

Reframing Mean-Spirited as Misunderstood

When a gift is upsetting, or perhaps just off-puttingly irrelevant, it can be tempting to assume mal-intent. It *feels* mean, so it must *be* mean. Checking those assumptions by looking for evidence to support them, or requesting that evidence, can help us sort out exactly what has happened so we can respond to reality rather than fantasy. Sure, there is such a thing as a mean-spirited gift. It is certainly hard for me to imagine how, for example, a father could think it would be a good idea to send his adult daughter a book about weight loss for her birthday. Preachy gifts are rarely welcomed, especially when they carry unsolicited criticism and judgment.

I believe mean-spirited gifts are rare, that most missteps are just misunderstandings. "Great relationship" doesn't always equal "great gift." Jessica in Seattle told me about her excitement as a young child when her mom gave her Skittles on her birthday, an entire bag of her favorite candy, all to herself. Joy! Except not quite. In Jessica's mind, her mom made a big mistake by buying the "tropical" bag instead of the "original" flavors. Jessica especially hated the banana ones, those imposters, masquerading as lemon! As an adult, Jessica remembers being quite upset in the moment, thinking and feeling, *You don't know me at all!* But it didn't turn out to be a big deal, even for Jessica. She got over it, outgrew it. It was just a bag of Skittles, after all. And all this happened in the context of a loving, supportive relationship, making it easier to let it go. Also in elementary school, Jessica was not a fan of breakfast. To encourage her to eat a good one before school every day, Jessica's mom told her that she would make her anything she wanted for breakfast and, as per Jessica's request, ended up making homemade mashed potatoes every morning for an entire year. As gifts go awry, let's remember to keep the whole relationship in mind.

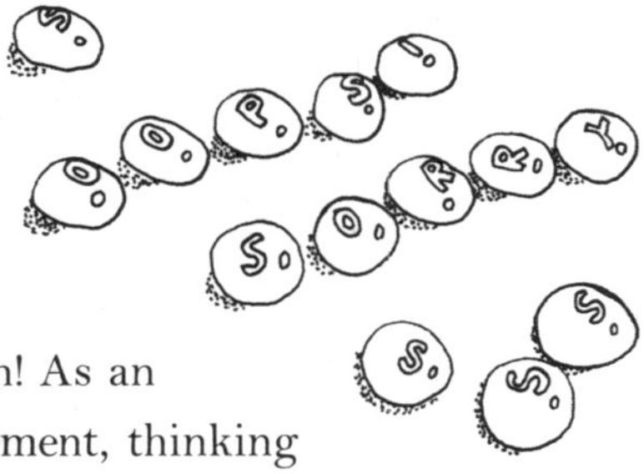

When our first reaction is offense, we can slow down and get curious. We can ask whether the gift is truly mean-spirited or merely lacking information. Is the gift a Trojan horse, purposely out to get you? Or is it a pretty pony that you just don't want—well-intentioned but unsuitable, like when, for example, a girlfriend gave her vegetarian boyfriend a leather jacket. She soon learned he didn't want to wear animals either. Oops! This was perhaps a bit unskillful, but it was not malicious. New relationships are especially prone to this kind of mistake. As receivers, we can be generous in helping givers connect the dots that are important to us, especially when the givers show us they care to know. When a gift is a mismatch for our values, and the relationship is dear to us, I suggest finding a way to let the giver know sooner rather than later.

Getting to know someone well shows us that we will never know them completely. That is okay. We need not understand someone completely to love them fully. We are all, by nature, mysteries to each other. The high-quality information intimate relationships generate makes it possible to attempt highly attuned gifts, to be wonderfully specific and even adventuresome. For instance, within the context of a twenty-year friendship between two fellows, one gave the other a gift certificate for a few sessions with a personal trainer. The friend had explicitly expressed that he wanted to work with one. The gift was based on inside information and seemed safe. The giver's encouragement was genuine, without any judgment about health or being in shape, but the giver told me he sensed that the gift nevertheless had managed to land with a tinge of something undesirable. The situation became a little prickly, and the troublesomeness of the gift started to show up in their friendship as touchiness and reactivity around other issues and conversation topics.

Finally, an opportunity to broach the subject appeared one day, and the recipient expressed both appreciation for the care in the gift and the fact that it had felt like too much pressure. Since they had been good friends for so long, their "marble jar" of trust held plenty of good will for their relationship to stumble and recover. (Vulnerability researcher Brené Brown explains that trust is earned and destroyed bit by bit, one small act at a time, like adding and removing marbles from a jar.)[1] The two friends' willingness to tolerate the discomfort of a sensitive conversation let them practice being vulnerable in their friendship; it also let them enjoy their friendship's resilience. The giver learned that he can be better at calibrating to his friend, knowing what is too little, too much, or just right; the recipient was reassured that his friend genuinely wanted to do better. When I asked the giver if it might have relieved some of the pressure if he had presented the gift as a homemade IOU coupon instead of prepaying for the trainer sessions, he said yes. The fact that he had already spent the money upped the ante. Even with the fumble, though, these fellows handled the situation so well that, by the end, they got to add yet another glass marble to their jar. The gift had transformed into something good.

Stay Curious and Speak Up

Curiosity feeds good conversation. A woman in a coffee shop told me she has way too many Christmas pajamas; her mom gives her a new pair every year, yet she wears them only on Christmas so it feels wasteful. I asked her if she pretended like she loved the new PJs every year. She said yes. I asked: "Is it time to speak up?" A recipient might decide to engage a giver or not based on whether the importance of the relationship warrants it, on how egregious a gift felt, and on their level of confidence in the giver's ability to receive feedback—to respond vs. react. If invited to engage, the giver, too, then gets to say yes or no or anything in between.

Practicing curiosity together can take many different forms, from a quick note via text message to a more complex conversation in person or over the phone. We can be loving of others and firm about our needs at the same time. We can help people learn to love us better through communicating directly. Upon the birth of Rebecca's first child, her nana delivered a big batch of homemade tortillas to nourish the new mother. Rebecca felt loved and supported by her favorite comfort food. After the birth of her second child, however, she got a Tupperware of sliced melon. How disappointing! And so, as the birth of Rebecca's third child neared, she chimed in with a simple, direct request of Nana: *I would love your tortillas after the birth.* And when the baby arrived, so did the tortillas. I think Rebecca's move was a classy one, essentially saying "no thanks, didn't love it" to the previous gift by communicating what she wanted this time. There was a foundation of love and care, so a simple request was all that was needed.

In some situations, an apology might feel appropriate, and it's never too late. My friend Kim spent a few years working for a nonprofit in Uganda after college. At the end of her time there, her Ugandan co-worker who had become a dear friend presented her with a bon voyage gift—a ceramic cow made by a local artisan. Already overwhelmed with packing and preparing to leave the country, Kim pictured trying to fit the large and heavy, and fragile, gift into her suitcase and turned it down, apologizing. Once home in the United States, though, she regretted the missed opportunity to honor their friendship by accepting it. A decade later, Kim's co-worker visited the States, and Kim finally got to express, *in person,* the depth of her regret around not accepting the gift. Sometimes life gives us a "take two," a second chance to express something that feels a bit unfinished. The friendship meant a lot to Kim, and she wanted to make that clear.

As we exercise our curiosity and negotiate our way through gifts that don't go well, we each get to decide what we are available for. Sometimes when the misstep is serious, a recipient might want to inform the giver, but without an emotional back-and-forth about it. This might sound like: *Hey, friend. I'm feeling the love in the gift from you, but moving forward, can you avoid anything that highlights my religion? I prefer not to discuss this further, but I need you to know because I value our relationship.*

Or the receiver might desire a more involved process of repair. In these cases, I suggest that the recipient schedule the chat so the giver, too, can reflect ahead of time and be emotionally prepared. This might sound like: *Hey, friend. Sweet of you to remember my birthday! I feel the love in your gift, but it's not working for me and I'm having some big feelings. I really value our relationship so I'd like to discuss, so we can understand each other better moving forward. Can we schedule a time to chat, maybe grab coffees and take a walk?*

Braving Difficult Conversations

Let's visit a few mindsets and practices that can help difficult conversations bring people together rather than pushing them apart. A vulnerable dialogue will likely go better if each person begins by assuming the best of intentions. It can be helpful to begin by saying as much. A recipient can acknowledge the giver's intention to be loving while also being clear that the gift did not work for them. Givers help create a welcoming space for this by assuring recipients that they are ready to learn. So delicate, right? Why would anyone even attempt such a thing? Because the relationship matters.

I aspire to Marshall B. Rosenberg's "language of life," in which he advises that each party take responsibility for their own actions and emotions, refraining from judgmental evaluations that undermine the generous spirit required for the mutual enrichment of life.[2] Recipients can try to identify their feelings, share them, and tell the gift giver specifically what didn't work for them about *this* gift situation, keeping to observable aspects of the specific event and their needs that went unmet. Givers can share their observations, feelings, and needs too. "I" statements work best. Questions and curiosity, not assumptions and accusations. Ultimately, articulating one's needs in the form of clear requests is key.

We can keep our integrity and be generous at the same time, giving people the benefit of the doubt until we know more. I suggest givers begin by saying something about what they had in mind and heart as they chose the gift; it might change everything. If anything about the gift did work well, I suggest recipients say so, and be specific, so the giver can have that feedback too. All of this might require some deep breaths from both parties. Maybe even breaking and resuming later. Anger, disappointment, and frustration might arise, but both parties can try to transform it into compassion and creative solutions.

If we give someone a gift and they would like to share something about how it didn't work for them, we must remember our original intention to wish them well. Our recipient has bothered to give us feedback, and they might have had to muster their courage to do so. Both parties can try to sustain an atmosphere where everyone feels safe speaking from the heart. We can be kind to ourselves, try not to take things personally, and get to work on making them better. When our recipient tells us how the gift felt, we must believe them and take their experience seriously even if it doesn't sync with our own experience or intention.

I understand why givers might get defensive. Their love got lost in translation. The key here is to proceed with care, and to try to weather the emotions of the moment. As part of a healthy repair process, givers can confirm their love is real while learning what would be a better vessel for their love next time. The trickiest part for givers is not to get lost in guilt or self-blame, but to reach for gratitude and appreciation. It is an honor to be privy to the contents of someone else's heart. The recipient is displaying that they think the relationship is worthy of an awkward or even difficult conversation.

As a recipient, when we summon the courage to speak up, and do so with kindness, we might be surprised at how well we are received. As a giver, when we welcome such honest speech, we might be equally surprised at how well it can go. When it comes to difficult conversations of any type, it can be helpful to remind ourselves that the discomfort and high emotion can be good signs. We might be on the brink of a breakthrough, of deepening our understanding.

Making Requests and Agreements with Love

A difficult conversation doesn't have to be a drag. Oftentimes, we can keep it light. The woman with all those Christmas pajamas hadn't spoken up so far because she didn't want to hurt her mom's feelings. In the coffee shop, we wondered if she might suggest a fun alternative that would feel great to her mom, such as an annual Christmas season brunch after which they'd go shopping together for a new garment that the daughter wanted to wear all year round, for years to come.

Communicating about a gift that lands poorly can get tricky as the gift increases in complexity or the relationship in importance. My heart goes out to everyone when this happens! Unless all parties can brave the difficult conversation, the course correction that is required becomes elusive.

In these reparative conversations, giver and receiver can remember that the goal is to make things better. In seeking to understand each other and repair any harm done, we can identify immediate remedies as well as more systemic ones, such as clarifying boundaries, making agreements, and setting intentions for the future. Making specific requests for behavioral changes that the other person can consider keeps us from getting lost in hurt feelings. An agreement based on clear requests can relieve the pressure to understand each other completely, or the full complexity behind a gift landing poorly. That may not be possible in just one conversation, or even ever. In the meantime, we can start to mend and reduce future harm. The repair might involve replacing the gift with another item, perhaps by the recipient pointing the giver to a wish list. Just as important is a change in future behavior, especially if a hot topic has surfaced. Learning from the situation shows that we can adjust to each other, even trust each other.

While keeping in mind that a gift is for the benefit of a recipient, on their terms, both parties can make requests for actions that will contribute to everyone's needs getting met. And both may agree or decline as need be. What I love most about Rosenberg's process is that a request for a change in behavior is made in such a way that the mood is not one of judgment or guilt, but one of collaboration. When we ask someone to change their behavior *as a gift to us* rather than out of guilt or shame, it's much easier to say yes. Why? It feels good to give a freewill offering to someone we care about, especially when we're not feeling attacked.

Well-intentioned givers who genuinely care about the relationship do their best to participate in processes of apology and repair when their areas of unawareness are revealed to them. Givers with good intentions also do their homework, revealing their awareness gaps before harm is done, or afterward, as the case may be. Recipients, too, can do their best. This includes tending to their own hurt feelings in whatever ways feel supportive to them, with or without the giver, and engaging in processes of repair only when they trust that those processes will contribute to their own wellness and not just compound the harm.

The vulnerable conversation can even precede the gift. A little foresight can sometimes prevent a problem before it exists. For instance, a daughter in Michigan knew her mom was making her a quilt as a gift. She loved the general idea but was concerned that she might not love the colors and fabrics, so she suggested that she accompany her mom to the fabric store to help choose the fabrics. Her mom was a little offended at first, but the daughter persisted. She told her mom that she wanted to love the quilt aesthetically in addition to loving it because it was made by her mom, so she would actually use it in her home and really enjoy it. The daughter made a good case, and her mom invited her into the creative process.

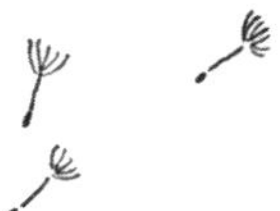

If we can make a robust habit of being vulnerable together, we can enjoy strong, resilient relationships. I try to show up to difficult conversations with good humor—and maybe cookies or flowers—as I do my best to make requests, set boundaries, and agree to new systems moving forward, ones that are good for everyone.

Beyond Yes or No

When someone gives us a gift, it is easy to think we must keep it. But when someone holds out a box with a bow and we take it into our hands, all we are really consenting to is opening the box to reveal the mystery that is inside. When an outstretched gift is not treated as an obligation, but an offer, then it is up to the recipient to decide whether they want it or not.

What's more, *accept* or *reject* are rarely our only options. It doesn't have to be all or nothing: Keep a gift or give it back. Any *no* can transform into a *yes* of sorts with a bit of creativity, goodwill, humor, and grace. We might decide that we feel good about only part of a gift, such as *yes* to a romantic picnic, but not in public, please. Or *yes* to this sweatshirt, but only in a different color or size. We can make adjustments, guiding the gift home: *Yes, if . . . Maybe when . . . Only with . . . Yes, but I need you to understand that . . . I'd feel better about it if . . .* Once a gift is out in the open space between us, we can adjust course.

Even when I "reject" a gift, that very rarely means literally giving it back to the person who gave it to me. I just keep it moving. There are a few exceptions. If the gift I didn't want might be sentimental to the giver, such as heirlooms, I would return it so the giver can decide who gets it next if it is not going to be me. One woman told me that she returned a teapot to the friend

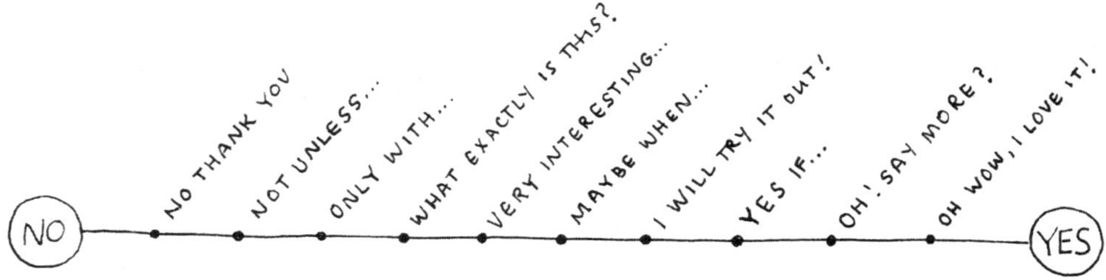

who gifted it to her because she felt lukewarm about it and her (very close) friend had shown much fondness for it during the bestowal. She knew she could just gift it back and their friendship would be fine. The friend would be delighted to have it. All good.

If your process reveals a desire to get rid of an unwanted gift that went home with you, I say go for it! Reminder: A true gift is an offer, an invitation. We can return the gift to the giver if that seems best, return it to the store if it was purchased, exchange it, donate it, regift it, or let it go ceremonially. A silly trinket might be fun to look at for a few weeks, even just for laughs. Hanging on to an unwanted gift for a little while might even lead us to change our mind. We can put gifts in limbo if we want to, into a "waiting room," just in case. We might realize, for example, that we can wear that ugly T-shirt as pajamas, enjoying the love in it without cramping our style in public. Gifts can grow on us.

We can get creative, saying yes and no at the same time. For example, if you end up with an heirloom chair from your great-grandmother and you love the wood but not the fabric, reupholster it into a chair that you will love. A friend of mine rescued the gift of an ugly lamp from her mother simply by changing where she placed it in her home. Her mom thought she had stumbled upon a lamp by my friend's favorite vintage lamp company, but in my friend's eyes, it didn't look anything like the brand she loved. She responded to this unwanted gift with both a *yes* and a *no* by keeping the lamp in her guest room, where she doesn't have to look at it daily, but her mother can enjoy it when she visits, a nod to the love in the lamp.

"I saw this and thought of you." A lovely sentiment, but what if the gifts that come with the sentiment begin to swamp the recipient? I spoke with a young woman who shared her frustration at the many gifts her mother sent her, things her mother had picked up when she thought of her daughter. How could she let the mother know that her love was appreciated but the gifts were unwanted? The woman and I tried to come up with a tender solution, one that might encourage the mother's expressions of love, but without all the purchases. We got curious. Could she ask her mom to just snap photos of these items and text them to her with the same message?—*I saw this and thought of you.* The daughter could promise to speak up whenever the item was truly something she wanted to own.

We also wondered whether the daughter could subtly transform the nature of the game with a gift of her own. We made a game plan. The daughter would keep an eye out for lovely things in the world, including wonderful things not in stores, that reminded her of her mom and then text her mom a photo and "thinking of you" note whenever she found one. For some future birthday, she could make her mom a keepsake book of the series of photos that she had sent to her in this spirit. Might this be a gentler way to give her mom feedback? Maybe her mom would join in the fun of the new game?

Make It Better, No Conversation Required

A vulnerable conversation isn't the only way to repair a gift gone poorly; sometimes, a direct conversation isn't even necessary. A giver might just do better next time. Like Gabriela did when she organized a farewell party for an important co-worker who was leaving their company. Previously, she had given him "a day off" for his birthday, thoughtfully arranging for other people at the office to cover for him on his special day. He enjoyed his day off, but later on, Gabriela learned that he didn't feel directly celebrated by the officemates. He also did not fully understand her role in coordinating his day off. Since he didn't understand the trouble she went to for him, her care was lost in translation. Oops! They never directly discussed the small gaffe, but when he announced that he would be leaving the company, Gabriela dove in on designing a party for him. Even though it was a goodbye party and nowhere near his birthday on the calendar, she had the bakery write "Happy Birthday!" in icing on the cake. Gabriela had registered his mild disappointment at the previous gift and stepped up to meet him in the way he wanted to be met.

Giving with Humility

As mentioned earlier, gift recipients are not the only ones who can initiate a feedback process. Givers can let their recipients know that they are open to feedback. In fact, a recipient might be more likely to speak up if a giver has put in the effort and vulnerability to broach the subject, making it clear that they welcome dialogue. For instance, *Hey, friend. I'm all ears if you have any feedback about the gift I gave you, or tips for next time.* Or, *I kinda went out on a limb with that gift for you; I'm curious how it felt if you're inspired to share.* If directly following up about a particular gift isn't a good fit, another approach is to ask more broadly for feedback, such as asking someone about gifts from you they've loved in the past, and why. You can also ask them about the best and worst gifts they've ever received. Another angle, ask them what their "love language" is and to tell you a good story about someone speaking it to them fluently.

Humility can also show up at the bestowal, to help catch a gift before it goes awry. A little can go a long way, and there's certainly no need to preemptively apologize for a terrible gift before you have real data. We can, however, prepare the ground for openness and authenticity by including a receipt or inviting the recipient to keep it moving, if needed.

Include a gift receipt. If the gift was purchased, the giver can include the receipt with it (sealed in an elegant envelope) in case the recipient would prefer to exchange it for something else from the same shop or service provider. I like the tone this sets. The inclusion of the receipt expresses humility around the giver's selection and encourages a recipient to guide the gift home by exchanging it for something else if they so desire.

Invite people to "keep it moving." What if, as givers, we preemptively gave permission for our recipients to get rid of a gift they don't want? What if we said this aloud or jotted the phrase on our gift tags until it became a new norm? I can hear people, en masse, sighing in relief, giddy at the notion. What a load off! Givers can try their best, acknowledge their own limitations, and let a gift go. Receivers, in turn, can try their best to receive a gift, then let it go, too, if that's what feels best.

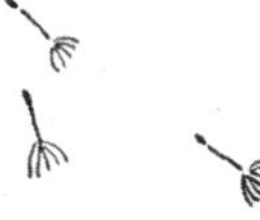

Heal It Forward

What if the giver is unwilling or unable to engage in the way the receiver would like them to? When it doesn't feel appropriate to process a gift together, a recipient can still create a space for themselves to heal from the situation. If we want company, we can invite trusted souls into that healing space with us. We can talk it out with a friend or therapist, journal about it, or shake it out on the dance floor.

Sometimes healing from an upsetting experience, gift or otherwise, comes from unexpected sources on extended timelines. It might not involve the people originally involved. A woman told me a disappointing gift story from her childhood. On her mom's birthday, she had excitedly presented her mom with a birthday card she had made especially for her. She remembers her mom's harsh reaction, word for word: "You're too cheap to buy me a card?" The woman never got the repair and healing that she longed for from her mom, but that doesn't mean she never found a way to ease that painful moment. Sitting with me sixty-some years later, she opened a large keepsake tin and showed me the treasure inside—a hundred or more handmade cards, letters, and drawings, all made for her over the course of many years by her own children. The healing here, from the direction of her children instead of her mother, is of course not the same as what she would have liked with her mother, but it did give loving attention to that very old wound, mending whatever areas it could. And in the process she sent the message to her children that she values their handmade offerings.

We can patiently wait for healing to find us, or we can actively seek it out. Sometimes, we get lucky enough to just stumble upon it. I try to stay open to the kindness of the world, wherever and whenever I can find it, make it, or become a vessel for it. When we are feeling too hurt or lost to see the resources for healing that surround us, we can point them out to each other. When I lose hope, I rewatch my favorite clip from *Star Wars: The Force Awakens.* I pretend that interstellar tavern keeper Maz Kanata has just reached for my hand instead of Rey's. Then she tells it to me straight, "The belonging you seek is not behind you; it is ahead."

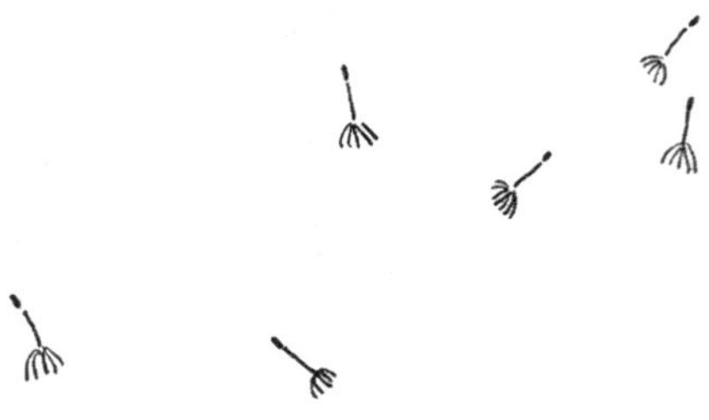

Keep Playing

Several years ago, my friend Myles received a Weber kettle grill from his dad for Christmas. The classic! Charcoal, not gas, and built to last. No doubt Myles's father envisioned years of festive backyard gatherings. The only problem? Myles does not like to barbecue. *Not at all.* After six years, he had yet to fire up that grill. For Myles, the gift being a mismatch for him didn't come with any emotional baggage or need for healing, but the gift itself was taking up precious space and gathering dust in his carport. Myles and I had only recently met at a friend's birthday party, but soon enough, I offered to show up at his house and whisk away the grill as part of my latest experiment—a removal service for unwanted gifts. I call it Let It Go Hauling. To my delight, he said yes.

I was excited to meet this grill that had become a bit of a superstar in my mind—a delicious story of a so-called "bad" gift. Myles led me to the spot where it sat—unused, untouched. I popped the trunk of my car and we started to move the grill, but it all felt too fast. I wanted more out of this moment, so we paused to admire the thick layer of dust on the lid. I suggested to Myles that he write any parting words into the dust with his finger. "Chow down," and into the trunk the grill went. Half-jokingly, I asked Myles if he wanted to do a little jig in the empty spot where the grill used to sit. Soon enough, he was tapping out a timestep and I was laughing, astonished that my new friend had a legit dance move at the ready. It turns out he had taken tap lessons his entire childhood! Then Myles pulled out his to-do list and crossed off "BBQ Craigslist," and I autographed the paper, making our ridiculousness official.

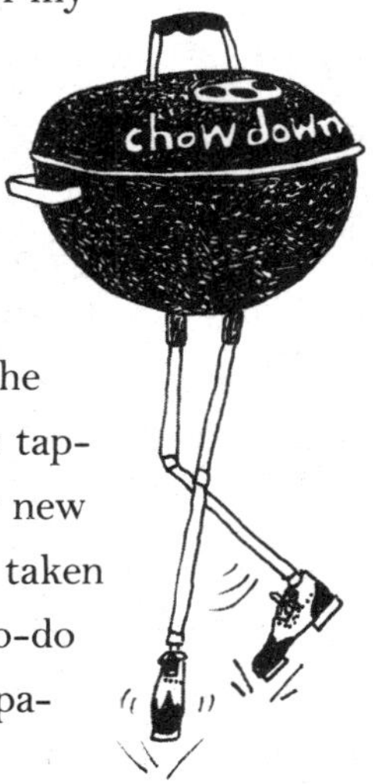

The Joy of Repair

The kiddos who made that birthday banner for me recently visited my art studio for a playdate. The younger one, as usual, made a beeline for my gumball machine. When the machine jammed, we pulled it down and took it apart with a screwdriver, everyone excited to see the inner workings. I noticed how old the gumballs were and announced that it was time to pitch them. And so the younger kiddo started to stuff his pockets! I was delighted to see his dreams coming true, but there was no way I was going to send him home to his parents with a hundred or more little sugar bombs. And so, I swooped up my friend, flipped him upside down, and the gumballs came pouring out! They shattered into pieces as they hit the floor. It was a big mess, but we had a good giggle.

I saved some of the shards I swept up that day in a jar on my desk as a souvenir. I didn't want to stop smiling about that sweet moment. I eventually wondered: What sort of fun could we have with all this broken, stale gum? Is there some other way to engage with it that won't spike our glucose to the moon? I remembered Yoko Ono's *Mend Piece*. And *kintsugi*. And *tikkun olam*. And this passage from Molly Martin's book about how to mend clothes: "To repair something (anything) in the modern world is a defiant act, which flies in the face of consumerist values and products."[3]

And so, the next time I joined family dinner at their house, I brought the jarful of gum shards, a bottle of glue, gold paint, and two gumballs from the fresh batch I had bought. Working over newspaper on their dining room table, we pieced the gumballs back together into delightful new multicolor configurations. And sealed the seams with metallic gold.

Reflect

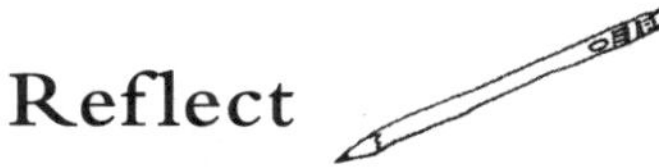

1. Can you think of any unwanted gifts you have received in which the love was still strong? Have you missed out on any love contained within undesirable gifts over the years? If so, can you claim the love today, finally receiving it?

2. With a hearty dose of curiosity, reflect upon a gift from the past that went poorly. Was the *impact* of the gift misaligned with the *intention*? Did the gift land as *mean-spirited*? Or was it maybe just *lacking information* or *underresourced*? How much of the upset that ensued was *caused* by the gift versus merely *activated* by it?

3. The next time you receive a gift you don't want, before getting rid of it, make a list of five different ways you could do so. Can you transform it or creatively reconceive it such that you want to keep it? Who would be the perfect person to redirect it toward? Is there a local organization that could benefit from it? For at least one of the ideas, design a ceremonial send-off.

4. Do you have any lingering hurt feelings associated with gifts given or received? If reflecting upon them reveals a desire to work through what happened, engage the other person in a process of repair and healing. What do you want them to understand? How can they make it better with you? How can they do better next time?

12

The World Is Round!

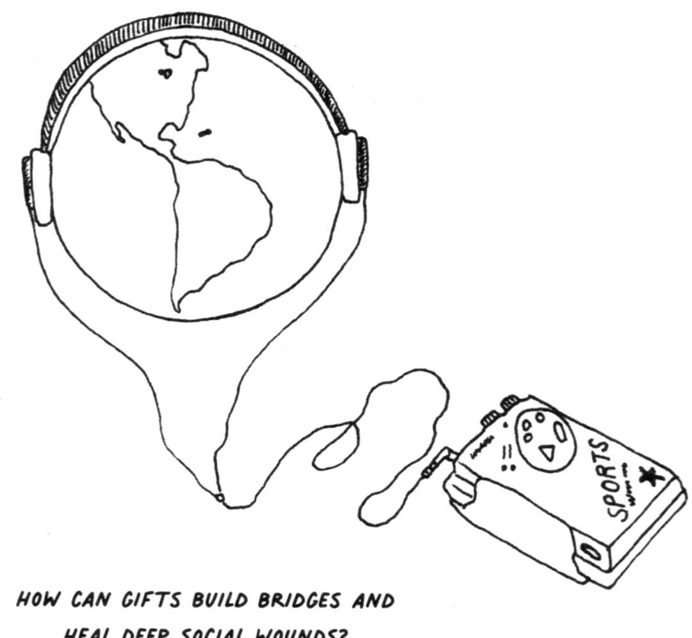

HOW CAN GIFTS BUILD BRIDGES AND
HEAL DEEP SOCIAL WOUNDS?

HOW CAN MY GIFTS HELP SUMMON A WORLD
IN WHICH EVERYONE FEELS WELCOME?

IN THE FACE OF FEAR AND HESITATION,
WHAT CAN A GIFT GIVER DO?

Look again at that dot. That's here. That's home. That's us.

—CARL SAGAN, *PALE BLUE DOT*

You Are Here

For hundreds of thousands of years, humanity has been a kaleidoscopic project of epic scale and intricate detail. Each culture—the language, food, architecture, textiles, clay vessels, songs, dances, and much more—has been crafted over many millennia in a co-creative response to the Earth itself. In this lively little corner of the universe we call home, matter and energy do-si-do themselves dizzy into a stunning variety of forms. Sunlight hits the periodic table, and it explodes into billions of tiny little beautiful pieces such as sand and raindrops, ferns and feathers, blueberries and tin pails with handles to *kuplink, kuplank, kuplunk* those blueberries into.[1] And the pieces have places. Wet as a rainforest. Dry as a desert. Colorful as a coral reef. Many of the pieces also have feet or wings or boats or other forms of mobility, such as seedpods catching a strong wind. Humanity's surviving and thriving have always been premised on coming together in new ways, cross-cultural and cross-species projects that respond creatively to the full range of being on this planet, and today's challenges show no different.

To solve the pickle humanity has gotten itself into, we are going to have to get very creative, and fast. The ecosphere is in crisis—fires, floods, disease, poverty, war. If we want to make it to the next century and beyond—all of us, and in relative peace—we must bridge difference at every scale, and I think gifts are a great if unexpected place to practice. Not being able to work together across difference is tearing the world apart and breaking our hearts along the way. Heck, it is even ruining Thanksgiving dinner.

I don't have all the answers, but I do have questions I care a lot about: *Can small acts of generosity contribute to the difficult and joyful work of bridging difference that this unprecedented moment of history requires? Might gifts help humanity remind itself that all its people belong here, that the circle of human concern is large enough for everyone?*

The Spaces Between Us

I am going to state the obvious because it is so easy to forget. We do not have direct access to other people's inner lives. Even the most attentive friend can miss the mark because people live distinct lives. We cannot ever know or predict everything about another human being, especially when the difference quotient is high. But isn't it the ultimate joy of relationship to learn and grow beyond our own perspective, getting to hang out with people who are not exactly like us?

The goal is not to *close* the gap between us. Closing the gap eclipses creative possibility by eliminating difference and reducing the diversity and complexity of the whole system. Instead, we can try to *bridge* the gap and remember that traffic on a bridge goes both ways. We can try to understand each other better while letting people be who they are, be who they want to be. Rather than trying to persuade someone else to become more like us, we can get curious about what it is like to be them. Any transformations that come can be the ones people choose for themselves, ones that organically emerge out of the creativity that activates when difference is accompanied by mutual curiosity in the context of compassion and trust. This is, put simply, one of the central pleasures of a great friendship or romance, is it not? Bit by bit, or sometimes suddenly, we become a new version of ourselves in the presence of someone else because they are able to say something or do something that we find interesting by virtue of their not being us.

I believe we can, and should, gift across difference. Every gift already does this to some degree. To do it well, we also need to ask: *When is it good for a gift to acknowledge identity and differences in identity? How will I engage with larger cultural contexts as I give? And, does* this person *want* this *from* me?

Othering vs. Honoring

The biggest mistake to make when it comes to giving gifts across significant difference involving group identities is to attempt to "see" someone, but to do so in a way that reduces a unique individual to a category. The result can be much worse than just giving a random all-purpose gift. Even if the giver is more or less on equal footing in terms of social power, the result can be an experience of being misunderstood, skipped over, even invisible. In other words, *unseen.* This is a mini version of the patterns of thought that conquer and colonize, that have dehumanized for centuries. To see people as individuals does not mean erasing or ignoring their group identities; it means not assuming their affiliations or reducing people to them. This of course shows up in big ways on a national and global scale, but we'll stick to gifts here.

One woman told me about receiving a panda plushie back in college from a new friend who, it seemed, thought she would like a panda because she was "Chinese," or perhaps just "Asian." The gift struck her as strange times two. First, she had been born and raised in California, a panda-less part of the world (in terms of natural habitat). Second, she was of 100 percent Vietnamese heritage, and there aren't pandas in Vietnam either; they mostly live in China. Nevertheless, if she had been a big fan of pandas and she had excitedly shared that fact with her friend, it might have been a good gift, but this gift was based on stereotype rather than observed interests. Her friend didn't know her well enough to know what her heritage was, so how could he possibly know she would want it highlighted?

As we cultivate our ability to pay attention to each other and give with empathy, such attention is going to reveal what we have in common as well as what makes us different. It is important to see difference. We can, and many of us already do, use these distinctions in positive ways. Seeing difference helps us acknowledge history, explain the present, cultivate solidarity, and point out co-creative possibility. But when is it appropriate for a gift to highlight such things? When does it help and when does it hurt?

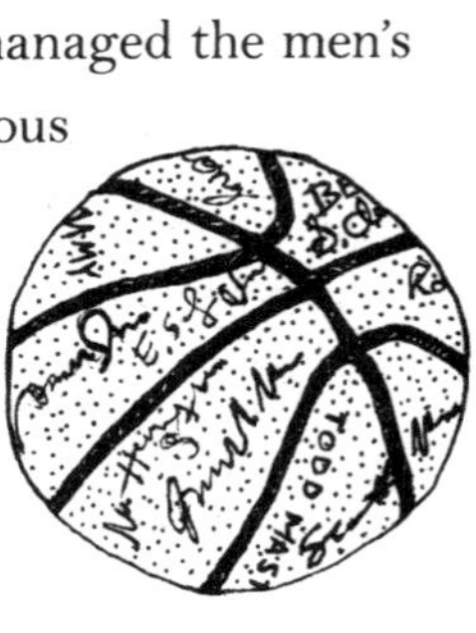

In some gift contexts, especially in close relationships, highlighting a difference between giver and receiver has the potential to honor and build trust. It can be part of being seen deeply, fully. In other contexts, calling attention to a difference—especially a sensitive one with a fraught history—holds the danger of *othering* rather than *honoring*, casting someone out rather than inviting them deeper into the realm of belonging. As a college student in Virginia in the late 1990s, a woman named Casey co-managed the men's basketball team with one of her (male) friends. It was a serious commitment, and they shared the responsibility. They both traveled with the team, dressed up for games, hauled the gear, and cheered on the players. Basketball was Casey's favorite sport. At the end of the season, the team's players surprised their managers with thank-you gifts. Casey's male co-manager received a basketball signed by all the players. Casey received a gift basket from Bath & Body Works. In her mind, the gift meant that, in their eyes, she was a girl more than she was a part of the team. It didn't matter whether she liked lotion and soaps; she did not want lotion and soaps *from them.*

Singular and Plural

Gifts are an opportunity to practice pluralism as we celebrate our similarities, honor our differences, savor our individuality, and tap into our common humanity. I think people feel the most seen when they honor each other as unparalleled, unrepeatable bits of creation. Perhaps it is just the Western individualist part of me speaking, but it seems to me that it is hard for people to feel like they matter if they are just one of many and the same as everybody else. Humans arrange and rearrange themselves, again and again, into all sorts of overlapping groups of identity and shared experience, and a person's particular intersection of affiliations is part of what makes them special.

Let's return to my courtship story, the one with the flowers being passed back and forth. A few months before Oscar's birthday, he mentioned his love for a type of decorative textile common in Central America and unfamiliar to me. These short, wide tapestries dangle from the interior top edges of windshields. He searched for one online but couldn't find a good example. So for his birthday, I improvised one with macramé. When Oscar had first told me about huge, wild mango trees growing all over El Salvador, with mangos free for the picking, he had said it wistfully. I have never seen someone enjoy a mango as much as this sweet man. We ate a lot of them together, sprinkled with lime and his mom's homemade *alguashte* (powdered squash seed). They

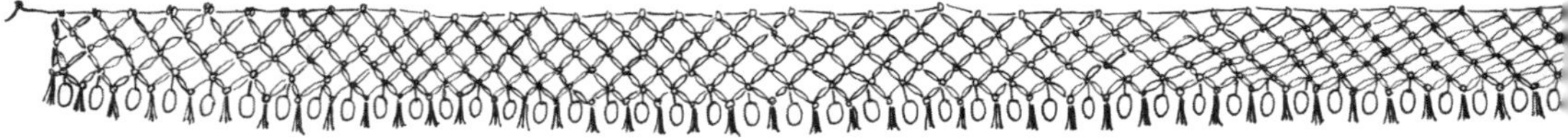

were a portal between where Oscar grew up and where he lives now. So with mangos in mind as I made the tapestry, I incorporated bright-orange oval beads for "mangos" and put them on "trees" by using green and brown cordage. I knew my beloved missed the tropical landscape of his childhood, that there was both joy and grief in the geography of his life story.

Telling other people our stories is an inherently vulnerable thing to do. We hold out something important to us and expose it to the elements. Leadership coach Charles Feltman helps me understand the gravity of this act when he writes, "Trust is choosing to make something important to you vulnerable to the actions of someone else."[2] Oscar trusted me with his love of mangos (easy) and with many other stories from his life (harder), a life that is both very different from and very similar to mine, depending on how you slice it. We didn't always agree or understand each other, especially working with two different native languages. By spotlighting some of his world in the form of a beautiful object for him, I hope I showed him that his stories were safe with me. Sacred, even. Audre Lorde's words come to mind: "The sharing of joy, whether physical, emotional, psychic, or intellectual, forms a bridge between the sharers which can be the basis for understanding much of what is not shared between them, and lessens the threat of their difference."[3] The macramé gift was a great success. Oscar wanted to install it immediately. We ran out to his truck with a jar of safety pins, climbed up into the cab, and pinned the mini mango forest up to the windshield.

Practice makes progress. The more we give, the more we grow. As I dream up gifts that I want to make and give, I can trust that my heart is in the right place, but I also want to know, *How good are my methods?* We can catch some unconscious errors by reconsidering our instincts as they pop up. The key is to summon our self-awareness and ask: *Is this gift idea the work of a trustworthy and wise heart, responding to the reality in front of me? Or is it the product of unconscious biases, social conditioning, and hurtful histories, thus embodying ideas that I don't agree with and actions that might cause harm despite my good intentions?*

When compared with the panda toy or the gift basket of bath products, I think the key distinction illustrated by my macramé gift for Oscar is that it didn't fill the gap between us with stereotypes and assumptions. I gave toward the specific ways my gift recipient chose to share his background and identity with me as we spent time together.

Accompanying Each Other

Many great gifts primarily reference something that is shared or the same, such as concert tickets to see a band both giver and receiver love. But I don't want to only and always gift toward what is the same because, over time, the subtext is that we can only connect because of what we have in common. I want some of my gifts to embody the idea that we can also love each other and thrive together because of what is different. Gifts remind us that we live not just for ourselves but for each other.

Without difference, if taken to the extreme, there can be no *from me* or *to you* at all. A complete merge into *one* eclipses relationship itself; there is no space to span. In my mind, a healthy society does not blur and blend its members into *one* but honors everyone's edges so we can coexist as *many*. As Octavio Paz writes, "Love, then, is represented in the form of a knot. A knot made of two intertwined freedoms."[4] The freedom piece is key. I agree with bell hooks: "Fear is the primary force upholding structures of domination. It promotes the desire for separation, the desire not to be known. When we are taught that safety lies always with sameness, then difference, of any kind, will appear as a threat."[5]

Practicing bridging difference in contexts where everyone feels safe and the stakes aren't too high builds both confidence and competence. My sweetie Oscar knew that I loved gifts of words. When my birthday rolled around, he reached toward this aspect of me with a creative spin on the greeting card form. He unraveled an entire vintage cassette tape, painted the ribbon white, then wrote a greeting on it and scrolled it back onto the wheels. I read the message along the narrow bottom edge of the cassette where the tape peeks out, rotating the reel with my fingertip!

Soon after, as we were driving to brunch together one day, the U2 song "One" came on the radio and Oscar and I immediately forgot what we were talking about and started singing along. We belted it out at the top of our lungs. Reflecting now, how apropos. "We're one, but we're not the same." He and I. Each whole, but still looking for love. *Carrying* each other, like in the song. *Carrying on* together—*andando de la mano.* Even though we grew up half a world away, we both knew all the words. In a way, we had listened to it together decades before on our matching Walkmans—me on my school bus in California and him in the middle of the twelve-year Salvadoran civil war, funded in part by the United States. But we were just kids back then. By chance, both of us had the bright yellow "sports" Walkman, the one with the lovely, squishy buttons. A few thousand miles apart, two kids who both loved to draw and swim and eat fruit put on their headphones and reached for that tiny green triangle with the tip of their finger: *PLAY.*

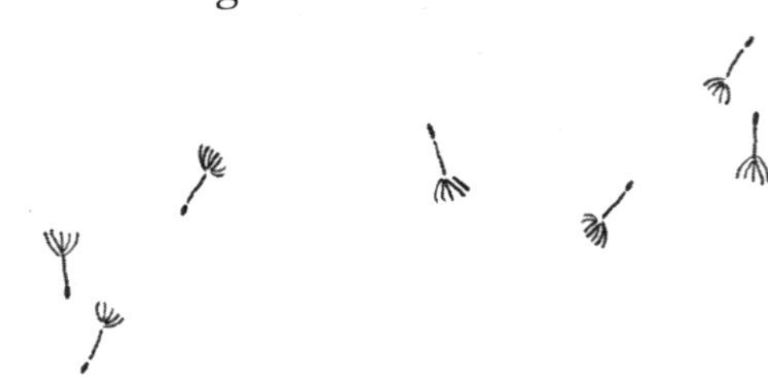

Gifts That Give Perspective

Cognitive empathy is commonly thought of as seeing the world through someone else's eyes, as perspective *taking*. But cognitive empathy has a secret sibling who is also an agent of positive relations in a diverse world—perspective *giving*. In addition to *seeing* a recipient, a gift can *show* something significant about a giver.

Lorie in Brooklyn told me she shares a little bit of her Italian heritage when she makes a huge batch of *struffoli*, also known as Italian honey balls, to share with her friends and acquaintances of many heritages. Since thoughtful gift givers inevitably focus on trying to see and support recipients, it is easy for them to forget that one of the things people want from us is to get to know *us* better, especially if the relationship is new or casual.

I once visited a group of children living in a foster home to teach them how to make origami flowers. A child came up to me at the end and quietly held out a tiny plastic Pokémon figure. He wanted me to have it, and I was honored. The gift celebrated our brief but beautiful time together. I had shared my love of origami. And his gesture shared something of him. It felt important for me to accept it, to take the toy. Doing so wordlessly announced that the feeling was mutual. With the Pokémon figure, the child chose to show himself to me in a very different way than if he had given me an origami flower. Spontaneously passing me the tiny purple monster from his pocket was a brilliant move. I didn't even know it was a Pokémon character—Gengar—until I researched it later, continuing the unspoken promise I made to the child as I received it: to expand my awareness to include him, to widen my circle.

To share something of ourselves can be a beautiful bid for connection,[6] a disclosure of our own heart that invites someone to see us and to show their heart too. In the world I want to usher into being, everyone's voice is heard and story honored. In this world, it is not always safe to share; what we want to show of ourselves depends on context. What's more, it's all in flux. When it feels safe and appropriate, I encourage all of us to show ourselves with our gifts, especially if there is something we are excited to share so that the people around us can understand us better.

Solidarity and Sanctuary

We have explored the desire to be seen and supported. As broadly true as this may be, people also have strong feelings about *whom* they are being seen by. To be seen is not always safe, or wished for. I'd like to reserve a space—a calm, nourishing sanctuary—for gifts that build solidarity through the comfort of shared identity. This kind of camaraderie can help us find the strength to persevere through all sorts of challenges.

A recipient in a tough spot might want to receive a particular gift only from someone who has experienced a similar difficulty. When Heidi in Tennessee was diagnosed with cancer in her forties, she received a hand-delivered care package from a cousin who had been through cancer treatment herself. Heidi welcomed her inside knowledge and tried-and-true recommendations, including a book called *Crazy Sexy Cancer Tips* by Kris Carr. Heidi laughed her way through the book and felt part of a powerful sisterhood.

Some gifts of solidarity touch upon identities that have been persecuted, oppressed, or otherwise treated unkindly. An exclusive gift based on shared experience can provide respite, a sense of hope, and even protection. Elizabeth in the Pacific Northwest once received such a gift at a basketry workshop. The gift giver was from a neighboring Indigenous tribe, and they did not share a language group, but Elizabeth told me that they have a big river in common, the one her tribe calls Píkul. The women chatted while they made baskets, and one of them surprised the group with a gift. With her fingertips, she placed one tiny seashell into each woman's palm, including Elizabeth's. It was a dentalium shell, or *'éxsex*, in Elizabeth's language.

'Éxsex is reminiscent of ivory in both color and shape, looking like a tiny elephant tusk. They are made by *Antalis pretiosa*, benthic sea creatures who, in centuries past, populated the West Coast from Alaska to Baja California. Their distinctive beauty and natural sparsity led to the shells' use as currency. When dancing with *Antalis pretiosa* in the form of regalia, the shells clink together, adding to the music. Elizabeth's new shell was left over from an heirloom piece of regalia that had been restrung.

Having never before touched a real 'éxsex shell, Elizabeth welcomed the tiny gift into her palm and felt the gravity of it all. "I saw my great-great-great-grandfather's necklaces in the shell as it warmed to my touch," she told me. "It's staggering to imagine a whole bridal costume or ceremony shirt, the weight of them, the sound they would make as the wearer moved." I learned from Elizabeth that modern dentalium goods are made with imported shells of a different species, and that the ancestral belts, costumes, and jewelry with native shells are mostly off-limits, on display in museums or private collections. Her shell is now part of her personal collection, the meaningful things that remind her who she is and her place on Earth.

The bestowal was a moment of shared recognition, each shell a *lively thing*—still humming with the music the shells made for generations. The recipients understood that the shells of 'éxsex are scarcer than ever today because of the lasting effects of colonial trade, modern waterway management methods, and ecological fragmentation. Elizabeth hopes 'éxsex might become more numerous again as the process of undamming the region's rivers progresses. Indeed, the largest river restoration project in US history, removing four dams from the Klamath River, was completed in 2024, allowing fish to swim freely again for the first time in a hundred years.

Co-Creating the World

Remember the hot, steaming dumplings my neighbor handed me at my front door? My neighbor's lovely gift had shared a little bit about her with me—her cooking, her cultural traditions. It had been an invitation to know her, even if just a little. I wanted to respond with something special from my own kitchen.

The artist in me perked up at a lecture by john a. powell, the director of the Othering & Belonging Institute, when he said that true belonging is co-created. He explained that *inclusion* merely makes a place at the majority's table for the minority to pull up a few chairs. In contrast, co-creation involves everyone from the get-go.[7] I wondered whether a gift for my neighbor might somehow emerge from a co-creative space in between us, even without our speaking to each other, since we don't share a language.

The answer ended up being literal. My neighbors grew shiso, an aromatic herb, along our shared driveway, between their onions and strawberries. My neighbor noticed me admiring their shiso one day and gestured for me to take some. And so now I wondered, *Could I make them a batch of shiso cookies?* I found a recipe and smiled when I saw that it also called for lemon zest. Their shiso plant and my lemon tree could go in on this gift together. I baked the cookies and put them in a canning jar with a few candied whole shiso leaves on top. On the gift tag, I wrote "lemon shiso cookies" and "I'm glad we're neighbors," knowing they could ask their son to translate for them if need be. My neighbor smiled, pointed at the cookies and then at me to ask if I had made them. I nodded. She seemed quite pleased.

Take Heart

On the whole, gift exchange is like a wonderfully slow, unrushed conversation. Between gifts, we can take our time to consider possibilities and to call upon our best selves. We can dream up gifts and start to play with ideas. We can get feedback, check our work, and sleep on it. We can do research, process emotions, and try to catch missteps before we make them.

Let's take heart. We can do this. To be courageous doesn't mean we don't feel fear; it means we go ahead and do something important even though fear is present. We can remember the three-ring diagram—*safety, challenge, overwhelm*—and try to stay at our growing edge. To do so includes calibrating our gifts to the level of trust in a relationship.

I took heart when I offered a gift to my cousin last winter. She'd recently had to put down her sweet pup, Juno, who was only five years old, because of a sudden illness. Juno was a service dog, trained specifically for—and with—my cousin, with a specialty in autism. Juno could tune in to my cousin's emotional state and help calm her. As needed, Juno would insist on eye contact and wait for evidence of my cousin's self-awareness. This highly attuned dog would sit on my cousin's feet if she sensed that something stronger was needed or even jump into her lap for full-body contact.

Wanting to offer my cousin a gift of solace after she lost Juno, I thought about a gift I'd made for her decades ago, when she was a child. I had sewn a miniature doll for her that looked like me, a "Mini Lea" to keep her company whenever it could be of help. I wondered if it would be comforting for my cousin to have a Mini Juno to carry in her pocket. Or would it be too sad? I hesitated. Losing Juno was devastating. But I didn't want to miss a great opportunity to send some love my cousin's way.

I decided to run the idea by my aunt first. She was uncertain; it might be too soon. A month later, while enjoying lunch together, my cousin brought up

Juno herself, so I asked her if this was an okay moment for me to share a creative idea related to Juno, or if that felt too tender. She gave me her blessing, so I asked her if I could make her a Mini Juno. I was ready for any answer, but she was delighted and said *yes.* I could tell that Mini Juno was already starting to work her magic. I ended up sewing five Mini Junos so my cousin could always have one handy—a whole pack of three-inch black Labs wearing their official service dog vests.

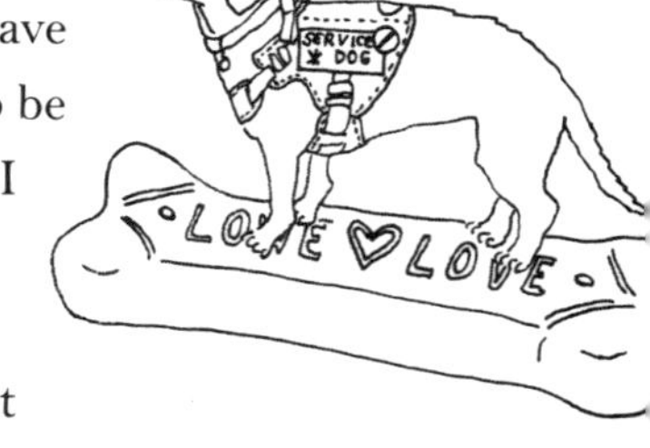

The Mini Junos bridged a fairly large gap. I have never had a dog, and I do not know what it is like to be on the inside of my cousin's autistic experience. But I had a gut feeling that we had a strong enough foundation to support this gift, and so it would be worth a try. Also, it is okay to be nervous. I've noticed that I am at my best when I have a few butterflies. Dread, no thanks. But *yes* to the flutter of uncertainty that comes with courage and the potential for growth.

Courage's best friend is self-compassion, and we would be wise to keep those two together. We can *make* mistakes without *being* mistakes. When a gift—or really anything we do—doesn't go how we hoped it would, we can celebrate our sincere and brave effort, remind ourselves of the goodness in our heart, and recommit to learning how to align intention with impact.

Revere the Earth

It's February 14, 1990, and I am waiting for the school bus with a backpack of handmade valentines for everyone in my class. Unbeknownst to me, Carl Sagan and his pals at NASA are also making a valentine of sorts, in the form of a photograph. On that day, the *Voyager 1* spacecraft was out beyond

Neptune, having been flying through space for twelve years. *Voyager 1* had already taken tens of thousands of photographs, sending new perspectives back to Earth, from Jupiter to Neptune. Before turning off its cameras permanently to save energy—*interstellar space or bust!*—mission control turned the camera back toward the center of the solar system to say goodbye, snapping a "family portrait" of planets that included the image of Earth that Carl Sagan would famously refer to as "the Pale Blue Dot." In the image, the Earth appears tiny and fragile, surrounded by a vast darkness. In Sagan's words, "a mote of dust suspended in a sunbeam."[8] I wonder: If the Earth itself is a mere mote, then what on earth am I? Once again, Carl Sagan points us home: "The vastness is bearable only through love."[9]

I recently sent a love letter into space—the space between me and another human. No need for NASA, just the USPS. Based on the film *Powers of Ten*, by Charles and Ray Eames, the stationery I crafted for this extra-special delivery consisted of a set of twenty-five nested envelopes. Each one was cut and folded from a still image of the film, with the outermost envelope displaying an illustration of Earth from millions of light-years away. The Milky Way is a mere speck from there, and Earth is nowhere in sight. My stationery would zoom in by a power of ten as each successively smaller envelope was opened—through darkness, into the spiraling arms of the Milky Way, past Saturn and Mars, and finally arriving at Earth, close enough to see a couple having a picnic in a park. My own tiny *Voyager*, launched from my desk.

While the roundness of planet Earth as an astronomical body takes care of itself—*thanks, gravity!*—the roundness of the human sphere requires maintenance. For me, being a good human means not only sharing this planet with a wide diversity of people, but also with a host of nonhuman beings and forces: plants, animals, fungi, molecules, minerals, and weather systems. There are many ways to revere life on Earth for the flourishing of all. The gift-giving opportunity here is to care how our gifts can remind us that we are earthlings, by our very essence, and can encourage us to pay attention to each other *and* the more-than-human world at once. Let's consider a few basics.

Air. A grandmother-to-be gathers balls of yarn in sky colors—cerulean, azure, robin's egg, light grey, dark grey, white. She is knitting the sky into a baby blanket, an ode to the atmosphere in honor of her grandbaby's time in the womb. Each day, the grandmother observes the weather, chooses colors to match, and then adds a small square patch of sky to the growing blanket. Bright blue and white for puffy clouds. Grey for a rainstorm. White for fog. One day, she sees a rainbow and adds a rainbow swatch. The result is a cozy calendar grid of sky excerpts, a souvenir of the grandmother's remembering to look up. The entire blanket sings "I see you" to both baby and sky.[10]

Soil. When I sent a singing telegram to a garden in Portland, Oregon, one summer, its human companion loved it too. My pen pal Polly and the delightfully rambunctious garden she cultivates gave Jen Forti of Bellagram Telegrams a warm welcome. Wearing a bellhop outfit with a music note on the cap, Jen lifted her ukulele and sang my custom message directly to Polly's backyard—a colorful, postage-stamp plot of Earth. *Dear Roses. Beloved Calendula. Borage, Phlomis, Foxglove. Dearest Nettles, Yarrow, Lemon Balm, and Lavender. My Darling Mycelia and Earthworms below. Sun above. THANK YOU.* In the spotlight of the sun, she then continued to serenade everyone with "World-Class Pollinator," a ditty by Tiffany Monk sung from the perspective of a bee. I wasn't able to interview the bees directly, but Polly called me immediately, swooning, all abuzz.

Polly sinks her heart (and hands) into the soil, tending and befriending the flora and fauna that are within her reach. The intention behind this cohabitation is the wellness of the whole system, and the joy of it all. Some of the garden's bounty becomes tinctures, teas, and balms in Polly's kitchen, which then wing their way to mailboxes near and far via her Herban Enclave subscription boxes. One of my favorite ways to care for the Earth is by taking good care of the Earth's good caretakers.

Water. I continue to wear the whale ring my parents gave me. The humpbacks, greys, and orcas are still not okay, but many still sing—and whistle and moan and knock and make other cryptic clicks. I can sense another reality nearby—perhaps the future—where humans have been humble, making way for their nonhuman kin. I envision a realm where use and abuse have relinquished their fearful grip and transformed into the lighter touch of trust, of creative accompaniment. If we make it, maybe someday humans will keep in better touch with the whales. Just imagine: a symphony for the sea. An orchestra poised on the end of a long pier, dressed to the nines. Musicians' hands hold instruments that the you and I of today don't recognize because humanity could conceive of them and craft them only after learning the languages of the whales. They make up for the sounds the *Homo sapiens* mouth cannot form but play the songs the human mind and heart can still fathom.

We Are One. We Are Many.

E pluribus unum. Out of many, one. The motto, first stamped into US coinage in 1795, did not intend to include all of us. In fact, originally the *many* in the Latin phrase referred to the many different states coming together into one nation, not individual citizens—much less individual inhabitants—coming together for the benefit of all. And, of course, at that time the nation was being governed by mostly the tiny Euro-descended male percentage of the population with power (and voting rights), to the exclusion of most of the people inhabiting the region—Indigenous people, enslaved people, women.

And yet, the motto is a subversive seed. Something to hold on to. Something we can hold each other to. The phrase sings from every new coin minted by the US Treasury, every coin passed from palm to palm or dropped into a tip jar. I believe that not only can the people living in the United States work together to wish each other well, but there is room enough for all of humanity and the other beings—all the green things and fantastic critters. We can form a great sphere of belonging, embracing difference rather than flattening it. Long ago, people feared they could sail right off the edge of the world, and I see why. Planet Earth is way too big for anyone to appreciate its curved, spherical edge from the surface, at least not on one's own. But when we all get together and compare notes, we know better. The world is round! And this is the only one we've got.

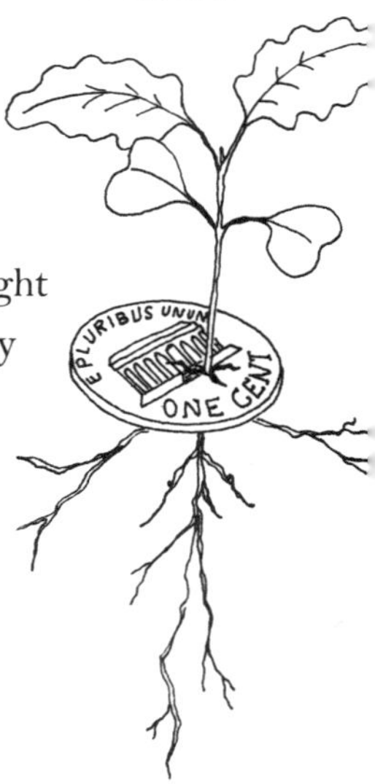

Survival of the Kindest

I love that the word *kind* is hiding inside *humankind.* I believe it is in our nature to tend and befriend—to push pause, think again, and when it appears safe to do so, work together for mutual benefit. I agree with Martin Luther King Jr.: "I am convinced that men hate each other because they fear each other. They fear each other because they don't know each other, and they don't know each other because they don't communicate with each other, and they don't communicate with each other because they are separated from each other."[11] I think good gifts, as creative gestures of care offered from the heart, can help us brave the uncertainty of difference without letting our old lizard brains push us around. We are mammals, deeply social beings with prefrontal cortexes that let us swap in curiosity for fear, returning us to our ability to act from a wise heart. Let's be who we are then—human and kind.

Reflect

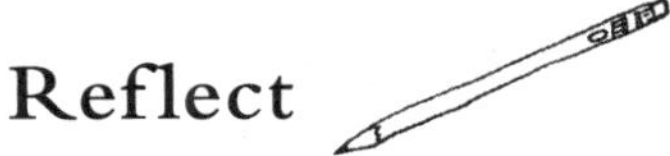

1. Does the framework of difference and diversity help explain why any of the gifts from your past landed poorly? This could be something you gave, received, or just witnessed. Did any of these gifts reach toward a person as a stereotype instead of a whole, complex person with a unique story?

2. In the context of a close relationship that has trust and safety, give a gift that honors an important difference between you and your recipient. Show them that you "see" them and care about them beyond what you have in common.

3. Consider the past few gifts you gave, asking whether they *showed* something about you, the giver, as they did a good turn for your recipient. In the future, is there anything about yourself you'd like to share by way of a gift?

4. Compose a gift for a human that also draws attention to the importance of the Earth, "seeing" the more-than-human world too.

CONCLUSION

Sincerely, Yours Truly

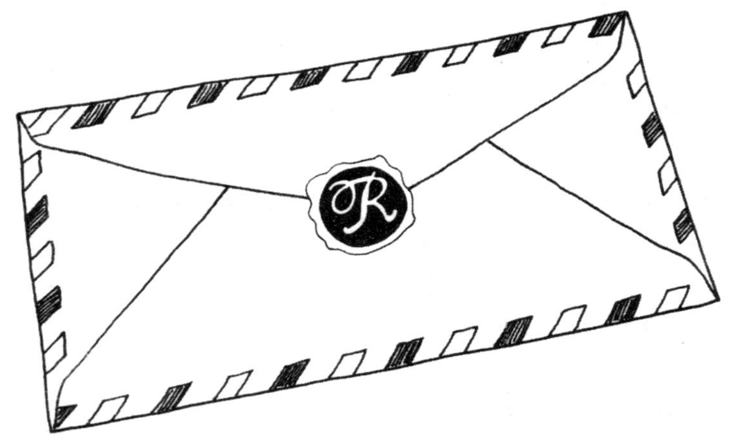

Till the gossamer thread you fling catch somewhere, O my soul.

—WALT WHITMAN, "A NOISELESS PATIENT SPIDER"

Reweaving the World

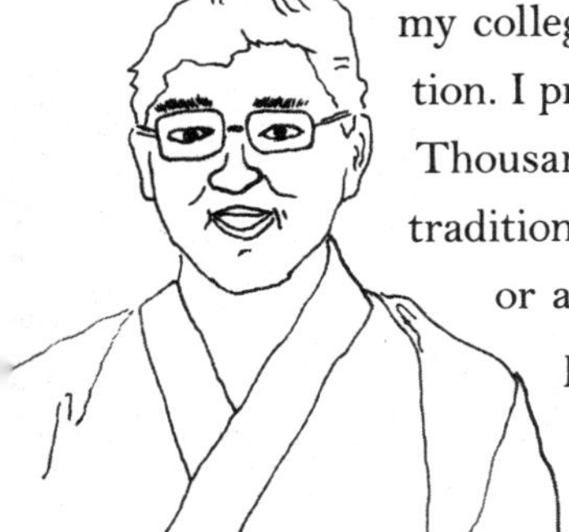

Yoroshiku onegai shimasu. With our palms pressed together, Takemoto Sensei welcomes me into the tearoom, Chikurakken, which translates to "a place to enjoy bamboo," among many other things. It is a gift box of sorts—big enough to hold the two of us, six and a half tatami mats, and the essential utensils for a tea gathering. Sensei, as everyone at my college called him, practices tea in the Yabunouchi tradition. I practice my own quirky kind of tea in my Tearoom of a Thousand Wonders here in Oakland, which is not Japanese or traditional but has an eclectic aesthetic more like a junk shop or a Joseph Cornell sculpture. Sensei and I like to compare notes, about tea and everything else—walking, umbrellas, mortality, trees, spices, his grandchildren, my love life—and have done so for more than twenty years. Sensei is full of surprises. He was certainly the only college professor of mine to do a somersault during a lecture! I showed up for office hours, again and again, with a pocketful of questions and a sense that, despite all my material privilege, something was missing. In class one day, Sensei gave me exactly what I longed for: a tangerine in the palm of my hand and an invitation to peel it. Mindfully.

One time, Sensei offered me a pair of scissors and said, giggling, "Go ahead. Try to cut yourself out of the universe." I laughed. I suddenly remembered my body and spent a moment contemplating my edges. What an absurd notion, as if we were paper dolls or discount coupons. Just cut along the dashed line, and you're out! The stranger thing, though, is that so many of us seem to walk around as if this were already the situation, as if we were separate, autonomous, alone. And perhaps at worst, as if we don't belong here on Earth at all. It is far from the truth, but not without reason. Being human can be a rough ride. What can inspire us to stay, to keep in touch—to reach for a roll of tape, a bottle of glue, or a spool of thread instead?

In 1869, John Muir wrote in his journal, perhaps after seeing a spiderweb glistening somewhere in the Sierras: "When we try to pick out anything by itself we find that it is bound fast by a thousand invisible cords that cannot be broken, to everything in the universe."[1] In his "Letter from Birmingham Jail" in 1963, Martin Luther King Jr. wrote something similar: "We are caught in an inescapable network of mutuality, tied in a single garment of destiny. Whatever affects one directly, affects all indirectly."[2] In 2024, writer and activist Rebecca Solnit picked up Muir's and King's loose ends in a widely circulated article: "Take care of yourself and remember that taking care of something else is an important part of taking care of yourself, because you are interwoven with the ten trillion things in this single garment of destiny that has been stained and torn, but is still being woven and mended and washed."[3] As for me, a deep bow to all of them and, even more, to the notion itself—this *garment of destiny* that belongs to all of us, and to which we all belong. The noun, though—the *garment*—isn't the heart of it. The heart is the *weaving*, always the verb. Most important is the *activity* keeping the garment intact, shimmering like silk in the sunlight.

Still, chatting with Sensei in his office, I have doubts, worries. I gently poke at the idea, *Are you sure we cannot cut ourselves out of the universe, that the cords cannot be broken?* What about this great unraveling? For isn't that precisely what humanity, some very powerful parts of it anyway, has been up to for the past few centuries (or longer), snipping cords left and right, willy-nilly, as if it doesn't matter? In response, Sensei turns to the sky, drawing my attention to the air, the atmosphere. I take a deep breath. I remember my body. In this moment, I am alive and in good company.

Sensei says we can accept things *as they are* and engage with whatever is here, or we can attempt—always unsuccessfully—to turn away from what is. Engagement is not always easy, thus the temptation to cut and run. When we attune to the web of our existential entanglement—in which the links can be clear or concealed, direct or roundabout, short or extensive—we understand that both the beauty and the suffering of the entire world are within reach. Sensei tells me he tries to have fun with it all, finding opportunities to *play*, to *see*, to *say wow*. (It is also important to *cry* and to *grieve*.) I try too. I know that when I find invitations hiding inside perceived limitations, I can roll with reality *as it is* rather than pushing against it, and things tend to turn out much better than I had feared. Hence, the shape of Sensei's somersault.

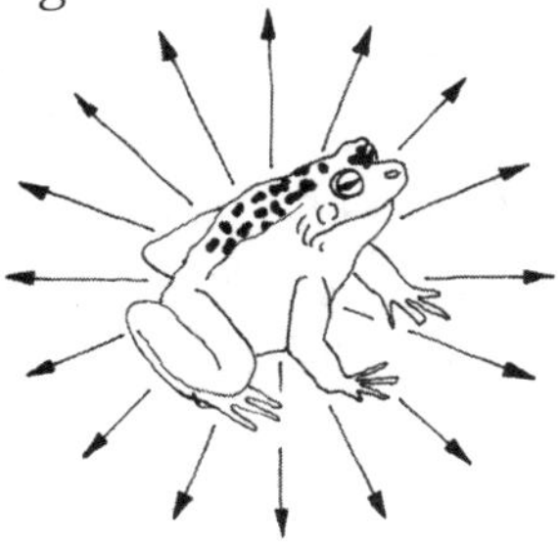

I invite you to reflect upon another important shape—your own. Draw your attention to your edges, the anatomical boundary of your body. While it can be tempting to define ourselves by what our skin holds in, let's shift our attention. In your imagination, expand your sense of being beyond your corporeal edges to include all your relations—all the people and beings you spend time with, places you go, things and experiences you give and receive, both consciously and unconsciously. What we truly are—and I think we all know this—is a radiating web of activity, spiraling out with no end in sight. As futurist architect Buckminster Fuller writes, "I seem to be a verb, an evolutionary process—an integral function of the universe."[4]

"Skin can divide us, or it can connect us to the universe." Well, Sensei, if you're going to put it like that, the choice is easy: *Connect me to the universe! Blast off!* Of course, I need not go anywhere else. The universe is right here, at my fingertips, just as it always has been. The hand-knit wool sweater I'm wearing right now is my space suit. Heck, the whorl patterns on my fingertips even look like tiny galaxies! (As do yours.) We are made of stardust, after all. I like how Carl Sagan puts it: "The nitrogen in our DNA, the calcium in our teeth, the iron in our blood, the carbon in our apple pies were made in the interiors of collapsing stars. We are made of starstuff."[5] And so, perhaps every gift tag's "to" and "from" are essentially this: *To: Stardust; From: Stardust.* It's not just a good gift that shimmers. *We* shimmer. As Sagan says, "We are a way for the cosmos to know itself."[6]

I do not believe it is too late to set down the scissors, to take a look around, and to attend to our webs—the people, living creatures, the landscapes and skyscapes we call home. No matter how the human story plays out in the next few centuries, every connection counts along the way. As Rebecca Solnit puts it, "The fact that we cannot save everything does not mean we cannot save anything, and everything we can save is worth saving."[7] I'm going to assume the verdict is still out and will be for at least the rest of my lifetime. There is much work to be done, and from many angles. We can make that work beautiful, joyful, fulfilling. Gestures of care in the form of good gifts, especially if we all do it together, can be a small part of the great healing that has already begun, a loving renunciation of the myth of separation. We can renew our vows to interdependence, reweaving the world one little corner at a time as if every moment matters. *Ichi-go ichi-e* in the tearoom with Sensei; each meeting, only once. You. Me. Here. Now.

Arigatō gozaimasu—"thank you very much." Translated literally: "It is difficult to exist without you." I cannot thank you enough, dear reader, because my gratitude is both too big and too small, especially because to say *you* is also to say *everything*—everything that has come together to make *this moment* possible, our meeting here on this page, this word, this punctuation mark. Sensei points out that, in a way, to say *thank you* suggests we are done, that this is where we part ways. But such parting is impossible because the true extent of our connection has always been irrevocable, even precedes the day we met. He suggests I say *sumimasen*, which means both "excuse me" and "it never ends." A relationship has no end, just as a tearoom has no real walls and a gift has no true edge, for there is no box, no ribbon, no bow large enough because there is no *thing* so small as to be contained by human hands.

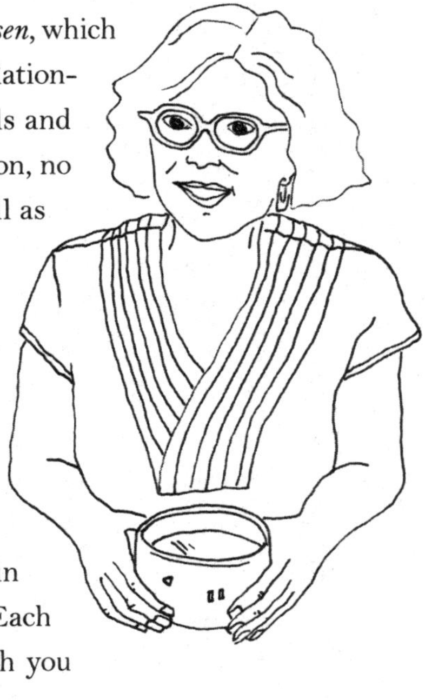

And so, I put my hand on my heart and say *sumimasen*—to everything. It has been my great honor and joy to bump into you here. Excuse me, thank you for reading, and I can never thank you enough because we are ongoing. It is not the nature of the invisible cords between us to break, but to just keep stretching, to keep shimmering in the light of the sun. Let's keep in touch. All of us. Each to each, gift by gift, moment to moment. I'll catch you around . . .

PS

M*ilk-witch. Monks-head. Irish daisy. Clock flower. Tell time. Blowball. Dandelion.* Resting like a bookmark between these two pages, imagine a dandelion, a long green stem with a tidy, delicate sphere of seeds at the top. Radial. Radiant. Spring fresh! Gently pick it up and draw it to your lips. Poised in your fingertips, set your intention to care for someone you love, to give them a good gift. Picture them standing a few yards in front of you. Make eye contact. Inhale deeply, and . . . *blow.*

One bursts into many, and the seeds are on their way! But don't just make a wish. Also *make your wish come true.* Do something about it. Follow up. If all goes well, your recipient can catch at least a few of the seeds and soak up the love and other benefits on offer. They might even grow those seeds out and keep them moving. *Oh look!* A few of the seeds are still stuck to the seed head. There is something in the gift for you too. Now. Soon. Farther down the road. I wonder what it will be, or become . . .

"Through the cracks one seed at a time, I give back what was never mine," goes the Humbird song.[8] A good gift can inspire us to be generous people whose hearts are ready to warm to others and pass goodness along. When a seed finds fertile ground, it takes root. But there is more. Ideally, the whole gesture—the original wish—is so abundant, so extra, that the peripheral seeds, the ones that the wind catches, find homes too. A good gift hits the ground running. And the thing about dandelions is that they don't quit. They are *makers.* They *make do.* They *make it up* like stems toward the sun, toward the stars. Seed to wind to root to sprout to bud to blossom to seed to wind . . . again and again.

RSVP—Tell Me a Story?

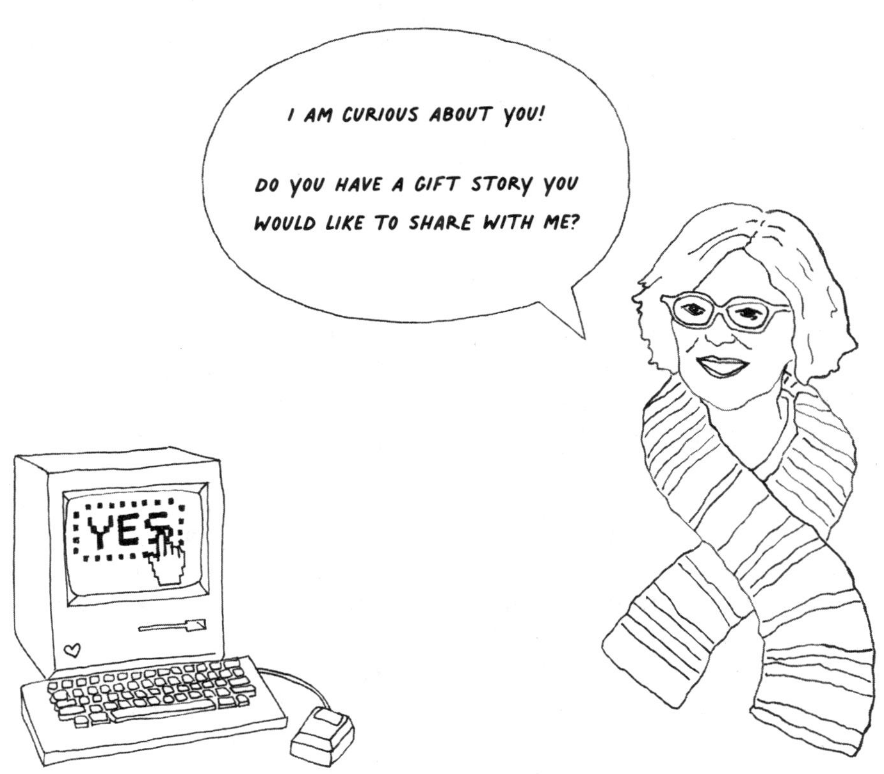

TELL ME ALL ABOUT IT AT THISISFORYOUBOOK.COM.

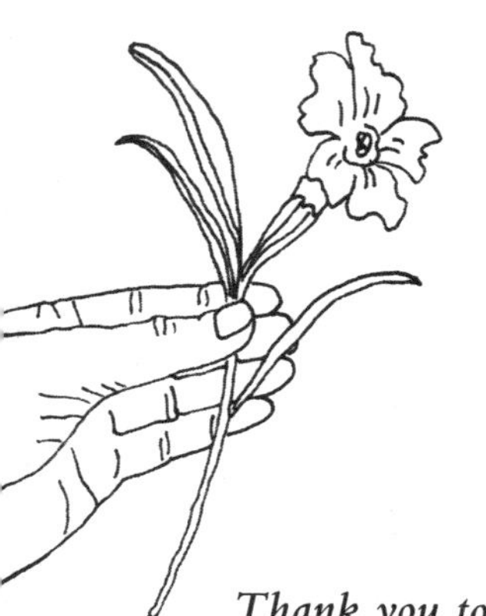

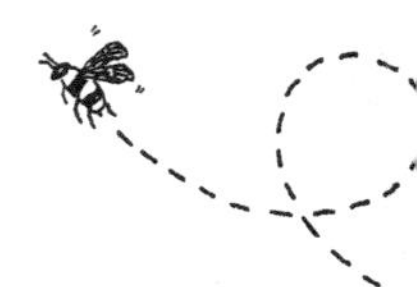

Thank You!

Thank you to my brilliant book team:

HARPERONE: DANIELLA WEXLER (FOR SEEING ME), STEPHANIE SMITH (FOR SEEING IT THROUGH WITH ENTHUSIASM), ANNA CALAME (ALWAYS NEARBY), ELINA COHEN (FOR BEAUTIFUL PAGES), CRISSIE MOLINA, JESSIE DOLCH, ELIZABETH MITCHELL, GHJULIA ROMITI, NINA GOMEZ, AND ALISON CERRI. MY AGENT: AMY RENNERT (FOR BELIEVING IN ME). MY WORKING EDITORS: GENINE LENTINE (FOR THE WAY YOU PAY ATTENTION), AYDEN LEROUX (FOR ALL THAT YOU NOTICE-THINK-FEEL-DO-ARE), LESLIE WELLS (FOR REIGNING IT IN). READERS (FOR EXPANDING MY VIEW): BRIT BARRON, SANDRA BOWLING, CHRISTINA TRAN, NASEEM ALAVI, MATTHEW STEIN, SOLANA RICE, AND ALBERT KONG.

Deep bow to my storytellers and conversation partners:

DAWN M. GROSS, SHERRY RICHERT BELUL, SONIA P., BLU MUCHA, LAIKA YOUNG O'BRIEN, MEGUMI LORNA INOUYE, ANNE HODDER-SHIPP, KAT VELLOS, IDA BENEDETTO, JEN FORTI, DONOVAN BEESON, LISA COUGHLIN, BRIAN FISHER, AMY ARMSTRONG, HELEN AND JOE HESKETH, BETTY LEWIS, NICOLE CACAL, DOMO, JOHN TSUKAYAMA, LAURA PESCETTI, HAYLEY, IRFAAN, HELEN SIMMONS, KATE, S. D. TURNER, ARIEL RICHARDSON, JESSICA IN SEATTLE, MICHAEL MCCANN AND ASHER EMMETT, GABRIELA BARROCAS, RUTH ANN GONZALES, ELI ZEMPER, DREW ZEMPER, SHARON AND SAM, EVE NESS, PAULA CONROY, JACQUELINE GORBUTT, ERIN FAE, TAMARA, ANDREA SCHER, TERRY AND CONNIE WELKER, ALEXIS MURPHY, DOMONIQUE MATTHEWS, TAMARA LATORRE, SANDY SILVERIA, HARSH SHAH AND LAURA MCDONALD, SUNITA SHAH, JOSHUA ROSENFELD, A. M. ALPIN, MAXINE WRIGHT, MATHEW SANDFORD, E.A.L., ANDREW EVANS, E.T., CANDACE, PATRICIA H., TASSOS STEVENS, CHILAN N., IAN, ROBOT, MADDY, SHIRLEY S., MARIE AND LAURA, KELLY TIERNEY, BRIAN R., ASHLIE M., EILEEN BIRD, BELINDA A., CHARLENE J. S., JANAE T. A., LAURA A., NIKKI GLOUDEMAN, MARGARET BLOOM, KENDRA B., CATHY C., REBECCA KEMP BRENT, CHRISTY C., REBECCA R. S., JANE GILLETTE, VAL B., MARGARET LINCOLN, CHRISTINA AMINI AND FAMILY, ALIA A., ELLAINE M.-S., CHRIS GUZOFSKI, LEA B., ANDREA KATZ, AMY M., NINA S., D.B., CYNTHIA R., LULU FLANAGAN, WILSON, KATEY O'BARA, CATHY HARKNESS, SAMANTHA BAER, DENISE, LINDA

CHRISCHILLES, ELIZABETH, KAREN Z., JOSEPH DEL PESCO, AUNTIE KARL, PANKAJ, HEIDI KRUEGER, MAYA LIU, MELANIE S., RENEE T., ANNE R., MEL LUNA, MELISSA CAMPBELL, NATALIA R., NEIL S., TANIA LOMBROZO, CLARE O., JOHANNE A., HELEN JUKES, MIM G. S., BILL GRASSE, ALI BUDNER, ANGELA MOFFETT, MARIAN CASTINADO, B. R. THOMPSON, BRENDA MYERS, DIANA LINEBACK, SARAH (O'FARRELL) MCCARTHY, RACHEL GELENIUS, TESS EVANS, LAURA LYNN ROTH, TRACY, LORIE, JEREMY REDLEAF, DEANNA DEATON, AMBLER, MEREDITH S., ZOË, LAURA CAPP, BRYAN VICTOR LIM, MYLES, KRISTEN M., KRISSY F., TOD B., BRIAN C., MY FRIEND IN EAST VANCOUVER, BRET VICTOR, SASHA M., DEBORAH W., FRED L., REBECCA E., ZACH METZGER (AND HIS GRANDMOM), MARIA AND IZHAR, KATE K., DAISY E., KAREN VAN HATCHER, MEGAN M., JENNY R., AHM, BURNING MAN DAN, AMANDA CHOI, BETH, CHARLENE MARGOT, D.M., ANDREA JOHNSTON, MARTHA A., MACKENZIE K., TAYLOR S., B.K.J., WENDI K., SARAH B. AND HER MOM, NATALIE, KARMIN, LISA (AND FIFI), ABBY, AND PEDRO!

Gratitude for my teachers and guides:

MY THERAPIST (FOR HOLDING SPACE FOR ALL OF IT), B.D., BETH PICKENS, ALIZA AND OPEN FLOOR, AMANDA RIEUX (FROM BERMUDA GRASS TO ALEGRÍA PARADES), MS. COOK (FOR YOUR CREATIVE HEART), TOM (FOR ENCOURAGING ME TO SHINE), SENSEI (FOR ALWAYS SAYING YES), MRS. SYKES (FOR CENTERING), MR. MASKER (FOR UNDERSTANDING), MAMA ELLIS (FOR KEEPING IN TOUCH), MRS. JOHNS (FOR ART LAB), MRS. GALLUP (FOR FOURTH GRADE).

Thank you, dear ones, near and far:

MY PARENTS (LOVING YOU ALWAYS), MY GRANDPARENTS (FOR LOVING ME SO), MY GREAT-GRANDPARENTS (AND THEIR HANDWORK), MY AUNT BETH AND AUNT C.C., ALLURE, OSCAR (POR ESTAR A MI LADO), AKIRA AND MAYA, MALCOLM, RHETT, JUSTINE, MATT, BIJOYA, BIDISHA, JOAN, ROSE, SARA, AYDEN, NASEEM, GENINE, SOLANA, POLLY, JANA, ELISE, NAOMI, GALE, CATHERINE, PAUL S., ANNA, ERIN, GEORGIA, SAM, AMY S., KYRIÉ, DONNA, JEFFREY, ESTHER, CHAIM, TALI, MILICENT, KENNY, ESTELLE, DAN, A.K.R., H.C., AMY A., MISHA, SYBIL, REBEKAH, RAPHI, J.B., KIMBERLY, ADRIENNE, MYLES, F.R., HELENA, PAUL G., PAM AND JOE, CASEY, JUSTIN, ELLEN, A.K., LENKA, R.A., MICHELLE, DANA, ANNIE, D.S., FARYN, BECKY, LENA, KEN, REBECCA, D.V., TIU, JASON, ABE, TANIA, CHRIS, VANESSA, PLUCKYPEA, AND MICHAEL.

With love for the places where I've found myself:

THE PACIFIC OCEAN, HUCKLEBERRY BOTANICAL PRESERVE, LAKE MERRITT, THE MORCOM ROSE GARDEN, THE TEAROOM OF A THOUSAND WONDERS, MY FARMER'S MARKET, THE UNCEDED

LAND OF THE MUWEKMA OHLONE, OAKLAND AND THE EAST BAY, WOODSONG, CHIKURAKKEN, WHITMAN COLLEGE, THE PALOUSE, THE COLUMBIA RIVER GORGE, THE CERAMICS BARN AT CATE SCHOOL, CATALINA ISLAND, MONTESSORI PRESCHOOL, HIGHWAY 128, THE ANDIRON SEASIDE INN, IN CAHOOTS RESIDENCY, THE LADY ANNE VICTORIAN INN, THE CHAI CABOOSE IN PORTLAND, BIG SUR, SIRENE, CLIO'S BOOKS, ORDINAIRE, WALDEN POND BOOKS, AND ALAMEDA POINT ANTIQUES FAIRE.

Thanks for the inspiring ideas and phenomenal company:

JAMES P. CARSE, PEMA CHÖDRÖN, NINA KATCHADOURIAN, JOSEPH CORNELL, TARA BRACH, MARY OLIVER, HENRY DAVID THOREAU, REBECCA SOLNIT, MR. ROGERS, ANNIE DILLARD, MARTIN HEIDEGGER, LEWIS HYDE, ROBIN WALL KIMMERER, SIMONE WEIL, GANDHI, BELL HOOKS, MARCEL MAUSS, *MARCEL THE SHELL WITH SHOES ON*, SENECA, IRIS MURDOCH, URSULA K. LE GUIN, MARIA POPOVA, M. C. RICHARDS, JOHN RAWLS, AUDRE LORDE, ESTHER PEREL, JOHN O'DONOHUE, ADRIENNE MAREE BROWN, JANE BENNETT, AMY LEACH, YOKO ONO, OCTAVIA BUTLER, KOBAYASHI ISSA, HAROLD (AND THE PURPLE CRAYON), DARIO ROBLETO, ODYSSEY WORKS, MICHAEL SWAINE, INGRID FETELL LEE, RAY AND CHARLES EAMES, KRISTA TIPPETT, AMY GOODMAN, EMILY DICKINSON, TIYA MILES, MARINA ABRAMOVIĆ, KRISTIN NEFF, GEORGIA O'KEEFFE, GARY SNYDER, JOHN A. POWELL, JOSÉ ANDRÉS AND WORLD CENTRAL KITCHEN, THE LONG NOW FOUNDATION, DAVID ABRAM, ROSS GAY, NEDRA GLOVER TAWWAB, JOHN MUIR, NASA, CARL SAGAN, JOHN KABAT-ZINN, MARSHALL B. ROSENBERG, KANDINSKY, PABLO NERUDA, WALT WHITMAN, RICHARD FEYNMAN, DONNA J. HARAWAY, DAVID GRAEBER, KENNETH MAUE, PRENTIS HEMPHILL, THICH NHAT HANH, TED PURVES, PRIYA PARKER, SUSAN DAVID, BRENÉ BROWN, WILL GUIDARA, LESLIE KNOPE, OLEG, U2, BOB MARLEY, TALKING HEADS, PAUL SIMON, HUMBIRD, *STAR TREK*, *CALVIN AND HOBBES*, *THE SOUND OF MUSIC*, THE GLASS FLOWERS, *THIS IS US*, *I LOVE LUCY*, WILLY WONKA, HELLO KITTY, THE USPS, *NATIONAL GEOGRAPHIC* MAGAZINE, EARTHSHIPS, BOWERBIRDS, SQUARE DANCING, ANTS, POLLINATORS, SPIDERS AND THEIR WEBS, SHEEP, TIDE POOLS, SEA URCHINS, SEA ANEMONES, ABALONE, WHALES, MAPLE SEEDPODS TWIRLING, DANDELIONS, CALIFORNIA POPPIES, FERNS, BORAGE, STICKY MONKEY-FLOWERS, MADRONES, OAKS, PHLOMIS, LEMON VERBENA, CEANOTHUS, POMEGRANATE SEASON, THE LEMON TREE IN MY YARD, WALLA WALLA SWEET ONIONS, TETRIS, *THE NEW YORK TIMES* GAMES, EBAY, COOL TOOLS, PATTERNS, TEXTURE, DETAIL, PERFORATION, POINTILLISM, PRISMS, KALEIDOSCOPES, MAGNIFYING GLASSES, CLAY, PAPER, YARN, CAST IRON, TWILL WEAVE, THE MICRON 005, CHOCOLATE, TEA, BUTTONS, DUST, SAND, STARS, SEEDS, SOIL, FUNGI, EARTHWORMS, MY MYCELIAL MIND, MY BODY (AND THE TRILLIONS OF BACTERIA IN MY GUT), CHILDREN EVERYWHERE, GRAVITY, WATER, OXYGEN, CALIFORNIA, THE EARTH, THE MOON, THE LIGHT OF THE SUN—INCLUDING THE SHADOWS IT CASTS AND THE LOVE THAT PERSEVERES THROUGH THE DARKNESS.

My Card Catalog

CHAPTER 1: WHAT IS A GIFT?

1. Arnold Lobel, *Frog and Toad Are Friends* (Harper & Row, 1970), 36.

2. Seneca, *How to Give: An Ancient Guide to Giving and Receiving*, trans. James S. Romm (Princeton Univ. Press, 2020), 67.

CHAPTER 2: RELATIONSHIPS IN MINIATURE

1. James P. Carse, *Finite and Infinite Games: A Vision of Life as Play and Possibility* (The Free Press, 1986), 75.

2. bell hooks, *All About Love: New Visions* (William Morrow, 2018), 67.

CHAPTER 3: GIFT IS A VERB

1. Seneca, *How to Give: An Ancient Guide to Giving and Receiving*, trans. James S. Romm (Princeton Univ. Press, 2020), 187.

2. Jonathan Fields, host, *Good Life Project*, podcast, "The Surprising Science About Relationships & Happiness | Robert Waldinger," Acast, January 12, 2023, 1:13:57, https://www.goodlifeproject.com/podcast/the-surprising-science-about-relationships-happiness-robert-waldinger.

3. David Graeber, *Toward an Anthropological Theory of Value: The False Coin of Our Own Dreams* (Palgrave Macmillan, 2001), 218–220; Lewis Hyde, *The Gift: Imagination and the Erotic Life of Property* (Vintage, 1999).

4. Lewis Hyde, *The Gift*, 128.

5. Fred Rogers, *The World According to Mister Rogers: Important Things to Remember* (Hyperion, 2003), 91.

6. Jon Kabat-Zinn, *Wherever You Go, There You Are: Mindfulness Meditation in Everyday Life* (Balance, 2005), 64.

7. James P. Carse, *Finite and Infinite Games: A Vision of Life as Play and Possibility* (The Free Press, 1986), 6.

CHAPTER 4: NOT FOR SALE

1. Henry David Thoreau, *Walden: An Annotated Edition*, ed. Walter Harding (Houghton Mifflin, 1995), 28.

2. Jenny Odell, *How to Do Nothing: Resisting the Attention Economy* (Melville House, 2019), xxiii.

CHAPTER 6: WORDS ARE WONDERFUL

1. Mary Oliver, *Dream Work* (Atlantic Monthly Press, 1986), 14.

2. Fred Backus, "Most Americans Haven't Written a Personal Letter on Paper in over Five Years," *CBS News*, October 11, 2021, https://www.cbsnews.com/news/most-americans-havent-written-a-personal-letter-on-paper-in-over-five-years.

CHAPTER 7: PEOPLE ARE PRECIOUS

1. Thomas Lewis, Fari Amini, and Richard Lannon, *A General Theory of Love* (Vintage, 2001), 63.

2. Nedra Glover Tawwab (@nedratawwab), "Choose who you surround yourself with wisely because it impacts mental health and life," Instagram, May 16, 2024, https://www.instagram.com/p/C7B_9izOKT4/.

3. Anne Hodder-Shipp, *Speaking from the Heart: 18 Languages for Modern Love* (Shoebox, 2023).

4. Priya Parker, *The Art of Gathering: How We Meet and Why It Matters* (Riverhead Books, 2018), 117.

5. Annie Dillard, *Pilgrim at Tinker Creek* (Perennial Library, 1985), 80.

6. Tiya Miles, *All That She Carried: The Journey of Ashley's Sack, a Black Family Keepsake* (Random House, 2022), 103.

CHAPTER 8: WISHING EACH OTHER WELL

1. bell hooks, *All About Love: New Visions* (William Morrow, 2018), 215.

2. C. S. Lewis, *The Voyage of the Dawn Treader* (Penguin Books, 1968), 159.

3. Mihaly Csikszentmihalyi, *Flow: The Psychology of Optimal Experience* (Harper Perennial, 2008), 52.

4. Henry David Thoreau, *Walden: An Annotated Edition*, ed. Walter Harding (Houghton Mifflin, 1995), 87.

5. "WCK Ramadan Kits Reach Displaced Palestinians," World Central Kitchen, March 21, 2024, https://wck.org/news/ramadan-kits.

6. Jimmy Kimmel, "Chef José Andrés on Providing Food During Crisis, World Central Kitchen & Who Invented Pizza," November 7, 2023, YouTube, 5:12, https://www.youtube.com/watch?v=APN57-e2xrw.

7. Prentis Hemphill, *What It Takes to Heal: How Transforming Ourselves Can Change the World* (Random House, 2024), 81.

CHAPTER 9: THE ART OF ATTENTION

1. Masters Of The Universe (@masters), "Sun-Man lights the first candle on the Kwanzaa kinara, representing Umoja (unity). In the words of Sun-Man, 'The sun shines brighter on all worlds when good people unite.' Happy #Kwanzaa!" Instagram, December 26, 2021, https://www.instagram.com/masters/p/CX9CKz-gpgg.

2. James Baldwin, *The Fire Next Time* (Vintage, 1992), 95.

CHAPTER 10: EVERYONE IS CREATIVE

1. Vladimir Arkhipov, *Home-Made: Contemporary Russian Folk Artifacts* (FUEL, 2006), 106.

2. Octavia E. Butler, "A Few Rules for Predicting the Future," *Essence*, May 2000, 164.

CHAPTER 11: OOPS! OUCH. NOW WHAT?

1. Brené Brown, *Daring Greatly: How the Courage to Be Vulnerable Transforms the Way We Live, Love, Parent, and Lead* (Avery, 2015), 47.

2. Marshall B. Rosenberg, *Nonviolent Communication: A Language of Life* (PuddleDancer Press, 2015).

3. Molly Martin, *The Art of Repair: Mindful Mending: How to Stitch Old Things to New Life* (Short Books, 2022), 14.

CHAPTER 12: THE WORLD IS ROUND!

1. Robert McCloskey, *Blueberries for Sal* (Viking Press, 1948), 8.

2. Charles Feltman, *The Thin Book of Trust: An Essential Primer for Building Trust at Work* (Thin Book, 2009), 7.

3. Audre Lorde, *Sister Outsider: Essays and Speeches* (Crossing Press, 2007), 56.

4. Octavio Paz, *The Double Flame: Love and Eroticism* (Harcourt Brace, 1996), 152.

5. bell hooks, *All About Love: New Visions* (William Morrow, 2018), 93.

6. John M. Gottman and Joan DeClaire, *The Relationship Cure: A 5 Step Guide to Strengthening Your Marriage, Family, and Friendships* (Harmony, 2002).

7. john a. powell, "On Belonging. . . ." in *The Power of Bridging: How to Build a World Where We All Belong* (Sounds True, 2024).

8. Carl Sagan, *Pale Blue Dot: A Vision of the Human Future in Space* (Random House, 1994), 8.

9. Carl Sagan, *Contact* (Simon & Schuster, 2016), 371.

10. Lea Redmond, *Knit the Sky* (Storey Publishing, 2015), 18.

11. Martin Luther King Jr., "An Address by the Rev. Martin Luther King," Cornell College, Mount Vernon, Iowa, October 15, 1962.

CONCLUSION: SINCERELY, YOURS TRULY

1. "John Muir Misquoted," Sierra Club, updated January 3, 2025, https://vault.sierraclub.org/john_muir_exhibit/writings/misquotes.aspx.

2. Martin Luther King Jr., "Letter from a Birmingham Jail," April 16, 1963, https://www.africa.upenn.edu/Articles_Gen/Letter_Birmingham.html.

3. Rebecca Solnit, "Authoritarians Like Trump Love Fear, Defeatism, Surrender. Do Not Give Them What They Want," *The Guardian*, November 9, 2024, https://www.theguardian.com/world/2024/nov/09/authoritarians-like-trump-love-fear-defeatism-surrender-do-not-give-them-what-they-want.

4. R. Buckminster Fuller, *I Seem to Be a Verb* (Bantam Books, 1970), 1.

5. Carl Sagan, *Cosmos* (Ballantine Books, 2013), 244.

6. *Cosmos: A Personal Journey*, season 1, episode 1, "The Shores of the Cosmic Ocean," directed by Adrian Malone, written by Carl Sagan, aired September 28, 1980, on PBS.

7. Solnit, "Authoritarians Like Trump."

8. "Song for the Seeds," track 1 on Humbird, *Right On*, Nettwerk, 2024.

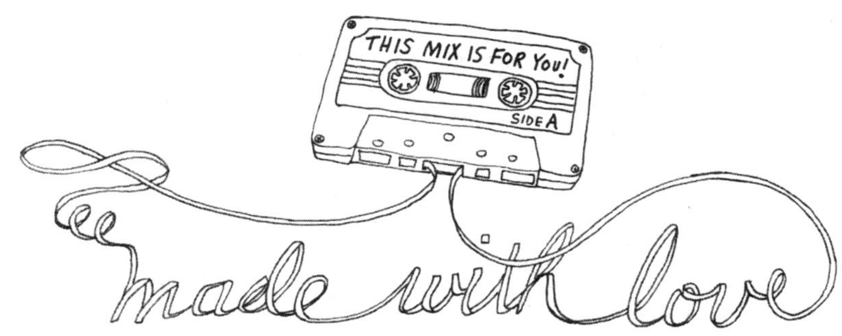

LEA REDMOND SEEKS THE EXTRAORDINARY HIDING IN THE ORDINARY AND WANTS TO SHARE IT WITH YOU. SHE MAKES THINGS, BOOKS, AND ACTIVITIES THAT INVITE HUMANS OF ALL AGES TO BE CURIOUS, PLAYFUL, AND KIND.

KEEP IN TOUCH WITH LEA AT **LEAREDMOND.COM**:

- REGISTER FOR GIFT DESIGN WORKSHOPS.
- FIND *THIS IS FOR YOU* SOUVENIRS.
- DOWNLOAD THE "MIXTAPE" SONG LIST.
- PURCHASE LEA'S BOOKS AND OTHER LIVELY THINGS.
- SEND A TINY LETTER OR PACKAGE VIA THE WSPS.
- SIGN UP FOR LEA'S EMAIL NEWSLETTER.

NOTES, IDEAS, CURIOSITIES:

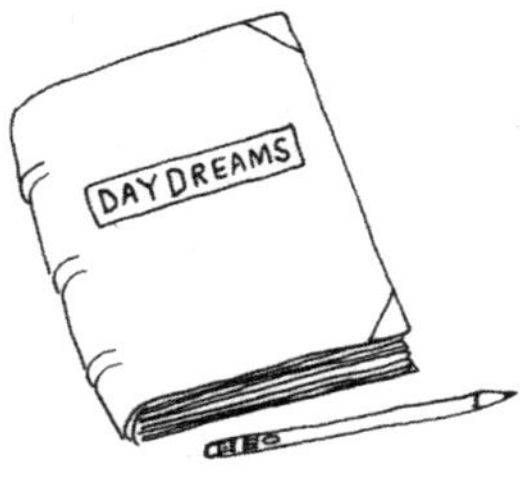

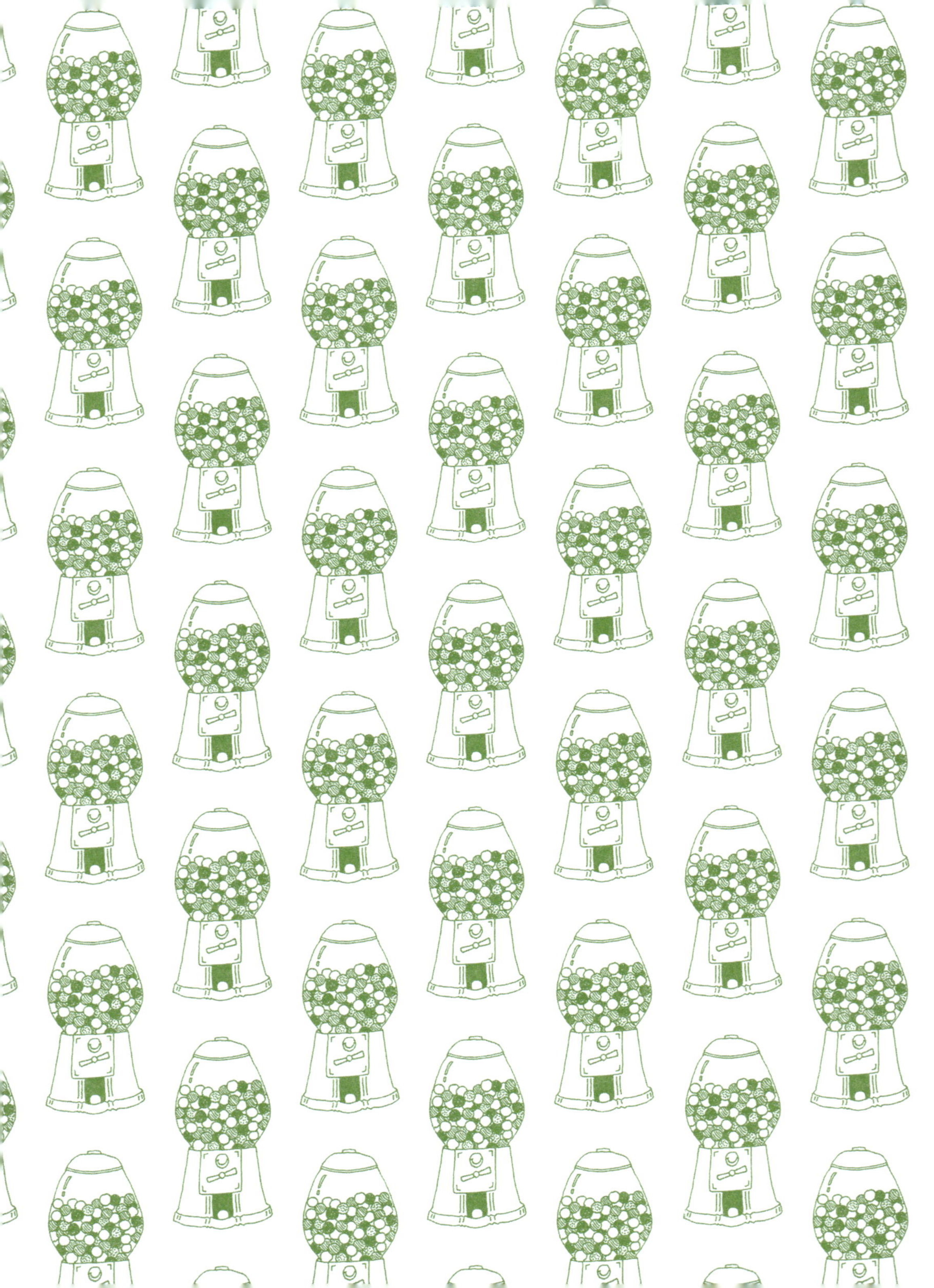